FileMaker® Pro 13

ABSOLUTE BEGINNER'S GUIDE

Tim Dietrich

800 East 96th Street,
Indianapolis, Indiana 46240

FileMaker® Pro 13 Absolute Beginner's Guide

ISBN-13: 978-0-7897-4884-3
ISBN-10: 0-7897-4884-3

Library of Congress Control Number: 2014953706

Printed in the United States of America

First Printing: December 2014

Trademarks

Warning and Disclaimer

Special Sales

For information about buying this title in bulk quantities, or for special sales opportunities (which may include electronic versions; custom cover designs; and content particular to your business, training goals, marketing focus, or branding interests), please contact our corporate sales department at corpsales@pearsoned.com or (800) 382-3419.

For government sales inquiries, please contact governmentsales@pearsoned.com.

For questions about sales outside the U.S., please contact international@pearsoned.com.

Editor-in-Chief
Greg Wiegand

Executive Editor
Rick Kughen

Development Editor
Ginny Munroe

Managing Editor
Sandra Schroeder

Project Editor
Mandie Frank

Copy Editor
Geneil Breeze

Indexer
Erika Millen

Proofreader
Paula Lowell

Technical Editor
Joe Fino

Editorial Assistant
Kristen Watterson

Interior Designer
Mark Shirar

Cover Designer
Matt Coleman

Compositor
Trina Wurst

Contents at a Glance

Table of Contents

Part 2: Beyond the Basics

About the Author

Tim Dietrich is an independent database professional who specializes in FileMaker Pro. He designs custom database solutions that help organizations solve problems and achieve goals. He also offers FileMaker training and coaching to groups and individuals, with courses designed for users at all skill levels. His clients range from small businesses to government agencies to Fortune 50 organizations.

Tim has been developing with FileMaker Pro since 1992, and he is a FileMaker 9, 10, 11, 12, and 13 Certified Developer. He holds a Bachelor of Science degree from Towson University, where he studied Computer Science with a concentration in Information Systems.

Tim lives in Richmond, Virginia, with his wife, Kelly, and their son, Alex. To learn more about the author, visit his website at: http://timdietrich.me.

Dedication

I want to dedicate this book to my wife, Kelly, and my son, Alex. I could not have written this book without your inspiration, support, and patience. I love you both.

Acknowledgments

A great big thank you to Joe Fino, who served as the Technical Editor on this book. Thanks, Joe, for your help with the book and for your friendship over these many years.

I would also like to thank the team at Target Marketing—especially Ellen von Reiser, Jay Nathanson, and Jim Nathanson. Thank you for giving me the opportunity to get back into the world of FileMaker when I needed it the most. I will never forget your kindness and generosity.

Thanks to Carole Jelen, my literary agent at Waterside Productions, for approaching me about this book. You presented me with a rare opportunity, and I can't thank you enough.

Thank you to the team at Pearson Education—especially Rick Kughen and Mandie Frank. I truly appreciate your guidance and patience as I learned the ins and outs of the publishing world.

And last but certainly not least, thanks to the talented team at FileMaker Inc. You never cease to amaze me with your innovative solutions and your ability to move the platform forward.

We Want to Hear from You!

As the reader of this book, *you* are our most important critic and commentator. We value your opinion and want to know what we're doing right, what we could do better, what areas you'd like to see us publish in, and any other words of wisdom you're willing to pass our way.

We welcome your comments. You can email or write to let us know what you did or didn't like about this book—as well as what we can do to make our books better.

Please note that we cannot help you with technical problems related to the topic of this book.

When you write, please be sure to include this book's title and author as well as your name and email address. We will carefully review your comments and share them with the author and editors who worked on the book.

Email: feedback@quepublishing.com

Mail: Que Publishing
       ATTN: Reader Feedback
       800 East 96th Street
       Indianapolis, IN 46240 USA

Reader Services

Visit our website and register this book at quepublishing.com/register for convenient access to any updates, downloads, or errata that might be available for this book.

About This Book

INTRODUCTION

Welcome to the *Absolute Beginner's Guide to FileMaker Pro 13*. If you want to learn as much about FileMaker Pro as possible and as quickly as possible, this book is for you.

One of the nice things about FileMaker Pro is that it can provide you with a lot of power without overwhelming you with complexity. If you have even the most basic computer skills, but no prior experience in developing databases, you can quickly learn how to use FileMaker Pro to create databases that meet your specific needs. Best of all, you don't need to learn a programming language to do so.

But don't let FileMaker's ease-of-use fool you into thinking that it is a "lightweight" database. That couldn't be further from the truth. Many businesses, organizations, and educational institutions use FileMaker to manage complex and large databases, from inventory and sales contacts to historic records, and everything in between. FileMaker powers Web sites and provides mobile users with the information they need anytime, anywhere.

If you're new to FileMaker Pro, this combination of ease-of-use and power is good news, because it means that FileMaker Pro can handle your database needs now and as they evolve, and the time that you use to learn about FileMaker will be well spent.

About This Book

The approach for writing this book and presenting what you need to know is a little different from what you might see in some of the other database books available and different from the other FileMaker books and training materials available. The challenge in presenting the material in this book was determining where to start and the best order in which to present it.

The best way to learn about FileMaker Pro is to first make you the most knowledgeable FileMaker Pro user possible. When you have a good handle on how FileMaker Pro databases work, you can go to the next level to create your own databases and share them with other users.

The material is presented in four parts:

In **Part I, "Getting to Know FileMaker Pro,"** you learn what databases are, what they can be used for, and why FileMaker Pro is the ideal database program to use to create and work with them. You learn about the FileMaker Pro application environment and discover the main functions and the various ways to perform them. You also create your first database and learn to work with data and navigate around your database.

Part II, "Beyond the Basics," introduces advanced techniques that you can use to make changes to FileMaker databases. For example, you will learn how to add new fields (including fields based on calculation formulas and special "container" fields that you can use to store many different types of digital files), make changes to the database's interface, create reports and charts, and more.

Part III, "Caring for and Sharing a Database," details the ways you can protect your database and share it with other users (including those on mobile devices). You will also learn techniques for backing up your databases, and how to tell when you're at a point where you should consider hosting your database with FileMaker Server.

In **Part IV, "Building Your Own Database,"** you will learn how to design a database that meets your specific needs. You'll first learn how to identify the tables, fields, and relationships that you will need in the database. And then, using the knowledge that you will have gained from the first three parts of the book, you will create your database from scratch.

Throughout the book, you find tips and tricks that I've discovered throughout 20+ years of using FileMaker Pro.

We have a lot to cover, so let's get started!

1

WELCOME TO FILEMAKER PRO

If you're interested in FileMaker Pro and have gone so far as to purchase this book, chances are you have a good idea of what a database is. As a matter of fact, you're probably anxious to launch FileMaker Pro and create a database to meet your specific needs. Don't worry—we get to that soon enough.

However, before we dive into FileMaker Pro, it is important that you truly understand what a database is. This background will help you understand the true power that FileMaker Pro provides and help you create your own databases more efficiently and effectively.

What Is a Database?

Whether you realize it or not, you likely interact with databases several times every day. When you use a credit card, your account and purchase information is retrieved from and stored in a database. When you search for something on Google, the results come from a database. The address book on your phone and even your email messages are all subtle examples of databases that you probably use all the time without even realizing it.

In the simplest terms, a *database* is a collection of related information. For example, a database being used to manage books would include information about the books, their authors, the publishers, the book categories, and so on. A database used to manage photographs might include information about the locations in which the photos were taken, the photographers and models involved, the equipment used, and perhaps even digital versions of the photographs. Databases store information in an organized, structured manner so that it can be retrieved, analyzed, and updated as quickly and easily as possible. Databases are models of things that exist in the real world, and a number of different types of models can be used. The most common model is the relational database model, which is the type of model used by FileMaker Pro.

In a relational database, information is stored in one or more *tables* that represent the various "things" that the database is being used to keep track of. The book database would include tables for the books, authors, publishers, and categories. The photography database would include tables for the photographs, locations, photographers, models, and equipment.

The tables in a relational database are made up of *rows* and *columns*. In FileMaker, we refer to rows as *records* and columns as *fields*.

Each row represents one occurrence of the "thing" that it represents. In the book database, we would see a row for each book in the collection. In the photography database, each row would represent a photograph in the collection.

The columns in a table represent attributes of the things being stored. As shown in Figure 1.1, in the photography database, the equipment table might include columns for the model number, manufacturer, the date it was purchased, the cost, and so on. As shown in Figure 1.2, in the book database, the table might include columns for title, author, publisher, and category.

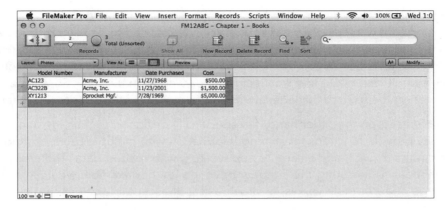

FIGURE 1.1

An equipment database might include columns for model number, manufacturer, date purchased, and cost. Notice that the each row represents a piece of equipment.

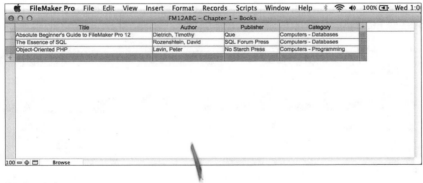

FIGURE 1.2

A database of books might include columns for the book title, author, publisher, and category. In this example, each row in the table represents a specific book.

Differences Between Databases and Spreadsheets

The rows and columns used to store information in relational databases seem a lot like the rows and columns that make up spreadsheets. In fact, at first glance, they seem so much alike that you might be wondering why you need databases at all. While they do appear to be similar, databases and spreadsheets are two entirely different things, intended for two entirely different purposes.

Spreadsheets are designed to help you analyze information, generate graphs, and experiment with "what if" scenarios. They are intended to be used by one person at a time and are usually limited with regard to the amount of information they can store. Spreadsheets do not provide functionality to help ensure the integrity of your data, and as a result, you might find inconsistencies and errors in the data. So while a spreadsheet can be used to manage information, it really isn't the right tool for that job.

Databases, on the other hand, are specifically designed to manage information. They provide functions for sharing information with multiple users, storing large amounts of data, and linking to and working with related data. The also provide functions for ensuring the integrity of your data. For example, you can specify a range of acceptable values, or provide lists of acceptable values that users can pick from, to help make the data accurate and consistent.

Databases also make it possible to view, work with, and present data in a variety of different ways. For example, you might work with data while viewing it as a list or as a form, or use it to generate reports, labels, or envelopes. Figures 1.3, 1.4, and 1.5 all show information from the same record, with the first figure showing the record as a form, the second showing it as part of a list, and the third as part of a list of address labels.

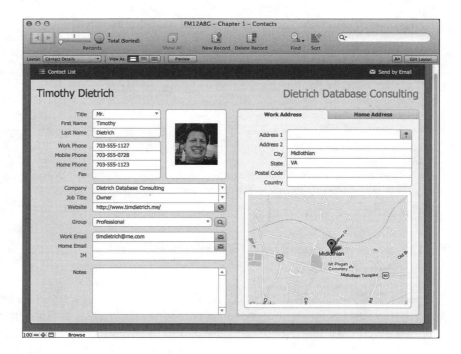

FIGURE 1.3

An example of a screen from a database used to manage contacts.

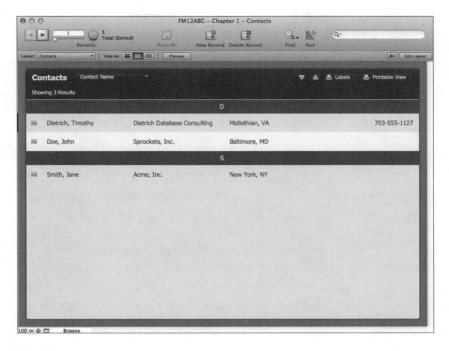

FIGURE 1.4

Another example of a screen from the same database.

Finally, databases typically provide functions for sharing data with other computer systems, including other types of relational databases and Web sites. Perhaps best of all, databases can share their data with other systems in real time, so that as soon as the data changes in your database, that change is reflected elsewhere. For example, a price change made in a product database would immediately be published on a Web site that uses that data.

Although it might help you to visualize database tables as if they are spreadsheets, keep in mind that databases and spreadsheets are two different things. Table 1.1 summarizes the differences between the two.

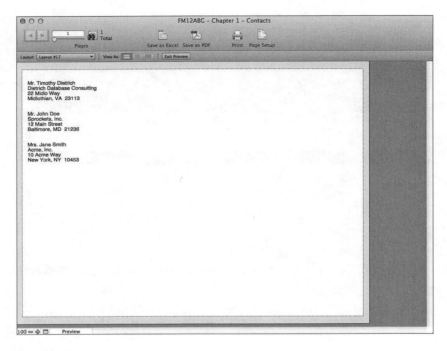

FIGURE 1.5

An example of an address label generated from the same database

TABLE 1.1 Differences Between Spreadsheets and Databases

Spreadsheets	Databases
Primarily used to perform calculations and analysis	Used to manage information and present it in various ways
Can be problematic if used by more than one person at a time	Can be accessed by multiple users at the same time, with built-in functions to prevent users from trying to change the same data at the same time
Limited with regard to the amount and types of data they can store	Can be used to store a large amount of data, and in various types, including text, dates, numbers, photos, movies, and other file types
Limited functionality to ensure the accuracy and reliability of data	Provide functions to ensure the accuracy and reliability of data

The Power of Databases

So far, we've talked about databases in general terms. You now know that databases are collections of related information, and that they store information in a way that makes it possible to retrieve it and update it quickly. But how can databases help you, exactly? Following is a list of features that can help you:

- **Forms**—With a database, you can set up forms to make adding and changing data easy. These forms might look like paper-based forms that you or your database's users are already accustomed to.

- **Rules**—You can set up rules so that the data being entered is consistent and accurate. For example, in a database used to manage orders, you might require that the order date be a valid date, that the price you're selling an item for is greater than your cost, or that the customer placing an order is set up in your database of customers. You might also require that certain data be provided, such as a customer's phone number or mailing address, or that the values in certain fields be unique (such as a customer's email address).

- **Relationships**—You can set up relationships between tables in your database, so that you can see related data in various places, and so that when something changes, you need to change it only in one place. For example, in the orders database described previously, when you are viewing a customer's order, you might also want to display that customer's address. If a customer's address changes, you would need to change it only in the Customers table, and the new address would automatically appear when you're looking at any orders that the customer has placed.

- **Records**—You can easily find records that meet your criteria. For example, maybe you want to see all customers that purchased a specific product. Or perhaps you want to see a list of your best customers, based on the total value of the orders that they placed this year. When you find the data that you are interested in, you can generate reports or graphs based on it.

- **Task automation**—You can automate repetitive or complex tasks. For example, suppose you need to generate a complex report every week, and there are multiple steps involved in generating it. You can make generating the report as easy as possible by "scripting" those steps.

- **Sharing capability**—You can also share your database so that multiple users can access it at the same time, and those users might even be in different locations. Continuing with the order database example, it might be that you have people taking orders in different branches around the country. A database makes it possible for each user to work with the data at the same time, and even prevent potential problems that might occur if multiple users try to update the same information at the exact same time.

- **Publishing capability**—You can publish your database to the Web. For example, you could give your customers a way to view the status of their orders, or their order history, through a secure Web site.

- **Data access**—You might want to provide your sales team, who are "out in the field," with access to data. For example, you might want to provide them with product information, inventory levels, and pricing, via their iPhones or iPads.

As you can see, databases—and FileMaker in particular—provide you with a lot of options. They let you manage, work with, and share information in exciting and powerful ways.

Why FileMaker?

In technical terms, FileMaker is a *relational database management system* (RDBMS). Other RDBMSes include SQL Server, Oracle, MySQL, and Microsoft Access. While all RDBMSes provide the tools and functions needed to create, manage, and use relational databases, FileMaker does so in ways a little different from the others.

FileMaker was designed to make setting up, managing, and using a database as easy as possible. In fact, it is so easy that it is possible for someone with little to no programming experience to develop her own databases, without having to learn a programming language. This makes FileMaker an ideal solution for individuals, small businesses, and workgroups that have limited IT resources.

As you see in Chapter 2, "Creating Your First Database," FileMaker provides built-in templates to help you quickly create databases for handling many common tasks, such as managing inventory and orders, tracking expenses, managing contacts, and more. You can customize those databases to meet your specific needs.

You can also easily create your own databases entirely from scratch. FileMaker provides an intuitive, graphical interface to make that process as easy as possible—and again, without needing to learn a programming language. For example, you can point and click to create scripts that automate common or repetitive tasks for you, or to create relationships between related tables. You can even use drag and drop tools to create powerful reports and a variety of different types of charts. And with FileMaker's new "layout themes," your solutions look like they are professionally designed.

FileMaker makes it easy to share your databases with other users—even if they don't own FileMaker themselves. With a single click, you make your database available to users who can access it using a Web browser. FileMaker also provides powerful security options, so that you can specify what users can see or do in your database.

Other RDBMSes aren't nearly as easy to use. Most require that you have programming experience. Their tools aren't nearly as friendly and intuitive as FileMaker's are. And if you're hoping to use one of those other RDBMSes to develop a database quickly, you might be in for a surprise.

Understanding the FileMaker Platform

FileMaker is actually a software platform that consists of FileMaker Pro, FileMaker Pro Advanced, FileMaker Go, and FileMaker Server. It's important that you understand the differences between the products. Table 1.2 lists some of the differences.

TABLE 1.2 The FileMaker Platform

Product	Purpose
FileMaker Pro	FileMaker Pro is used to create and work with FileMaker databases. It can be run on Macs or Windows-based PCs. This book will primarily focus on FileMaker Pro, although we will also discuss FileMaker Server and FileMaker Go.
FileMaker Pro Advanced	FileMaker Pro Advanced includes all of the tools and functionality found in FileMaker Pro, plus additional tools that a professional database developer will find helpful. For example, with FileMaker Pro Advanced, you can create custom menus and custom functions, use a special tool to help debug complicated scripts, and more. (If you don't have FileMaker Pro, don't worry. The examples in this book assume that you are using the standard version of FileMaker Pro.)
FileMaker Server	FileMaker Server is used to host databases, so that they are available to multiple simultaneous users in a safe and secure manner. It is intended to be run on a dedicated Mac or Windows-based server. While it isn't absolutely necessary that you host your databases using FileMaker Server, we will discuss why you might want to do so in a Chapter 16, "Sharing a Database."
FileMaker Go	FileMaker Go is used to access FileMaker databases using iOS-based mobile devices (such as iPhones, iPads, and iPad Touches). Unlike FileMaker Pro and FileMaker Pro Advanced, FileMaker Go cannot be used to create new FileMaker Pro databases, or to change the structure of existing databases. Instead, it can be used to access and work with data that is stored in existing FileMaker databases, whether those databases are on a server or on the mobile device itself. FileMaker Go is provided as a free application on the App Store. we will talk more about FileMaker Go in Chapter 17, "Taking Data with You."

NOTE   Databases created with FileMaker Pro running on a Mac can be opened by users running FileMaker Pro on a Windows-based computer, and vice versa.

 NOTE   As of the writing of this book, the latest version of FileMaker is version 13, so the official names of the products are FileMaker Pro 13, FileMaker Pro 13 Advanced, FileMaker Go 13, and FileMaker Server 13. However, throughout the book, we simply call them FileMaker Pro FileMaker Pro Advanced, FileMaker Go, and FileMaker Server.

What Can FileMaker Do for You?

You can use FileMaker Pro to create a wide variety of databases for use in your business or personal life.

For your business, you can create databases to keep track of several things, including

- Inventory or supplies
- A product catalog
- Customers
- Suppliers
- Orders
- Quotes and proposals

For you personal use, you might want to create databases to track the following:

- Your home inventory
- Your book, music, or movie collections
- Your baseball card collection
- Research notes for a school project that you're working on
- Members of a club that you belong to or manage

With FileMaker, the possibilities are endless. Once you begin using FileMaker Pro, you quickly discover other things that can use it for.

THE ABSOLUTE MINIMUM

This chapter provided you with some important background regarding databases in general. Here are the key points to remember:

- Databases are collections of related information.

- Relational databases organize information using a structure that consists of tables, rows, and columns.

- While databases and spreadsheets both use rows and columns to store data, they are different tools intended to perform two different sets of tasks.

- Relational databases are extremely powerful, and they give us the ability to manage, work with, and share information in exciting and powerful ways.

- FileMaker is different from other database software because it is easy to use and requires no formal IT training or programming experience.

- FileMaker is actually a family of software that includes FileMaker Pro/FileMaker Pro Advanced (which is used to create and work with FileMaker databases), FileMaker Server (which can be used to host FileMaker databases), and FileMaker Go (which provides iPhone, iPad, and iPod Touch users with a way to work with FileMaker databases from their mobile devices).

IN THIS CHAPTER

- Getting Started Tour
- FileMaker Quick Start
- Creating a Database Using a Starter Solution
- Saving and Closing a Database
- Quitting FileMaker

2

CREATING YOUR FIRST DATABASE

In Chapter 1, "Welcome to FileMaker Pro," you learned about databases in general, and about some of the powerful and amazing things you can do with databases created with FileMaker Pro. In this chapter, you launch FileMaker Pro and create your first database using a template (what FileMaker refers to as a *Starter Solution*). In upcoming chapters, you use this database to get to know your way around FileMaker, to learn important FileMaker concepts, and more.

Getting Started Tour

To get started, open FileMaker Pro. If this is the first time you have opened the application, you see the FileMaker Getting Started Tour, as shown in Figure 2.1.

FIGURE 2.1

FileMaker's Getting Started Tour.

This tour is an interactive introduction to some of the key features of FileMaker Pro. We discuss all the features covered in the tour in much more depth. However, if you want to take a few minutes to go through the tour, feel free to do so by clicking the Start the Tour button.

 TIP If you want to view the Getting Started Tour in the future, you can do so by selecting Help > Product Documentation > Getting Started Tour.

After you finish the Getting Started Tour, simply close either of the two windows.

FileMaker Quick Start

You now see the FileMaker Quick Start screen (see Figure 2.2). If you do not, select Quick Start Screen from the Help menu.

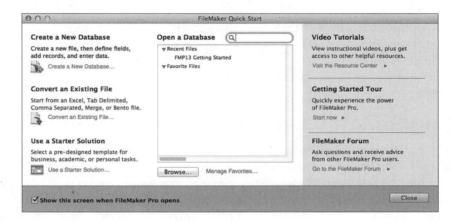

FIGURE 2.2

FileMaker's Quick Start screen.

The Quick Start screen does exactly what you might expect: It helps you to get started with FileMaker Pro as quickly as possible, regardless of whether you want to create a new database or work with an existing database. The Quick Start screen provides a lot of options, so let's take a moment to learn about them.

The leftmost column of the Quick Start screen provides three options for creating a new database:

- **Create a New Database** is used when you are creating a database from scratch. This involves creating your own tables, adding fields, setting up layouts, and more. We learn to do those types of things in Part II, "Beyond the Basics," and then create a database from scratch in Chapter 19, "Creating Your Database."

- **Convert an Existing File** enables you to create a FileMaker Pro 13 database based on data that already exists in another type of file. You can create a FileMaker database using data in an Excel spreadsheet, a tab or comma-separated text file, a dBase database, and a few other types of files.

- **Use a Starter Solution** is used when you want to create a new database based on a predesigned template that FileMaker provides. We use this option later in this chapter to create your first database.

In the middle of the Quick Start screen, you see a list of databases that you have worked with in the past. (If you are just getting started with FileMaker Pro, the list might be empty.) Below the list is a Browse button that you can use to navigate to and open a database, as well as a link that you can use to manage your favorite FileMaker database files. We discuss favorites in Chapter 3, "Exploring FileMaker Pro."

The rightmost column of the Quick Start screen provides links to three helpful FileMaker Pro resources, including Video Tutorials, the Getting Started Tour, and the FileMaker Forums. The FileMaker Forums are a Web site where you can get help and advice from members of the FileMaker community.

Creating a Database Using a Starter Solution

The easiest way to create a new FileMaker Pro database is to use a Starter Solution. *Starter Solutions* are predefined database templates designed to meet several common needs, such as managing contacts, inventory, and so on. Databases created from Starter Solutions can be used as is, or customized to meet your specific needs. These Starter Solutions have been professionally developed, so they are good examples that you can use to learn how to create your own databases.

Let's take a quick look at the Starter Solutions available. Click the Use a Starter Solution link, and the Starter Solution window opens (see Figure 2.3).

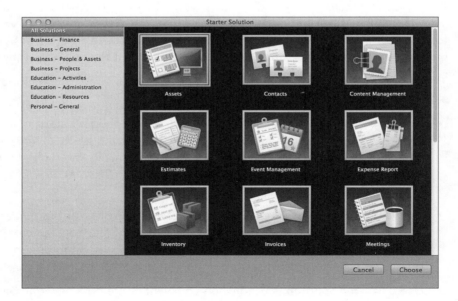

FIGURE 2.3

FileMaker's Starter Solutions.

The Starter Solutions are divided into three general categories: Business, Education, and Personal. The Business and Education Starter Solutions are also subcategorized. An All Solutions category is also provided, and it lists all the Starter Solutions available.

Click on a category in the leftmost column of the Starter Solution window to see the types of Starter Solutions available.

Now, let's use a Starter Solution to create your first FileMaker Pro database. Throughout this book, we use the Contacts solution. However, I encourage you to also explore the other Starter Solutions.

The Contacts Starter Solution is listed in several categories, including Business - People & Assets, Education - Administration, Personal - General, and of course, All Solutions. Once you have located it, either double-click it or select it and click the Choose button.

Next, a dialog box displays, and you are asked to provide a name for the new database and a location to save it to (see Figure 2.4). Let's use the name that FileMaker Pro suggests (which is a name relevant to the Starter Solution that you selected), and save it in the suggested location (which is typically the Documents folder on your hard drive). Click the Save button. Your new database is created, and a new FileMaker window opens displaying the new database.

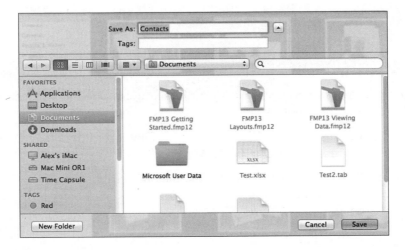

FIGURE 2.4

Dialog window used to name a new database and specify its location.

Congratulations! You just created your first FileMaker Pro database! I'm sure you are anxious to start using your new database, and we do that in Chapter 3. But at this point, let's learn how to close a FileMaker database.

Saving and Closing a Database

Unlike many other applications, when you close a FileMaker database, there is no need to save your database file before closing it or quitting FileMaker Pro. When you close a database, all the changes that you have made to it are saved automatically. This includes any changes made to the structure of the database (the tables, fields, and relationships), the screens/layouts that you created, as well as changes made to the data stored in the database.

There are several ways to close a FileMaker database:

- Use the File > Close menu command.

- Use a keyboard shortcut. On a Mac, it is Command+W. On a Windows-based computer, it is Ctrl+W.

- Close the last window that you opened to the database.

 NOTE When you close a database, all the windows that you have open to that database are closed. You do not need to close each window individually.

When you close a database, FileMaker Pro remains open, as do any other databases that you happen to have open. However, if you quit FileMaker Pro, then all the databases close at that time.

Quitting FileMaker

When you are finished using FileMaker Pro, you can quit the application using one of the following methods:

- On a Mac, use the FileMaker Pro > Quit FileMaker Pro command. On Windows, use File > Quit FileMaker Pro.

- Use a keyboard shortcut. On a Mac, the shortcut is Command+Q. On a Windows-based computer, it is Ctrl+Q.

Let's quit FileMaker Pro now. In Chapter 3, we start FileMaker Pro again, open the Contacts database created in this chapter, and start working with it.

THE ABSOLUTE MINIMUM

In this chapter, you launched FileMaker Pro and created your first FileMaker Pro database using a Starter Solution. Here are some key points to remember:

- FileMaker Pro's Quick Start window provides access to several important functions and resources. From the Quick Start window, you can create new databases, open existing databases, and access helpful FileMaker-related resources.

- FileMaker Pro includes several database templates called Starter Solutions. You can use Starter Solutions to quickly create databases that address common business, education, and personal needs.

- Unlike other applications, when you close a FileMaker database, all your changes are automatically saved for you. There is no need to save your work before closing the file.

3

EXPLORING FILEMAKER PRO

Now that you have a database to work with, we can begin to explore the FileMaker Pro environment. To do so, we open the database, and then work our way from the top of the screen to the bottom, starting with the menu commands, then the Status Toolbar, and then the content area.

Opening a FileMaker Pro Database

In Chapter 2, "Creating Your First Database," you learned several ways to create a new FileMaker Pro database, and you created your first database using a Starter Solution. In this chapter, you learn how to open an existing database.

To get started, open FileMaker Pro to display the FileMaker Quick Start screen (see Figure 3.1). If it does not display, select Quick Start Screen from the Help menu. The screen should look much like it did when we used it in Chapter 2.

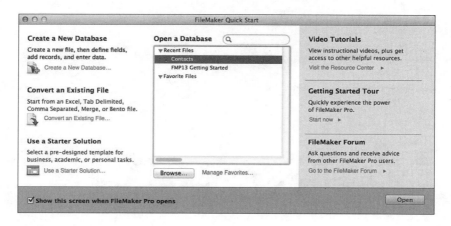

FIGURE 3.1

FileMaker's Quick Start screen, with the Contacts database listed as one of the Recent Files.

Opening a Recently Used Database

Notice that in the center of the screen, in the Open a Database area, that a database is now listed under Recent Files. The fastest way to open a database that you recently worked with is to locate it in the Recent Files list and double-click it. Alternatively, you can view a list of recent files by selecting the Open Recent command from the File menu.

Opening Other Databases

If the database that you want to use isn't one that you used recently, there are other ways to locate and open it.

One method to locate the file is to browse or search for it on your hard drive. When you find the file, double-click it to open it in FileMaker Pro.

Another method to locate the file is to browse for it from within FileMaker Pro. To do so, click the Browse button in the Quick Start window, or select the Open command from the File menu. The Open File window displays, and you can use it to locate the file. When you find the file, double-click to open it.

The methods discussed assume that the database you want to work with is located on your computer. However, you can also open databases hosted on other computers. You learn how to do that in Chapter 16, "Sharing a Database."

TIP   FileMaker Pro provides a convenient way for you to access your "favorite" databases. A list of your favorite databases is available in the Quick Start menu (located below the list of Recent Files), or you can access the list by selecting the Open Favorite command from the File menu. To manage your favorites, either click the Manage Favorites link in the Quick Start window, or select File > Open Favorite > Manage Favorites. Click the + button to locate and add a database to your list of favorites. To remove a favorite from the list, select it, and then click the - button.

Menu Commands

Now that your Contacts database is open, let's explore the FileMaker environment and learn to navigate around a database. Like other applications that you work with, FileMaker Pro provides easy access of its functionality via the menu bar at the top of the screen. The menus available when you first open a FileMaker Pro database include File, Edit, View, Insert, Format, Records, Scripts, Window, and Help. Let's examine each of these menus to see the commands that they provide access to.

NOTE   As you examine FileMaker's menus, you might notice that some commands are dimmed or "grayed" out. This indicates that the command is not available at the moment, either because it is not applicable, or because you do not have the privileges needed to use the command. We talk about privilege sets in Chapter 14, "Protecting a Database."

TIP   FileMaker Pro provides keyboard shortcuts for many of its commands. As you explore the menus, you see symbols next to commands for which a shortcut is supported. For example, next to the Records > New Record command, you can see the Command symbol followed by the letter N (if you are using a Mac), or Ctrl+N (if you are using a Windows-based computer). To see a list of the keyboard shortcuts that FileMaker Pro supports, choose Keyboard Shortcuts from the Help menu.

The File Menu

The File menu (see Figure 3.2) includes commands used to create new databases, open existing databases, close databases, and more. A number of these commands are similar to options available on the FileMaker Quick Start screen. However, the File menu provides several additional commands that you need when a database is open, including Close, Manage, Sharing, and a few others.

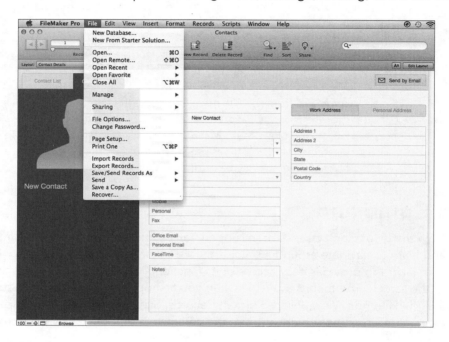

FIGURE 3.2

FileMaker's File menu.

The Edit Menu

The commands available via the Edit menu (see Figure 3.3) are used to work with data in fields. For example, there are commands that you can use to copy and paste values into fields, to clear field values, to spell check text entered into a field, to export the contents of a field to another file, and more.

FIGURE 3.3

FileMaker's Edit menu.

The View Menu

The View menu (see Figure 3.4) includes commands that affect the way that you see and work with a database.

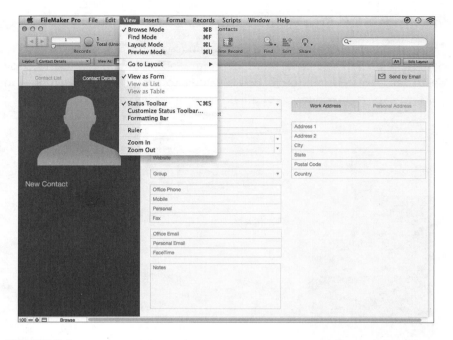

FIGURE 3.4

FileMaker's View menu.

Modes and Layouts

The first four commands listed under the View menu are used to change the mode that you are working in. When you are working with a FileMaker Pro database, you are always in one of four modes: Browse mode, Find mode, Layout mode, and Preview mode.

Browse mode is used to work with the data in a database. In Browse mode, you can add, update, and delete records. When you are working with a FileMaker Pro database, you spend the majority of your time in Browse mode. In fact, when you first open a database, FileMaker is in Browse mode.

Find mode is used to query the database and to work with a set of records that meet specific criteria. In FileMaker Pro, this process is often referred to as *performing a find*, and the set of records you are working with is known as the *found set*.

NOTE   In FileMaker Pro, the set of records that you are currently working with is the *found set*. For example, suppose that you have a table that contains several hundred records, and you perform a find on that table such that only 25 of the records meet your criteria. In that case, your found set would consist of only those 25 records. We talk more about the found set concept in Chapter 6, "Finding Records."

The forms and reports that you use to work with and view data in FileMaker Pro databases are referred to as layouts. You use *Layout mode* to create, change, and delete layouts. Layouts are covered in depth in Chapter 11, "Working with Layouts."

Preview mode allows you to see what a layout would look like if you were to print it or save it as a PDF document. When you are in Preview mode, you can see data, but you cannot change it.

TIP   If you are ever unsure as to what mode you are in, look in the bottom-left corner of the window. There you see the name of the mode that you are currently in.

We talk more about FileMaker's modes, and switch back and forth between them, throughout the course of this book. However, let's continue to explore FileMaker in Browse mode.

NOTE   When you change modes, the menu commands (as well as the contents of the Status Toolbar, which we discuss in a moment) change as well. The menu commands displayed are those applicable to the mode that you are in. For example, when you are in Browse mode, the menu commands available are applicable to working with data (such as those to add or delete a record), while the menu commands available when you're in Find mode are those applicable to filtering data. In this chapter, we focus on the menus available when you're in Browse mode.

In addition to providing commands to change modes, the View menu also provides the Go To Layout command, which is used to change the layout that you are working on. In our Contacts database, you can see eight layouts available to choose from, and that they have been grouped into folders (Desktop, iPad, iPhone, and Web). The check mark that appears next to Desktop > Contact Details indicates the layout that you are currently on.

TIP   The name of the layout that you are working on is also listed in the bottom-left corner of the Status Toolbar. That name is actually a button, and clicking it opens a drop-down menu that you can use to navigate between layouts.

Layout Views

Three of the commands listed under the View menu are used to change the way records are displayed on the current layout. You can view data on a layout in three different ways.

In *Form view*, data is displayed from only one record at a time. This is the view most often used when entering data.

In *List view*, data from the records in the found set is displayed in a continuous list. You can scroll up and down through the list of records to see their data. This is the view that you typically use to review multiple records at one time.

In *Table view*, data from the records in the found set is presented as a table. The rows of the table represent the records, while the columns represent fields. Table view is similar to what you see when working with a spreadsheet.

Hiding and Displaying Toolbars

The View menu also provides commands that you can use to change the FileMaker Pro window. For example, you can choose to show or hide the status and formatting toolbars.

Zooming In and Out

You can use the Zoom In and Zoom Out commands to adjust the scale at which you see the layout. The scale is normally 100%. However, you can zoom in and out to change the scale to as low as 25% and to as high as 400%.

TIP   The number in the lower-left corner of the window indicates the scale at which you are currently viewing the screen's contents, and the minus and plus buttons can be used to zoom out and zoom in, respectively.

The Insert Menu

The commands available under the Insert menu (see Figure 3.5) help you put values and files into fields. These commands make it easy for you to insert the current date or time, the user's name, and more.

FileMaker Pro supports a special type of field known as a *container*, into which you can place entire files, including pictures, movies, sounds, PDF files, and more. The Insert menu includes a few commands that enable you to insert the files. We discuss container fields in Chapter 9, "Working with Fields."

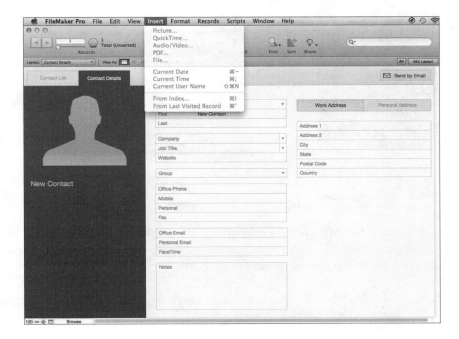

FIGURE 3.5

FileMaker's Insert menu.

The Format Menu

In FileMaker Pro, text that has been entered into a field can be formatted. You can use the commands listed under the Format menu (see Figure 3.6) to change the font, size, style, alignment, line spacing, and color of values entered into a field.

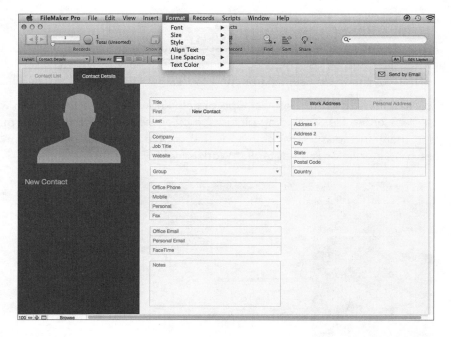

FIGURE 3.6

FileMaker's Format menu.

It is important to note that the formatting you apply to a value in a field applies only to the record that you are on when you apply the formatting. The formatting does not apply to other records in the table.

 TIP You can also change the format of text by using the formatting bar, which appears below the Status Toolbar. If you don't see it, you can enable it by selecting Formatting Bar from the View menu, or by clicking the "Aa" button located toward the bottom-right corner of the Status Toolbar.

The Records Menu

The commands available under the Records menu (see Figure 3.7) help you to work with and navigate between records in a table. This menu includes commands for adding a new record, duplicating an existing record, and deleting a record (or a group of records).

The Go To Record submenu includes additional commands used navigate to the previous or next record, or to jump directly to a specific record (based on its position in the found set).

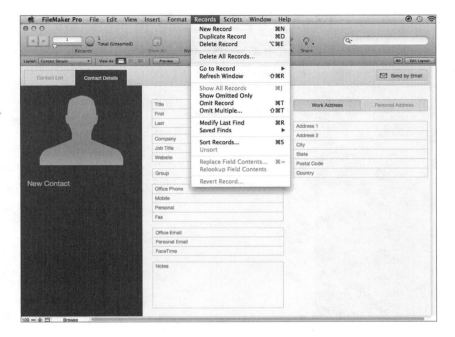

FIGURE 3.7

FileMaker's Records menu.

The Records menu also includes commands that can be used to change the found set. For example, you can see commands that can be used to omit one or more records, to modify the last find that you performed, to perform a find whose criteria you have saved, to sort records, and more. We cover the find-related commands in Chapter 6.

The Scripts Menu

Chapter 1, "Welcome to FileMaker Pro," mentioned that one of the benefits of using a database is that repetitive or complex tasks can be automated. The example given was one where a report needs to be generated on a weekly basis, and multiple steps are involved in doing so. In FileMaker Pro, you can create a script to automate that process.

The Scripts menu (see Figure 3.8) provides access to the command that we use to create, update, delete, and organize scripts. It can also be used to provide easy access to certain scripts via the menu itself. we discuss scripts in detail in Chapter 13, "Automating Tasks with Scripts."

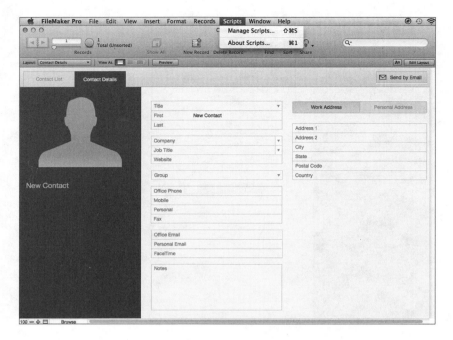

FIGURE 3.8

FileMaker's Scripts menu.

The Window Menu

When working in FileMaker Pro, you might want to work with several FileMaker databases at the same time—and FileMaker Pro supports doing so. In fact, you might use a database that references related data in another FileMaker database, and that database might open up automatically without your even realizing it.

When you open multiple databases, each opens in its own window. And that's where the Window menu comes into play (see Figure 3.9). From that menu, you can open windows, hide windows, reposition windows, and see a list of any open windows so that you can navigate between them.

The first command listed under the Window menu is New Window. When you select this option, a new window is created based on the window that you are currently on. In other words, you can use this feature to open two (or more) windows to the same database. The new window uses the same layout, mode, found set, and sort order that the original has. However, in the new window, you can navigate to another layout, change the found set and sort order, and so on—and the original window's state remains unchanged. This is a helpful, powerful feature of FileMaker Pro. It's as if you were running two copies of FileMaker at the same time!

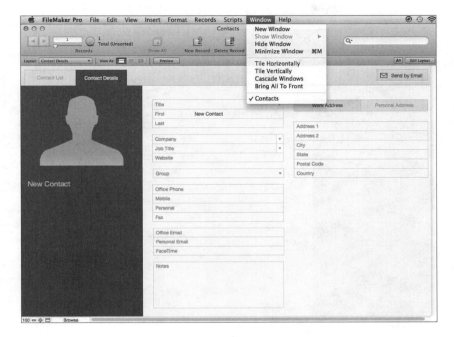

FIGURE 3.9

FileMaker's Window menu.

When you select the Hide Window command, the current window disappears, and it might appear that you have closed the window. However, the window is still open; you can see it listed under the Window > Show Window submenu.

The Tile Horizontally, Tile Vertically, Cascade Windows, and Bring All To Front commands all automatically reposition the windows that you have open. You might find these to be helpful when you have several windows open and want to quickly see the contents of each one.

Finally, at the bottom of the Window menu, you see a list of the windows that you have open. The check mark next to one of the windows indicates the window that you are currently viewing. You can jump to another window by selecting it from this list.

The Help Menu

FileMaker Pro's Help menu (see Figure 3.10) provides access to a number of resources that are helpful as you use FileMaker Pro, and even more helpful as you begin to develop your own databases.

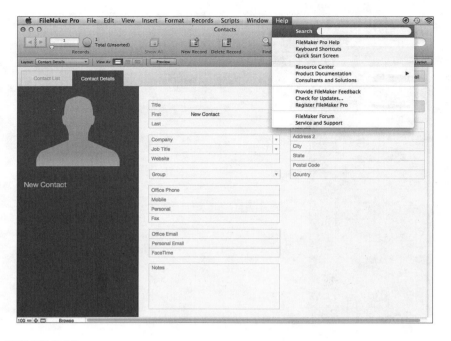

FIGURE 3.10

FileMaker's Help menu.

The Help menu includes a search function that you use to look up topics in FileMaker's built-in help system. You can also browse the contents of the help system by selecting the FileMaker Pro Help command.

The Help menu also provides links to several online resources, including the FileMaker Resource Center and FileMaker Forum (which is also available on the Quick Start screen).

One of the more interesting commands available via the Help menu is Check for Updates. You can use this command to see whether you are running the latest version of FileMaker Pro, and if not, you can jump directly to a Web page to learn more about and download any available updates.

 TIP   You can have FileMaker Pro automatically check for updates by setting the application's preferences. To do so, first open up the Preferences dialog window. (On a Mac, this is available via FileMaker Pro > Preferences. On a Windows-based computer, use File > Preferences.) The preferences that you need to set are listed in the Application area of the General tab.

The Status Toolbar

Below the menu commands, and at the top of window, is FileMaker's Status Toolbar (shown in Figure 3.11). It includes navigation controls for moving between records and layouts, information about the records you are working with, as well as buttons that you can use to perform some of the more commonly used commands.

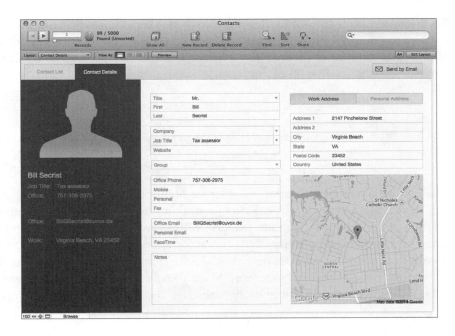

FIGURE 3.11

The Status Toolbar displayed in Browse mode.

   NOTE   Like the menu bar, the contents of the Status Toolbar change depending on the mode that you are working in. In this section, we cover the Status Bar as it appears and functions when you're in Browse mode.

Moving Between Records

In the leftmost corner of the Status Toolbar, you see what FileMaker refers to as "the book." The left page acts as a button that you can click to go to the previous record, and the right page acts as a button that takes you to the next record.

The number next to the book indicates the number of the record you are currently on, based on its position in the found set. The number is actually a field, and you can type into it to jump directly to a specific record in the list of records you are working with. (For example, enter "3" to jump to the third record.) Below the current record number field is a slider that you can use to move between records.

Information About the Found Set

To the right of the current record number field is a pie chart that graphically depicts the number of records that you are viewing in the found set, compared to the total number of records in the table. The chart might appear as an empty circle if you are viewing all of the records in the table.

 TIP If you want to see the records omitted from your found set, you can click the pie chart in the Status Bar. Doing so changes your found set to the records that had been omitted. Click the pie chart again to return to your original found set. (This is equivalent to performing the Records > Show Omitted Only command.)

Next to the pie chart is another number (or numbers, depending on your found set). If you see a single number listed here, that number indicates the number of records in the table that you are working with. However, if you see two numbers listed and separated by a backslash character, the number to the left indicates the number of records in your found set, while the number to the right is the number of records in the table. For example, "7 / 35" indicates that your found set consists of 7 records out of a total of 35 records in the table.

Below the number is either the word "Total" (indicating that you are looking at all records in the table), or "Found" (indicating that you are looking at only a portion of the records in the table). And finally, next to "Total" or "Found" is a word in parentheses. That word either is "Unsorted" (which indicates that the records you are viewing are in no particular order), "Sorted" (which indicates that the records are in a particular order), or "Semi-Sorted" (which indicates that some of the records are sorted, and some are not). We discuss the concept of sorting records in Chapter 7.

The Status Toolbar Buttons

Also included in the Status Toolbar are buttons that you can use to perform some of the more commonly used FileMaker Pro commands. For example, you see buttons for performing tasks such as adding a record, deleting a record, performing a find, and sorting records.

NOTE Like the menu commands listed in the menu bar, there may be times where buttons in the Status Bar appear to be "grayed out." In those cases, either the commands that the buttons represent are not applicable at that time, or you do not have the privileges needed to use those commands, so the buttons have been disabled. For example, the Show All button changes your found set so that it includes all the records in the table. If your found set already includes all the records in the table, then the Show All button is disabled.

 TIP If you are not sure what a button does, hover your mouse over it for a second. A tooltip appears and explains what the button does.

 TIP You might find that you use certain FileMaker Pro commands frequently, and they are not available as buttons in the Status Toolbar. If that's the case, you can customize the Status Toolbar to add icons for those commands. To do so, use the View > Customize Status Toolbar menu item.

Quick Find

The final component of the Status Toolbar is the Quick Find field. We discuss Quick Find in detail in Chapter 6. However, here is a brief overview of this powerful FileMaker function.

There are times when you want to find records that meet specific criteria. For example, in your Contacts database, you might be interested in seeing the records of people who live in the state of Virginia. In that case, you would perform a find by entering Find mode, typing "Virginia" into the State field, and performing the find. In that example, our criteria were specific. We only wanted records where "Virginia" was the value in the State field.

However, at other times we might want to locate records that contain a certain keyword, and it might appear in any number of fields. For example, suppose that we are interested in all records that contain the keyword "Acme." In that case, we could simply enter "Acme" into the Quick Find field, press the Return key, and FileMaker finds the records where "Acme" appears in the Company field, the Notes field, and so on. Without the Quick Find function, we would need to perform a much more complex find, or series of finds, to locate the matching records.

Additional Tools

The bottom row of the Status Toolbar includes additional tools that you might find helpful.

First, there's the Layout pop-up menu. As I mentioned earlier, you can use this to determine what layout you are currently working on and to quickly move to another layout.

Three small View As buttons are listed next, and they correspond to the three layout views described earlier in this chapter. From left to right, the buttons can be used to change to Form, List, or Table view.

The Preview button can be used to quickly view the layout in Preview mode.

The bottom right-hand corner of the Status Toolbar includes a button that you can use to toggle the display of the Formatting Bar (which provides buttons that you can use to format text in a field). You also see an Edit Layout button, which serves as a shortcut to place you into Layout mode.

The Content Area

Below the Status Toolbar is the content area. This is the area in which you work with data, view reports, perform finds, and more.

THE ABSOLUTE MINIMUM

In this chapter, we began exploring the FileMaker Pro application environment, including the many different commands available. Here are the key points to remember:

- It is common for FileMaker Pro's commands to be accessible in several different ways and in several locations, including the command menus, as keyboard shortcuts, as buttons in the Status Toolbar, and more.

- In FileMaker Pro, the forms and reports that we use to work with and view data are called layouts.

- When working with a FileMaker database, there are four different modes that you work in. You use Browse mode to work with data, Find mode to find records that meet certain criteria, Layout mode to work with layouts, and Preview mode to see what your layout will look like if you print it.

- It is possible to work with multiple FileMaker databases at the same time, and when doing so, each database appears in its own window. It is also possible to work on the same database in multiple windows.

4

WORKING WITH RECORDS

In Chapter 3, "Exploring FileMaker Pro," you became familiar with the FileMaker Pro application environment. You learned about the commands that FileMaker Pro provides and the various ways that you can access them.

In this chapter, you use what you learned to explore and work with the database you created. You change, add, and delete records; navigate through records and layouts; and much more. This chapter provides you a more thorough understanding of how to use a FileMaker Pro database.

Changing an Existing Record

When you created the Contacts database, FileMaker Pro automatically added the first record for you. With the exception of the First Name field, the record is empty. Let's change that record by entering data in the fields.

1. Click the Title field. A drop-down menu displays. Here, you can select a title. Select a value from the list. Notice that the field has a thin highlight around it. That's how you can tell which field you are in.

2. Click the First Name field. Enter your first name in the field.

3. Click the Last Name field and enter your last name.

4. Save the changes that you made to the record. In database terms, we refer to the act of saving changes to a record as *committing the changes*. To commit your changes, click anywhere in the content area of the window where a field or button isn't present.

Adding a New Record

Let's add a new record to the database. As you might have guessed, FileMaker Pro provides several ways to add records, including

- Click the New Record button in the Status Toolbar.
- Select the New Record command from the Records menu.
- Use a keyboard shortcut. On a Mac, the shortcut is Command+N, and in Windows, it is Ctrl+N.

After you choose one of the previous methods, a new record is created. Again, with the exception of the First Name field, the fields are blank. Click the fields to enter some values.

Duplicating a Record

In some cases, you might want to create a new record based on values from an existing record. This is called *duplicating* a record.

There are a couple of ways to duplicate a record:

- Select the Duplicate Record command from the Records menu.
- Use the keyboard shortcut. On a Mac, the shortcut is Command+D, and in Windows, it is Ctrl+D.

When duplicating a record, a new record is created with values from the original record. Of course, you can make changes to the duplicate record if you need to do so.

Canceling Changes to a Record

Suppose that you start to make changes to a record, and then realize that you don't want to make those changes after all. As long as you haven't committed the changes (by clicking outside a field in the content area of the screen), you can cancel (or undo) your changes.

To do so, select the Revert Record command from the Records menu. A dialog box displays (see Figure 4.1) and asks whether you really want to revert all changes to this record since it was last entered.

FIGURE 4.1

The dialog box that displays when you attempt to revert changes to a record.

Click the Revert button, and the record is set back to the values that it had when you started making changes to it.

If the Revert Record command is grayed out, this is an indication that the changes you made to the record have already been committed. Unfortunately, at that point there is no easy way to revert the record to its initial values.

TIP The Revert Record command also comes in handy when you start to create a new record and then change your mind. Instead of saving the new record, you can cancel it by selecting the Revert Record command.

Moving Between Fields

So far, when adding or changing values in fields, you have moved between the fields by clicking them. That works, but can be tedious. Fortunately, there is a much easier way to move between fields. In FileMaker Pro, the Tab key can be used to move from one field to the next. Similarly, you can use Shift+Tab to move to the previous field.

As you tab between fields on a layout, FileMaker usually determines which field to place you in based on the field to the right of the current field, or, if there is no field to the right, to the field below the current field. However, as you see in Chapter 11, "Working with Layouts," you can specify the order in which fields are entered as you tab through them.

Moving Between Records

If you haven't already done so, create a few additional test records. We need them to demonstrate how to move between records.

 TIP   Remember that you can easily see the number of records in the table by looking at the Status Toolbar. The number that appears to the right of the pie chart indicates the number of records in the table.

In Chapter 3, "Exploring FileMaker Pro," we discussed several components of the Status Toolbar that can be used to move between records. Let's use those to move between the test records you created.

First, let's use the book (the navigation control in the leftmost area of the Status Toolbar) to move between records. Simply click the left-hand page of the book to move to the previous record, and click the right-hand page to move to the next record.

Notice that as you move between records, the number of the record displayed changes in the Status Toolbar. As discussed in Chapter 3, that number is the current record's position within the set of records that you are working with. If you want to go directly to another record, simply enter a number into the current record field. For example, to go to the fourth record, enter the number 4 and press the Enter or Return key.

You can also navigate between records by using the slider control that appears below the current record number field. Click on it and drag it to move from one record to another. This can be helpful when browsing through a large set of records and trying to familiarize yourself with them.

Deleting a Record

So far, we added new records and made changes to existing records. Now let's delete a record.

To do so, first navigate to the record that you want to delete.

CAUTION   Before deleting a record, always confirm that you really are on the record that you want to delete. Once a record has been deleted, there is no way to restore it.

Next, use the Delete Record command to start the process of deleting the record. To do so, use one of these methods:

- Click the Delete Record button in the Status Toolbar.

- Select the Delete Record command from the Records menu.

- Use a keyboard shortcut. On a Mac, the shortcut is Command+E. On Windows, it is Ctrl+E.

Before deleting a record, FileMaker Pro wants to be sure that you really do want to delete it. When you choose the Delete Record command, a dialog box displays (see Figure 4.2) and asks whether you want to permanently delete this entire record.

FIGURE 4.2

The dialog box that displays when you choose to delete a record.

If you are certain that you want to delete the record, click the Delete button. Otherwise, click Cancel, and no harm is done.

Deleting Multiple Records

FileMaker Pro also provides a command for deleting multiple records at one time. The command, located under the Records menu, displays differently depending on the current set of records that you are viewing.

If you are viewing all the records in the table, the command is listed as Delete All Records. Otherwise, it is listed as Delete Found Records.

If you select either of those commands, a dialog box displays and asks whether you really want to delete the records. The message in the dialog box also differs depending on the set of records being viewed. If you are about to delete all records in the table, the message reads, "Permanently delete ALL *N* records?"

(where *N* is the total number of records in the table; see Figure 4.3). Otherwise, it reads "Permanently delete ALL *N* records in the current found set?" (where *N* is the number of records in the found set).

FIGURE 4.3

The dialog box that displays when you choose to delete multiple records at the same time.

If you are certain that you want to delete the records, click the Delete All button. Otherwise, click Cancel.

CAUTION   Deleting multiple records is a potentially dangerous thing to do. That is why there are no shortcuts for these commands. Always check to see that your current found set contains only the records that you want to delete, because there is no "undo" for this type of operation.

Moving Between Layouts

So far, all the changes made to the database have been done using the same layout. However, when you work with a FileMaker Pro database, you typically end up using multiple layouts so that you can view your data in alternative ways and work with data in other tables.

In FileMaker Pro, there are several ways to move between layouts.

- Click the Layout field in the Status Toolbar. A menu of available layouts displays from which you can select the layout that you want to move to.

- Use the Go to Layout command, located in the View menu.

- Click on a button that has been set up in the content area for moving to another layout. For example, in the Contacts database that we are working with, clicking the Contact List button (located in the top-left corner of the screen) takes you to the Desktop > Contacts layout.

Use one of the preceding methods to change to the Desktop > Contacts layout. This layout is designed to display the contact records in a list.

Changing Layout Views

In Chapter 3, I mentioned three different ways to view records on a layout: Form view, List view, and Table view. To change the view, click on one of the three view buttons in the Status Toolbar or select a command from the View menu.

The layout we are working with now displays multiple records at the same time. Therefore, this layout displays records in List view. The layout we were previously working with displayed only one record at a time. It was displaying records in Form view.

Experiment with the different view options, and notice how the appearance of the layout changes. On the current layout, displaying the records in Form view isn't much help to us. However, click the button to change to Table view, and you see that the records are now displayed as a spreadsheet-like table.

To experiment with views further, change back to the layout we were originally using (Desktop > Contact Details).

 TIP   The view that you want to use depends on the layout you are working with and what you want to do with the records. In cases where you need to make changes to a large number of records, it might be helpful to view the records as a table.

When you view a layout in Table view, some additional functions are available that you might not realize. For example, notice that the field names are used as the column headers. You can click on a column name to easily sort the records based on the values in that column. You can also hover over a column header, and an arrow appears to the right of the column name. Click on that arrow, and a menu of additional options is displayed.

THE ABSOLUTE MINIMUM

In this chapter, we continued to explore FileMaker Pro by working with records and navigating between layouts. Here are the key points to remember:

- There are several different ways to open a FileMaker database. You can choose it from a list of recent databases that you worked with. You can locate the database on your computer's hard drive. And you can choose from a list of your favorite databases.

- FileMaker Pro provides commands that make it easy to add new records and duplicate existing records.

- In FileMaker Pro, you move between fields either by clicking in them directly or by using the Tab key.

- Changes that you make to records are automatically saved when you click anywhere in the content area of the window (where a field or button isn't present).

- You can cancel any changes made to a record by using the Revert Record command under the Records menu. However, you can only do so if the changes that you want to undo have not already been committed.

- You can delete a single record or multiple records at one time. Regardless, you need be careful when deleting records, as there is no way to undo the deletion of records.

- You can view a database in many different ways either by changing the layout that you are working in or by changing the manner in which records appear in a layout.

5

IMPORTING RECORDS

In the previous chapter, you learned how to manually add records to a FileMaker database. However, there may be times when the data that you want to add to your database already exists in another file, such as data in a spreadsheet or in another type of file exported from another application. To avoid manually entering those records, you can use FileMaker's import function to enter them for you.

In this chapter, you import a large number of records into your Contacts database. If you haven't already done so, open the Contacts database now.

NOTE You can download a file containing sample contacts from this book's website, located here: www.informit.com/title/9780789748843

Preparing for the Import

FileMaker can only import data into one table at a time. Therefore, before you import records, you must first determine the table you want to import the records into, and then navigate to a layout based on that table. Your Contacts database includes only one table (Contacts). Therefore, any layout will do.

To begin the import process, select File > Import Records > File. The Open File dialog window displays (see Figure 5.1).

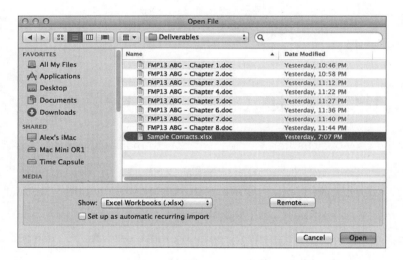

FIGURE 5.1

The Open File dialog window, from which you can select a file to import records from.

Selecting the Source File

Using the Open File window, locate the sample data file (Sample Contacts.xlsx). You can filter the files that appear in the window by selecting a file type from the Show menu, which is located at the bottom of the window.

File Types Supported

FileMaker's import function can be used to add records from a number of different types of files, including tab-separated files, comma-separated files, merge files, Microsoft Excel spreadsheets, and dBase files. Of course, you can also import records from other FileMaker Pro databases.

Once you have located the file that you want to import from, click the Open button, located in the bottom-right corner of the window. The Import Field Mapping dialog window displays, as shown in Figure 5.2.

FIGURE 5.2

The Import Field Mapping window with improperly aligned source and target fields.

Field Mapping

The purpose of the Import Field Mapping window is to align the fields in the source file with the fields in the table that you are importing into. Let's take a moment to explore the window.

The top portion of the window displays a table of fields. The fields listed on the left side of the window are the fields in the file that you are importing records from, which we refer to as the source fields. The fields listed on the right are the fields in the table that you are importing into, which we refer to as the target fields.

Notice a few differences between the fields in the source file and those in the Contacts database. First, there are a fewer number of fields in the source file. Second, the names of the fields in the source file are different from those in the target table. And finally, the order in which the fields appear in the two lists is also different. As a result of these differences, you are going to need to be careful when aligning the source and destination fields.

To align a field, click and drag the target field, and when it is aligned with the source field, release the mouse button. For example, drag the target field named First so that it aligns with the source field named First Name. Similarly, locate the Last target field and align it with the source field named Last Name. Repeat this process until all the source and target fields are properly aligned (see Figure 5.3).

 NOTE   As you are aligning the source and target fields, be sure that the icon between the columns is the "Import this field" icon, which appears as two dots and a right arrow. This is how you indicate that the data in the source field should be imported into the destination field. To toggle between the "Import this field" and the "Don't import this field" icon, click on the icon between the columns.

FIGURE 5.3

The Import Field Mapping window with the source and target fields properly aligned.

Below the table of fields are two functions that can sometimes help to align the fields. To the left is a tool that looks similar to the "book" in the Status Toolbar. You can use this book's pages to navigate between the records in the source file, giving you an opportunity to preview the source data. Next to the book are two numbers. One shows the number of the record that you are previewing, and the second indicates the number of records that are in the source file.

To the right is the Arrange By drop-down menu that you can use to have FileMaker attempt to arrange the target fields for you. The options available include matching names, last order, creation order, field names, field types, and custom import order. The matching names option is available only if the source file is another FileMaker database. By selecting one of these options, FileMaker changes the order of the target fields.

Selecting an Import Action

At the bottom of the Import Field Mapping window is the Import Action field, which has three options. The option that you choose determines how FileMaker handles the records as they are imported into the database. The options are Add New Records, Update Existing Records in Found Set, and Update Matching Records in Found Set.

When the Add New Records option is selected, FileMaker creates a new record in the target table for every record in the source file. However, there is one exception. If the source file is another FileMaker database, only the records in the current found set of the selected table are imported.

When the Update Existing Records in Found Set option is selected, FileMaker replaces data in the target table with data from the source file. Data from each record in the source file replaces data in the corresponding record in the found set of the target table. Therefore, data from the first record of the source file replaces data in the first record of the target table; data from the second record of the source file replaces data in the second record of the target table, and so on.

 CAUTION   Be careful when using the Update Existing Records in Found Set option, as it can be confusing and potentially dangerous. The important thing to remember about this option is that it simply replaces data in the target table. Unlike the Update Matching Records in Found Set option discussed next, this option makes no attempt to update matching records.

It is possible that the number of records in the source file is different from the number of records in the current found set of the target table. In that case, you have two options. You can either have FileMaker ignore the extra records, or add them. To have FileMaker add the extra records, select the Add Remaining Data as New Records check box. In cases where there are fewer records in the source file, FileMaker replaces as many records in the target as it can, and leaves the remaining records unchanged.

When the Update Matching Records in Found Set option is used, records in the target table are updated using data from matching records in the source file. You indicate how the records between the source file and the target table match by setting up one or more pairs of matching fields in a manner similar to how you previously aligned the fields.

To set up the pairs, you first align the matching fields as you did earlier. You then click the right arrow that appears in the column between the source and target fields. The right arrow is replaced with a two-sided arrow, indicating that the two fields are a part of the matching criteria.

You should keep a couple of things in mind when using this option. First, only the records in the current found set of the target table are considered as the records are matched and imported. Therefore, if the current found set does not consist of the entire set of records in the table, there is a chance that a record in the source file that would have been matched to a record (had it been in the found set) will not be updated.

Also keep in mind that in setting up the match criteria between the source file and the target table, the fields that you choose are important. You need to be absolutely certain that the fields that you choose will result in a proper match.

For example, suppose that you receive a file with updated phone numbers for the contacts in your database. If you were to set up the match criteria only on the last name fields, as the records are imported, records might be updated incorrectly. You might end up with the phone number for someone named "William Smith" getting improperly matched and imported into a record for someone named "John Smith." However, if you were to match on both the first and last name fields—or better yet, on a combination of the first name, last name, and ZIP code fields—then the matching will be much more accurate.

Finally, like the Update Existing Records in Found Set option discussed previously, you can choose to use the Add Remaining Data as New Records option with this option as well. If you do, then any records in the source file that do not match up with records in the found set of the target table are added to the target table. In other words, FileMaker updates records where a match is found and adds any records where no match is found.

There is one additional import option that you need to consider—the Don't Import First Record option. If the first record in the source file isn't actually data but is instead the names of the fields in that file, use this option to skip the first record. (The first record in the Sample Contacts.xlsx sample data does include field names, so you will want to select the Don't Import First Record option.)

Importing the Sample Data

Let's continue the process of importing the sample data into your Contacts database. To do so, be sure that the source and target fields are aligned properly, that the Add New Records option is selected, and that the Don't Import First Record option is checked. Then click the Import button.

Import Options Dialog Window

Next, depending on how the fields in the target table have been set up, the Import Options dialog window might appear (see Figure 5.4).

FIGURE 5.4

The Import Options dialog window.

If one or more of the fields in the target table have Auto-Enter options set, this dialog displays. We cover Auto-Enter field options in Chapter 9, "Working with Fields." For now, think of them as fields whose values are automatically set when a record is added to the table. This Import Options dialog window gives you an opportunity to override the Auto-Enter options as records are imported.

In this case, you are not importing into fields that have Auto-Enter options, so you should check the Perform Auto-Enter Options While Importing check box. To continue with the import process, simply click the Import button.

As records are imported into the target table, the Import progress window displays, showing the number of records that remain to be imported (see Figure 5.5). If you want to stop the import process for any reason, you can click the Cancel button to do so. (Keep in mind, however, that if you do cancel the import, any records that have already been imported will remain in the target table.)

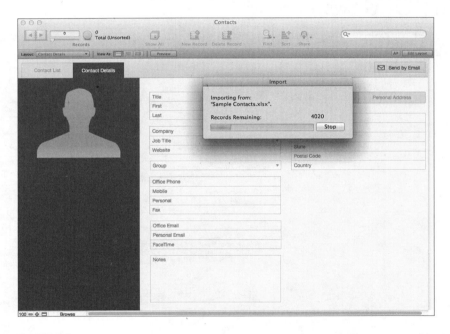

FIGURE 5.5

The Import progress window.

Import Summary Window

When the import process is complete, the Import Summary window displays, as shown in Figure 5.6.

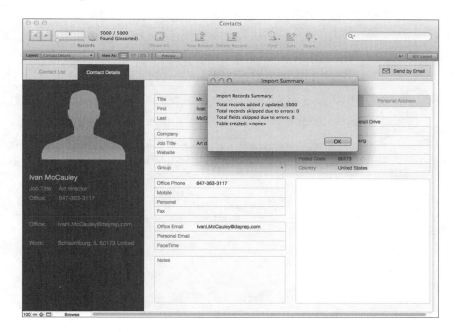

FIGURE 5.6

The Import Summary window.

This window displays the results of the import process, including the number of records added or updated, as well as the number of records or fields that could not be imported for any reason. Click OK to close the Import Summary window.

Your Contacts database should now include approximately 5,000 records.

As you can see, FileMaker's import function is powerful and has the potential to save you a lot of time. Imagine the time it would have taken you to manually enter those 5,000 records!

THE ABSOLUTE MINIMUM

In this chapter, you learned to use FileMaker's powerful import function to load records into a database. Here are the key points to remember:

- Before importing records into a FileMaker database, you need to take a few steps to prepare for the import. You need to be certain that you have navigated to a layout based on the table that you are importing records into. If you are replacing data in existing records or updating matching records, you want to be certain that your found set includes the records that you want to replace or update.

- FileMaker's import function supports a number of popular file formats, including delimited data files, Microsoft Excel files, as well as other FileMaker databases.

- The import function can be used to add new records to a table, to replace values in existing records, or to update matching records.

6

FINDING RECORDS

In Chapter 3, "Exploring FileMaker Pro," you were introduced to the FileMaker concept known as the *found set*. This is the set of records you are working with at any given time. For example, suppose that you are using your Contacts database, and only want to work with contacts that reside in the state of Virginia. Using FileMaker's commands for filtering data, you can locate those records. That set of records would be your found set.

FileMaker Pro provides several different methods for you to filter records. In FileMaker terms, the act of filtering data is often referred to as *performing a find*. In this chapter, you learn about the various ways that you can perform a find and do so using your Contacts database.

Using Quick Find

One of fastest and most convenient ways to perform a find is to use FileMaker's Quick Find tool (see Figure 6.1). With Quick Find, you can enter a keyword or phrase to filter on, and FileMaker searches for that criteria across multiple fields at the same time.

Let's give Quick Find a try. If you haven't already done so, open your Contacts database. Then change to the Desktop > Contacts layout.

The Quick Find tool is located in the rightmost area of the Status Toolbar. Click the field, and enter the text that you want to search for. For example, type **Smith** and then press the Return or Enter key.

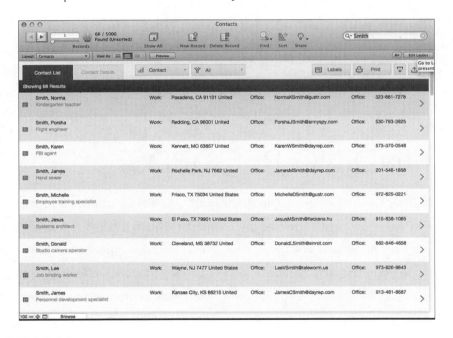

FIGURE 6.1

The FileMaker Quick Find tool.

The found set changes and consists only of those records that contain "Smith" in one of the fields being displayed on the layout. If you browse through the records, you find that in many of the records the word "Smith" appears in the Last Name field.

However, you might also see that for some of the contacts, the word "Smith" is part of the street address or city name. As you can see, FileMaker looked for the word in multiple fields and does so at one time. This is what makes Quick Find different from other types of finds that you can perform.

If you enter multiple values into the Quick Find field, FileMaker locates records where both values are present. For example, perform a Quick Find for the phrase "smith pa." The found set consists of records where "smith" and "pa" are found in the fields, regardless of whether those values are found in the same fields or in multiple fields.

Let's perform a Quick Find for "Smith" once again. Note the number of records that are found.

Next, change to the Desktop > Contact Details layout. This layout includes several additional fields not present on the Desktop > Contacts layout. Perform a Quick Find for "Smith" and notice that this time, more records are found than were on the other layout. This is because "Smith" is found in fields present on this layout but not present on the previous layout.

A few notes about the Quick Find function:

- If you perform a Quick Find and nothing is found, a dialog box displays the message, "No records match this find criteria." Clicking OK dismisses the dialog box, and your found set remains unchanged.

- Notice that there is an icon with both a magnifying glass and down arrow in the left-hand portion of the Quick Find field. You can click on that icon to see the ten most recent Quick Finds you have performed, and you can select from that list to perform a Quick Find again.

 TIP   As you see in Chapter 11, "Working with Layouts," when you are setting up layouts, you can specify what fields should and should not be included when Quick Finds are performed. In other words, it is possible for a field to appear on a layout and be excluded when Quick Finds are performed.

Entering Find Mode

You have seen that FileMaker's Quick Find tool is a flexible, convenient way to perform a find. You can use it to search across multiple fields at the same time.

However, there might be times when you want to perform a find with more specific criteria. For example, you might want to locate contacts in the state of Virginia. Or you might want an even more detailed find, such as contacts located in Virginia, Maryland, or Pennsylvania, and whose last names start with Smith. In those cases, you want to perform the find using FileMaker's Find mode.

You can enter Find mode in four ways:

- Select View > Find Mode.

- Use a keyboard shortcut—Command+F on a Mac or Ctrl+F on Windows.

- Click the Find button in the Status Toolbar.

- Select Find from the mode menu (located in the bottom left-hand corner of the screen).

Enter Find mode now. After you do so, the screen changes significantly (see Figure 6.2). For example, the Status Toolbar changes, and the buttons on it are different from those you have seen when using FileMaker in Browse mode.

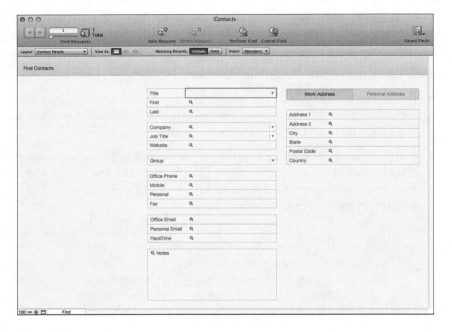

FIGURE 6.2

A layout displayed in Find mode.

Perhaps most importantly, notice that the fields on the layout no longer contain data, as if you are working with a blank record. However, the fields do include a magnifying glass symbol, which is FileMaker's way of indicating that it is in Find mode.

Performing Basic Finds

Let's use Find mode to perform a few basic finds.

If you are not already in Find mode, enter it now, and then change to the Details layout (Desktop > Contact Details layout). Then, in the Last Name field, enter **roberts** and click the Perform Find button in the Status Toolbar. FileMaker performs the find and returns you to Browse mode so that you can work with the records it has found. Figure 6.3 shows the first record that was imported into the database.

FIGURE 6.3

The results of performing a find for contacts with last names that start with "roberts."

 NOTE   When you enter Find mode, the Status Toolbar changes to include buttons for commands relevant to performing finds. For example, you see buttons for commands such as New Request, Perform Find, and Cancel Find.

Take a moment to browse through the records in the found set. As you can see, FileMaker found records that either contain or start with the value that you entered. Also notice that the capitalization of what you entered is irrelevant. (You can search for "Roberts" or "roberts" and receive the same found set.)

Suppose that you want to find contacts where the last name matches "Roberts" exactly. FileMaker provides a number of search operators for just this type of scenario. Enter Find mode again and click the Last Name field. Next, in the lower portion of the Status Toolbar, click on the Insert: Operators menu, and select the = math whole word (or match empty) operator. FileMaker places an equals sign in the Last Name field. Now enter **Roberts** behind that equal sign, and click the Perform Find button in the Status Toolbar.

Notice that this time FileMaker finds fewer records. Browsing through the records in the found set reveals that only contacts whose last name is "Roberts" were found. The contacts whose last names start with "Roberts" (such as "Robertson") have not been included.

As you might have noticed, the Operators menu, shown in Figure 6.4, includes several other options. For example, you can use operators to find records whose values are less than or greater than values that you specify, or those whose values fall within a specified range.

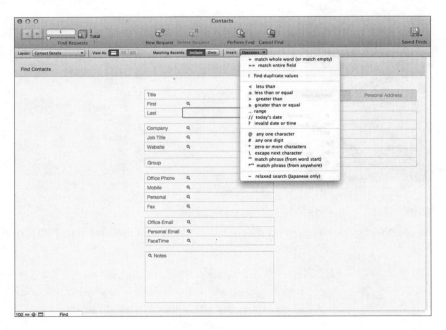

FIGURE 6.4

The Operators menu, available below the Status Toolbar in Find mode.

For example, suppose that you are interested in sending a letter to contacts whose ZIP codes are between 20000 and 21000. Enter Find mode, and click the Work Address Postal Code field. Type **20000...21000** into the field, and then click the Perform Find button. Browse through the records, and you see that the found set includes contacts whose ZIP codes fall within that range.

 TIP FileMaker provides a convenient way to see and select from the values present in a field. Select the Insert > From Index command, or use Command+I (Mac) or Ctrl+I (Windows), and the View Index dialog window appears. An index of the values in the current field is displayed from which you can select a value. This command is available in both Browse and Find modes.

Performing "and" Finds

The finds that you performed thus far have been with criteria in a single field. However, you can also perform finds with criteria in multiple fields. We refer to this as performing an "and" find.

For example, suppose that you are interested in finding all contacts whose last name starts with "Jones" and whose work address is in the state of Texas. To perform this find, enter Find mode, enter **Jones** in the Last Name field, and enter **TX** in the State field. Then click the Perform Find button. The records in the found set are those that meet both of the criteria.

"And" finds can include as many criteria as needed. For example, you could perform a find for contacts whose first name starts with "A," whose last name starts with "Jones," and who live in the state of Texas.

Performing "or" Finds

You learned how to perform "and" finds, where records must meet all the criteria specified in multiple fields. However, suppose that you want to perform an "or" find, where the records must meet either one set of criteria or another.

For example, suppose that you are interested in finding all the contacts whose work addresses are either in Maryland or Virginia (an "or" find). To perform this find, enter Find mode and enter **MD** in the State field. Then in the Status Toolbar, click the New Request button. Notice that the Status Toolbar's "book" tool changes, indicating that you are now on the second of two find requests. The second find request is blank. Enter **VA** in the State field and then click the Perform Find button.

As you browse through the records in the found set, you see that the contacts work in either Maryland or Virginia. If you want to find contacts in Maryland, Virginia, or New York, you can perform a similar find and simply add a third find request.

Performing Finds That Omit Records

At this point, you have learned how to perform "and" and "or" finds. Let's take a look at another fairly common type of find that you'll likely want to perform.

Suppose that you are interested in finding all contacts whose last name begins with "Jones" except for those who work in the state of Ohio. To perform this find, you need to use two find requests, just as you did previously with the "or" find. Enter Find mode now, and type **Jones** into the Last Name field. Next, click the New Request button in the Status Toolbar, and type **OH** in the State field.

At this point, if you were to perform the find, you would be performing an "or" find and would end up with a found set consisting of contacts whose last name begins with "Jones" or who work in Ohio. That's not what you are aiming for.

Instead, you want FileMaker to find the contacts whose last name starts with "Jones" and then omit those who work in Ohio. To indicate that the records that match the second request should be omitted, you need to click the Omit button located in the Matching Records area of the Status Toolbar. Then click the Perform Find button.

Notice that the records that are found meet your criteria. These are the contacts whose last name begins with Jones. However, none of the Joneses who work in Ohio are included in the found set.

 NOTE When performing finds that use the Omit option, the order in which you set up the find requests is important. Be sure that the requests that specify the records you do want to include in the found set are set up first, followed by the requests that indicate the records to be omitted. Otherwise, the results that you get might not be what you are expecting.

Finds That Return No Records

So far, the finds that you performed have all resulted in a found set. In other words, records were found that meet the criteria you specified. Let's see what happens if you perform a find where no records match your criteria.

To do so, enter Find mode. In the State field, enter **ZZ**, and then click the Perform Find button. FileMaker responds with a dialog box that states, "No records match this find criteria." You can click the Modify Find button to change your criteria and try again, or click Cancel, and your found set is unchanged.

Modifying the Last Find

Let's suppose that you perform a find—perhaps a somewhat complicated find—and then realize that you want to repeat that find with a few changes to it. Rather than entering your find criteria from scratch, you can use FileMaker's Modify Last Find command.

To modify the last find, either select Records > Modify Last Find or use the keyboard shortcut (Command+R on a Mac, Ctrl+R on Windows). FileMaker enters Find mode and restores any of the criteria that you used to perform the most recent find, regardless of how complicated that find was. You can then adjust your criteria, add additional find requests, delete find requests, and so on. And when you are ready, simply perform the find as you normally would.

Using Saved Finds

The Modify Last Find command is convenient, but only if the find that you want to work with is the most recent find that you performed. But what if you want to work with an older find? Or better yet, what if you find (no pun intended) that you are performing the same find repeatedly? Well, FileMaker takes these cases into account as well and makes it easy to handle both of them.

Let's start with the first case, where you want to perform a find that you did earlier. From the Records menu, select Saved Finds. A submenu displays, as shown in Figure 6.5. In that menu, towards the bottom, you see up to ten recent finds that you have performed. Select one from the list, and FileMaker performs that find. Then if you want to make a change to that find, use the Modify Last Find command. You see that all the criteria you used are restored.

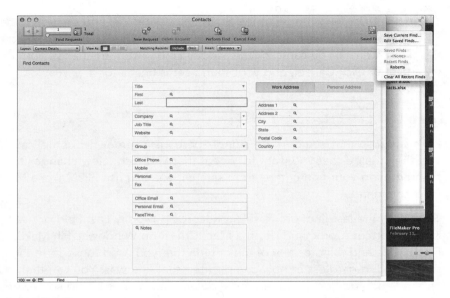

FIGURE 6.5

The Saved Finds menu.

Next, let's address the case where you are performing the same find repeatedly and want to save it. First, perform the find that you want to save. Next, from the Records menu, select Saved Finds, and then select Save Current Find. The Specify Options for the Saved Find dialog window displays (see Figure 6.6).

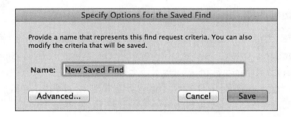

FIGURE 6.6

The Specify Options for the Saved Find dialog window.

You can use this window to name the saved find and more easily identify it later. FileMaker usually does a good job of naming the saved find for you, and you can use the name it comes up with if you want. Next, click the Save button. Then, when you want to use the saved find, you can select it from the Records > Saved Finds menu.

A few notes about saved finds:

- There are two ways to view the list of saved finds and recent finds. As you saw previously, when you're in Browse mode, you can select Records > Saved Finds. However, when you are in Find mode, you can access the list by clicking on the Saved Finds button that appears in the Status Toolbar.

- In cases where the database that you are working with is being used by multiple users, your lists of saved and recent finds are yours alone. Other users have their own list of saved finds. Unfortunately, there is no easy way for you to share a saved find with another user.

Using Fast Match

You have now seen several ways in which you can find records using FileMaker Pro. You used the Quick Find tool, Find mode, and both Saved and Recent Finds.

There is one additional method for finding records that you might find handy. This one, like Quick Find, is available to you only when you are in Browse mode. FileMaker refers to it as Fast Match. You can use Fast Match to find records that meet multiple, potentially complex, criteria.

Perhaps the best way to explain how Fast Match works is through an example. In your Contacts database, navigate to the Desktop > Contact Details layout. Then perform a find for contacts who work in the state of Ohio. Make a note of the number of records in the found set.

Then browse through the records in the found set and select a contact. (It doesn't matter which one.) Next, right-click in the City field. A contextual menu displays, and it includes several options. Three of those options are find-related: Find Matching Records, Constrain Found Set, and Extend Found Set. These are the Fast Match options that FileMaker provides.

Select the Constrain Found Set option from the menu. You then see that the found set has changed and that you are now viewing fewer records than you had been. FileMaker reduced ("constrained") the found set to only contacts who work in the state of Ohio and specifically to those who work in the city of the contact you selected.

Let's look at another example. This time, start by performing a find for contacts whose last names start with "Smith." Again, make note of the number of records in the found set.

Next, right-click the State field for one of the contacts, and this time select Extend Found Set. Your found set changes again. If you browse through the records, you see that the found set now includes contacts whose last names start with "Smith" or who live in the state that you selected.

Finally, let's explore the final Fast Match option. Select any record in the found set, right-click the Postal Code field, and then select the Find Matching Records option from the contextual menu. This time, the found set includes only those records whose postal codes match the one that you selected.

Showing Omitted Records

Sometimes, after performing a find, you might be interested to see the records not in your found set. FileMaker refers to these as the *omitted records* and provides two ways to view them:

- From the Records menu, select Show Omitted Only.

- In the Status Toolbar, click the pie chart.

When you choose to view the omitted records, your found set is replaced with the records not in the previous found set. To return to the original found set, simply perform Show Omitted Only command again.

 TIP   In some cases, when you are having difficulty determining how best to perform a complicated find, you might want to try a different approach. Instead of performing a find for the records that you do want to see, find the records that you do not want to see. Then use the Show Omitted Only command to locate the records that you actually do want to see!

Finding All Records

You have now learned several ways to perform finds in FileMaker Pro, and to filter the found set based on your criteria. However, suppose that you want to work with all the records in a table. There are several ways to do so:

- Click the Show All button in the Status Toolbar.

- Select Records > Show All Records.

- Use the Command+J keyboard shortcut on Macs, or the Ctrl+J shortcut on Windows.

Updating Multiple Records at One Time

Regardless of how you perform a find, you ultimately end up with a found set that consists of only those records you are interested in. Once you have the found set that you want to work with, you can do several things with it.

In Chapter 5, "Importing Records," you learned how to import records into FileMaker Pro. You might recall that the during the import process you can specify an Import Action. Two of those options are Update Existing Records in Found Set and Update Matching Records in Found Set. When using either of those two actions, only the found set records are impacted by the import.

As you see in Chapter 8, "Exporting Records," the found set also determines the behavior of FileMaker's export function. Only the records in the current found set are exported.

A couple of other interesting FileMaker functions are particularly helpful when used on a found set. One of them is the Replace Field Contents command. It gives you a way to update values in a field across all records in the found set at one time.

For example, suppose that the contacts in Postal Code 23222 currently have their City names set to Richmond, when they should actually be set to Midlothian. To correct this problem, you first perform a find for contacts in the 23222 Postal Code. Next, click the City field for any of the contacts in the found set and change it to Midlothian. Then with the cursor still in the City field, select the Records > Replace Field Contents. The Replace Field Contents dialog window displays (see Figure 6.7).

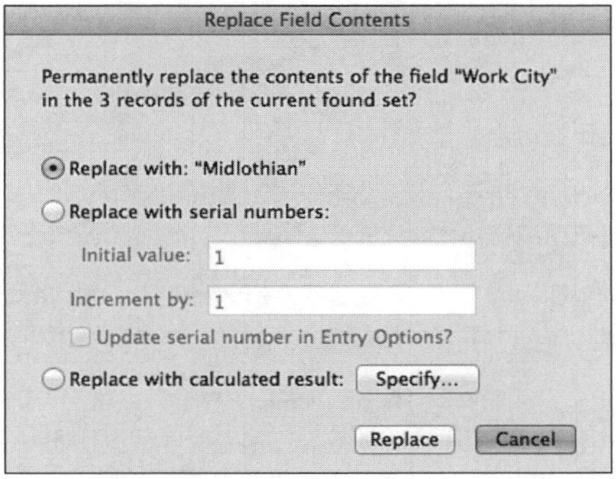

FIGURE 6.7

The Replace Field Contents dialog window.

This window gives you several options, including three different ways that the values in the field can be updated. In this example, use the first option Replace with: "Midlothian." To update the cities in all records in the found set, click the Replace button. The dialog window then closes, and the change is made. If you browse through the records in the found set, you see that the values in the City field for all records in the found set have been set to Midlothian. (That's a real time-saver, isn't it?)

A couple of notes about the Replace Field Contents command:

- The function works only on one field at a time. If you need to update multiple fields across the found set, use the Replace Field Contents command multiple times.

- There is no "undo" for the Replace Field Contents function. Therefore, before using it, make absolutely certain that you have the correct found set that you want to work with and that you are in the correct field that you want to update.

- In our example, the value we used is a simple text value. The Replace Field Contents dialog window provides two other options that you can use to specify the value that should be used. Replace with Serial Numbers gives you a way to assign serial numbers across the found set, and to specify both the initial value and the increment value. (For example, you could assign serial numbers, starting at 100, and incrementing by 10.) The other option, Replace with Calculated Result, gives you a way to assign values based on calculations. For example, you could use this option to replace the values in the Last Name field with their upper case equivalents. (You learn more about calculations and FileMaker's calculation engine in Chapter 10, "Working with Calculations.")

THE ABSOLUTE MINIMUM

In this chapter, you learned how to perform finds in FileMaker Pro. Here are the key points to remember:

- FileMaker provides several different ways to find records, and the best way depends on the type of find that you want to perform.

- The Quick Find function gives you an easy, convenient way to look for records that contain one or more values, regardless of what fields those values appear in.

- You can use Find mode to perform a variety of different types of finds, including finds with multiple requests (which you can use to perform "and" and "or" finds) and requests that indicate which records should be omitted from the found set.

- The Replace Field Contents command can be used to update values in a field across all records in the found set.

7

SORTING RECORDS

When working in a FileMaker database, there might be times when you want to work with or present records in a particular order. We refer to the process of reordering records as *sorting*. In this chapter, you learn how to sort records.

FileMaker provides a number of different ways for you to sort records. The most commonly used method is the Sort Records command.

The Sort Records Command

Let's use the Sort Records command to sort the records in your Contacts database. If you do not already have the database open, do so now. Then navigate to the Desktop > Contacts layout.

To access the Sort Records command, either click the Sort button on the Status Toolbar, select Sort Records from the Records menu, or use the Command+S (Mac) or Ctrl+S (Windows) keyboard shortcut. You then see the Sort Records dialog window.

The Sort Records Window

The top-left side of the window includes a list of the fields that you can sort on. By default, this list includes only those fields displayed on the current layout. You can click the Current Layout menu, located above the list of fields, to select Current Table. Doing this refreshes the field list, and you see all fields in the table, regardless of whether they appear on the current layout.

The list on the right includes the fields that you have selected to sort on, which FileMaker refers to as the Sort Order. You can add a field to the Sort Order by selecting it in the list on the left and selecting the Move button, or by double-clicking it. To remove a field from the Sort Order, either click it and select the Clear button, or double-click it. You can also click the Clear All button to completely reset the Sort Order and start from scratch.

For each field listed in the Sort Order, you can indicate whether it should be sorted in ascending or descending order. For example, you can sort the contact records in ascending order by last name, and secondarily in descending order by first name. To specify the sort order, click on a field in the Sort Order list, and then click either the Ascending Order or Descending Order radio button in the area below the two lists.

For our example, let's sort by state, last name, and first name. If you already have fields in the Sort Order, start by clearing it. Then locate Work State in the field list and double-click. Do the same for Last Name (the field is actually named Last), and for First Name (First). Note that these fields are not visible on the current layout. Therefore, be sure to select Current Table from the menu above the field list. Figure 7.1 shows the Sort Records window with the fields set properly.

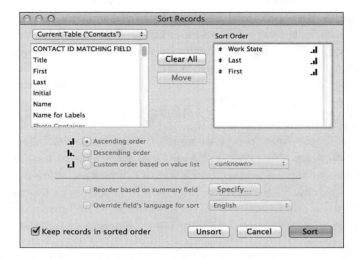

FIGURE 7.1

The Sort Records dialog window.

When you have finished setting up the sort order, click the Sort button. FileMaker then sorts the records. If you browse through the records, you see that the records are now in the desired order.

Impact of the Sort Order

There are several FileMaker functions whose behavior is impacted by the sort order of the found set. As you see in Chapter 8, "Exporting Records," one of those functions, the Export function, uses the sort order to determine the order in which records are exported from FileMaker into another file. Also, as you see in Chapter 16, "Sharing a Database," there are several reporting options whose behavior changes based on the sort order.

A few notes about the Sort Records command:

- When sorting records, you can indicate whether a field in the Sort Order should be sorted in ascending or descending order. However, there is also a third option. Custom Order Based on Value List gives you the ability to sort using a special order that meets your needs. For example, suppose that you have a database that is being used to track clothing, and that one of the fields in the Clothes table is Size. The values in that field might be Small,

Medium, Large, XL, and XXL. If you were to sort the field in ascending order, the records would be sorted alphabetically (Medium, Large, Small, XL, XXL) but not really in increasing order by size. With the Custom Order sort option, you could sort based on a value list that consists of the size values, and the records would then be sorted properly. (You learn more about value lists in Chapter 9, "Working with Fields.")

- In the bottom-left corner of the Sort Records dialog window is a Keep Records in Sorted Order check box. When that option is checked, and a sort is performed, FileMaker continues to present records in that sort order, even if new records are added, or if existing records are updated. If you uncheck this box, new records always appear at the bottom of the found set, and any changes made to existing records do not have an impact on their position in the list. In other words, you might end up with a "semi-sorted" set of records.

In addition to the Sort Records function, you can sort records in two other ways:

- In Browse mode, you can right-click a field and select Sort Ascending, Sort Descending, or Sort By Value List from the contextual menu to sort on that field.

- If you are viewing a layout in Table view, you can click on the arrow that appears in the rightmost portion of a field's column header. You can then select Sort Ascending, Sort Descending, or Sort By Value List to sort on that field.

THE ABSOLUTE MINIMUM

In this chapter, you learned to use FileMaker's sort function to change the order in which records appear. Here are the key points to remember:

- When sorting records, you can choose to sort fields in ascending or descending order, or based on more complicated sort order (using the Custom Order Based on Value List option).

- The order in which records are sorted has an impact on how some of FileMaker's other functions behave. For example, when exporting records, the order in which those records are exported is determined based on the current sort order.

- Sorting records does not permanently change the order in which records are physically stored in a table. You might need to re-sort records as new records are added to a table, as records are updated, or as records are deleted.

8

EXPORTING RECORDS

In Chapter 5, "Importing Records," you learned how to use FileMaker's import function to load records into a database using data stored in other files. FileMaker provides a similar function that you can use to get data out of a FileMaker database, so that it can be used in other applications. That function is the export function.

In this chapter, you export data from your Contacts database to a file in a different format. If you don't already have your Contacts database open, go ahead and open it now.

Preparing to Export

When exporting data from FileMaker, the table from which records are exported is determined based on the layout that you are on when you perform the export. Your Contacts database consists of a single table (Contacts). Therefore, in this example, any layout will do.

When you export data from FileMaker, only the records that are in the current found set are included in the exported file. Therefore, before using the export function, you should first find the records that you want to export. (In this exercise, let's assume that you want to export all of the contacts.)

Finally, the order in which the records are exported depends on the order in which the records in your found set are currently sorted. Therefore, if you want the records to be exported in a certain order, you should sort them before exporting.

Performing the Export

Once the found set has been prepared, you are ready to export the records. To do so, select File > Export Records. The Export Records to File dialog window displays (see Figure 8.1).

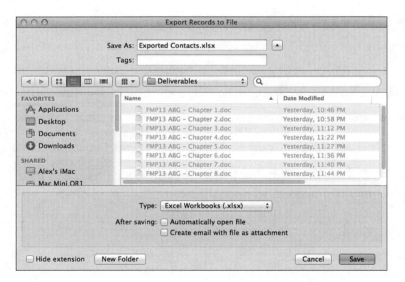

FIGURE 8.1

The Export Records to File dialog window.

This window looks similar to the Open File dialog window that displays when you import records, and it works in much the same way. You use this window to specify the name and location of the file you want to export the records to.

Supported File Types

Like the import function, FileMaker's export function supports saving data to a number of file types. This includes tab and comma-separated files, dBase files, merge files, HTML tables, XML files, and Microsoft Excel workbooks.

For this exercise, let's export the records to a Microsoft Excel workbook. Select the Excel Workbooks (.xlsx) option from the Type menu (located at the bottom of the window). Notice that when you select a file type, FileMaker automatically renames the file in the Save As field for you using the selected file type's file extension.

 TIP   Two additional options are available on the Export Records to File dialog window that might come in handy. The Automatically Open File option opens the exported file for you as soon as it is created. The Create Email with File as Attachment option attaches the exported file to an email message for you, so that you can easily send it to someone else.

Excel Options Window

Next, click the Save button. Because you chose to export the records to an Excel workbook, the Excel Options window displays (as shown in Figure 8.2). You can use this window to provide additional information about the worksheet that will be created, including the worksheet name, title, subject, and author. There is also an option to use the names of the exported fields as the column names in the first row of the spreadsheet. If you want to take a moment to provide values for the Excel Options, feel free to do so. However, this is entirely optional.

When you are ready, click the Continue button.

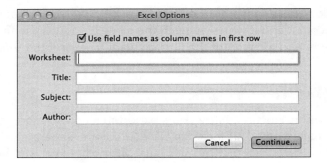

FIGURE 8.2

The Excel Options window.

Specify the Field Order for the Export Window

The final step in the export process is to specify the fields that you want to export, and the Specify Field Order for Export window, which displays next, is where you do that (see Figure 8.3).

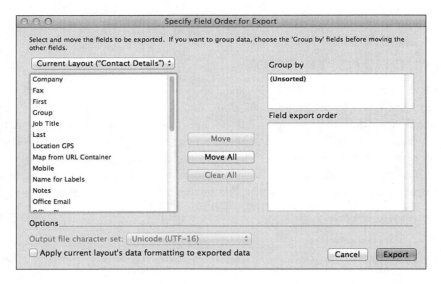

FIGURE 8.3

The Specify Field Order for Export window.

The left side of this window includes the fields available to be exported. The fields listed in the Field Export Order box are those that have been selected.

The list of fields includes all the fields that appear on the layout that you were on when you started the export process. To export fields not on the current layout, or to export fields from related tables, select a table from the menu that appears above the list of fields. Upon doing so, the list of fields updates to display fields available in that table.

To include a field in the export, either double-click it, or select it and click the Move button that appears between the two lists. Also, you can easily move all the fields to the Field export list by clicking the Move All button, and use the Clear All button to remove all the fields from the list.

To change the order in which the fields are to be exported, you can drag and drop the fields in the Field Export Order box. For this example, let's select the following fields: Company, First, Last, and Work Phone.

Additional Export Options

Three additional options are available on the Specify Field Order for Export window that we do not use in this example but that are worth mentioning:

- The Group By area is located above the Field export order and can be used to group records in the exported file. This option is available only in cases where the records in the found set have been sorted. When selecting this option, the values of records that fall into the same group appear only once in the expired file. (When in doubt, do not select any of the Group By fields.)

- The Output File Character Set is applicable only when exporting records to certain file types (such as HTML). This option should be used when you want the exported file to be created using an alternate character set (such as Japanese or Chinese).

- The Apply Current Layout's Data Formatting to Exported Data option can be used if you want the number, date, and time values in the exported file to be formatted in the same way they are on the current layout. For example, if one of the fields being exported is a number, and that field is formatted as currency on the layout, then the field is exported using that same currency format.

The Export Progress Window

When you are ready to export the records, click the Export button.

An Export progress window displays, showing the number of records that remain to be exported. When the process completes, the progress window closes. You then find the exported file with the name that you specified and in the location that you specified.

THE ABSOLUTE MINIMUM

In this chapter, you learned to use FileMaker's powerful import and export functions to get records into and out of a database. Here are the key points to remember:

- FileMaker's export function supports a number of popular file formats, including delimited data files, Microsoft Excel files, and other FileMaker databases.

- When you're exporting records, only records in the current found set are included.

- Records are exported based on the current sort order of the found set.

9

WORKING WITH FIELDS

Now that you have completed Part I, "Getting to Know FileMaker Pro," you should be familiar with databases in general, and FileMaker Pro in particular. You have the all the skills you need to go "beyond the basics" and learn how to make changes to FileMaker databases.

In this chapter, you learn more about fields. You discover the many different types of fields that FileMaker supports and their options. You also learn to add, change, and delete fields by making changes to the Contacts database that you created in Part I.

Understanding Field Types

As you learned in Part I, you can create FileMaker databases to keep track of a wide variety of things. You can create databases to track people, projects, inventory, invoices, and just about anything else that you can dream up.

The attributes of those types of things can vary significantly. For example, the Contacts database that you created in Part I tracked attributes such as first and last names, phone numbers, addresses, and so on. In an inventory database, you might track part numbers, product descriptions, prices, quantities, and perhaps photos of the products. An invoicing database might track invoice totals, dates, and more.

For you to create databases that track such a wide variety of things, FileMaker provides support for a number of different types of fields. And depending on the type of data that you need to keep track of, one of those field types might be more applicable than the others.

FileMaker supports the eight types of fields listed and described in Table 9.1: Text, Numbers, Dates, Times, Timestamps, Containers, Calculations, and Summaries. Each field type is intended to be used to store a certain type of data, and as a result, they each behave in different ways.

TABLE 9.1   Field Types

Field Type	Description
Text	Text fields can be used to store nearly any value, regardless of whether the value is made of letters or numbers. You can even put a date into a field that has been set up as a text field. And don't worry about entering "too much" into a text field: They can hold up to 2GB of data!
	You might be asking yourself, "If text fields can do all of that, why should I even worry about the other field types?" And that's a good question.
	The problem is that there might be times when you want to do something with a value entered into a field. For example, you might want to use the value in a calculation that expects the value to be a number, or in a calculation that expects a date. In those cases, if the field were set up as text, you cannot be certain that FileMaker knows what to do when the value is not the expected type, and the results can be unexpected.
Number	Fields set up as numbers are used to store numeric values, including both integers and decimals. It is possible to enter non-numeric values into number fields. However, in cases where FileMaker is expecting the value to be a number and it isn't one, the value will be ignored. And, just like text fields, the values that can be entered into number fields can be large. Values can be up to 800 digits long, with 400 digits of precision on either side of the decimal point.

Field Type	Description
Date	Date fields are used to store date values. FileMaker supports date values that go as far back as 1/1/0001, and as far into the future as 12/31/4000. Unlike number fields (into which FileMaker allows you to enter non-numeric values), the values entered into date fields must be valid dates. If you try to enter anything other than a valid date, FileMaker displays a dialog box indicating that the value is not acceptable.
Time	Fields set up as times are interesting in that they can be used to store a specific time (ex: 3:11 PM), or a time duration (ex: 1:45). Like date fields, FileMaker is somewhat picky about the values that can be entered into a time field. If you enter a value that FileMaker cannot work with, a dialog box appears to let you know.
Timestamp	Timestamps are used to store a value that consists of both date and time components. For example, 2/1/2013 3:16 PM. Like date fields, the date portion of values stored in timestamp fields must be a valid date between 1/1/0001 and 12/31/4000. And like time fields, the time portion must be a valid time or duration.
Container	Perhaps the most interesting type of field that FileMaker supports is the container field. This special field type can be used to store nearly any type of digital file that you can imagine, including images, documents, movies, Word documents, Excel spreadsheets, and so on. For example, in your Contacts database, there is a container field set up to store photos of the contacts. You learn more about container fields in Chapter 11, "Working with Layouts," when you learn to create layouts.
Calculation	One of the most powerful features of FileMaker Pro is its capability to perform calculations using data stored in the database. Fields set up as calculations are one of the ways that you can use this feature. You can set up calculation fields so that FileMaker automatically applies a formula to arrive at a certain value. For example, in a database being used to store inventory, an Items table might include fields for Quantity On Hand and Unit Value. In this table, you might add a calculated field to multiply the Quantity On Hand field with the value in the Unit Value field to arrive at the Total Value on hand for each item. One of the things that makes calculation fields different from other field types is that you cannot type into them. If you try to do so, FileMaker opens a dialog box and lets you know that the value cannot be modified. We cover calculations in great depth and discuss many different ways that you can use them in FileMaker databases, in Chapter 10, "Working with Calculations."
Summary	Summary fields are somewhat like calculation fields in that they are used to have FileMaker automatically determine values for you. However, with summary fields, the values that FileMaker calculates are aggregates of the values stored in the found set of records that you are working with. For example, in an Invoices database, you might create a summary field to calculate that grand total of all invoices in the found set. You use summary fields when you learn to create reports in Chapter 12, "Creating Reports and Charts."

Adding Fields

Now that you know the various types of fields that FileMaker supports, let's add a couple of fields to your Contacts database. If you have not already done so, open the database now.

There are several ways to add new fields to a FileMaker database. In this chapter, you use the more traditional and straightforward method. We discuss another option for adding fields in Chapter 11.

To make changes to the tables, fields, and relationships in a FileMaker database, you use FileMaker's Manage Database function. To do so, select File > Manage > Database. The Manage Database dialog window displays (see Figure 9.1).

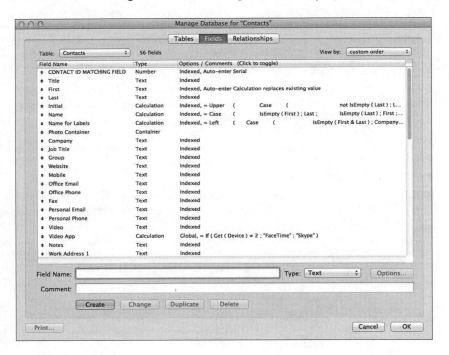

FIGURE 9.1

The FileMaker Manage Database window.

Notice that the window includes three tabs: Tables, Fields, and Relationships. The Fields tab should be selected. If not, select it now.

Let's take a look at what this window includes. Toward the top of the window is a drop-down menu from which you can select one of the tables in a database. In your Contacts database, there is only one table (named "Contacts"), so that is your only option. If the database consisted of multiple tables (as many databases do), you would see those tables listed here as well, and selecting one of them would show the fields that make up that table.

The majority of this window includes a table that lists all the fields in the selected table, including their names, types, and options. (Note that you can click the header of the Options / Comments column to toggle between what is displayed in the column.)

At the bottom of the fields table are fields that you can use to add fields or make changes to existing fields. Let's use this area of the window to add a field to the table.

Suppose that you want to start tracking the income of your contacts. To do so, add a field called Income by following these steps:

1. Click the Field Name field, and enter **Income**.

2. To the right of the Field Name field is a Type drop-down field. The type of values that we're planning to store in this field are numbers. Therefore, select Number from the menu.

3. Below the Field Name field is a Comment field. You can use this field to optionally make a note about the field itself, which might come in handy in the future should you forget what you intended the field to be used for (or should you have another developer work on the database). Add a comment such as "Estimated yearly income."

4. To add the field, click the Create button at the bottom of the window.

You can see the new field added to the list of fields.

Changing the Field Order

Notice that the new field appears at the bottom of the list of fields. If you want to change the order in which the fields are displayed, you have a few options.

- You can click on one of the table's column headers. For example, clicking on the Field Name column header sorts the fields by their names, clicking on Type sorts them by their type, and so on.

- You can select an option from the View By menu, which is located above the list of fields and to the right. You see options that include creation order, field name, field type, and custom order.

To place the fields in an order that isn't based on their names, types, or creation dates, you can use the up/down arrow icons located next to the fields and manually arrange the fields in an order that works for you. Doing so will automatically change the View By menu to custom order. Selecting custom order in the future returns the list to that same order.

Field Options

In addition to the various types of fields that FileMaker supports, it also supports a variety of field options. For example, you can set up a field so that when a new record is added it automatically gets set to a certain value. There are also options that can be used to restrict the values that can be entered into a field. Let's explore these options by adding some additional fields to the Contacts database.

Auto-Enter Options

You can use FileMaker's Auto-Enter field options, which are displayed in Figure 9.2, so that when a new record is created the field's value is automatically set for you. Table 9.2 lists the Auto-Enter options available.

TABLE 9.2   Auto-Enter Field Options

Option	Description
Creation Date	The field is set to the date on which the record was created.
Creation Time	The field is set to the time the record was created.
Creation Timestamp	The field is set to the date and time that the record was created.
Creation Name	The field is set to the name of the person who created the record. This value is determined based on the User Name value set in the FileMaker Pro preferences.
Creation Account Name	The field is set to the account name that the person who created the record was logged in with when the record was created. We discuss account names when we review FileMaker security in Chapter 12.
Modification Date	The field is set to the date on which the record was last modified.
Modification Time	The field is set to the time at which the record was last modified.
Modification Timestamp	The field is set to the date and time at which the record was last modified.
Modification Name	The field is set to the name of the person who last modified the record. Again, this value is determined based on the User Name value set in the FileMaker Pro preferences.
Modification Account Name	The account name that the person who last modified the record was logged in with when the record was created.
Serial Number	The field is set to the value in the Next Value box. FileMaker then automatically updates the value in the Next Value box by incrementing it based on the value in the Increment By box. So, for example, you might set up a Part Number field so that the next record created is assigned 100, and the record created after that is assigned 110, then 120, and so on. To do so, you set Next Value to 100, and Increment By to 10.

Option	Description
	You can use the Generate options to specify when a serial number should be assigned to a new record. The serial number can either be assigned as soon as the record is created (On Creation), or when the record is actually committed (On Commit). The difference between those two options is subtle, yet important. Suppose that a field is set up to have a serial number assigned when the record is created (On Creation), that the Next Value will be 27, and that the field is set to Increment By 1. When a new record is created, the field is set to 27, and FileMaker updates the Next Value for the field to 28. However, if the user cancels the creation of that record (using the Records > Revert Record command), FileMaker does not set the Next Value back to 27, and it remains set to 28. When the next record is created, the field is set to 28. Therefore, it might appear that a record is missing.
Value from Last Visited Record	The field is set to the value that was in the same field of the last record you were on. This option might be helpful if you are entering a number of records whose values are only changing slightly.
Data	The field is set to a specific value that you specify, and that value can be up to 255 characters long.
Calculated Value	The field is set to a value based on a formula that you specify. Earlier in this chapter, I mentioned that calculations can be used in many different ways, and this is one of them. We cover calculations in Chapter 10. When you set up a field so that it is auto-entered with the result of a calculation, you can also set an additional option titled Do Not Replace Existing Value of Field (If Any). When you select that option, FileMaker sets the field (using the calculation) only when the record is created. If you do not select that option, then FileMaker updates the value in that field whenever the result of the calculation changes.
Looked-Up Value	The field is set based on a value that is "looked-up" from a field in a related table. For example, suppose that you have a database used to track contacts, and it includes a Contacts table and a ZIP Codes table. The Contacts table includes fields for Name, Street Address, City, State, and ZIP Code. The ZIP Codes table includes fields for ZIP Code, City and State, and has been loaded with information for all the ZIP codes in the United States. And finally, a relationship exists between the Contacts and ZIP Codes table, based on ZIP Code. In the Contacts table, you could set up the City field so that it is auto-matically set to the value stored in the City field in the related ZIP Code record. You could do the same for the State field. This would save users time as they add new contacts and might help to ensure that the values in the City and State fields are correct and consistent.

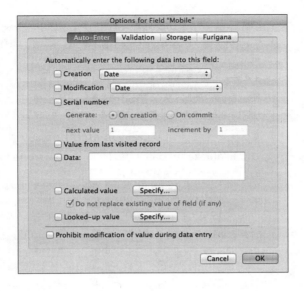

FIGURE 9.2

Auto-Enter options.

 NOTE In some cases, the field options available depend on the field's type. For example, date fields cannot be set up to use the Serial Number Auto-Enter options that other field types can be configured with. Also, in the case of calculation fields, no field options are available.

Let's add a few fields to the Contacts database and configure them with Auto-Enter options.

In the database, there are already three fields that can be used to keep track of contact phone numbers. One is used to track office phone numbers, another tracks mobile phone numbers, and the last one tracks personal phone numbers. It might be helpful to add another field that indicates which of those phone numbers a contact prefers to be contacted with.

To add this field, follow these steps:

1. Click the Field Name field and enter **Preferred Phone Type**.

2. The type of values that we plan to store in this field are words (Office, Mobile, or Personal). Therefore, select Text from the menu.

3. For the field comment, enter the following: **The phone number that the contact prefers to be contacted with.**

4. Click the Create button to add the new field. The field appears in the list of fields and is selected in the list. (If it is not selected, locate the new field and click on it.)

5. With the new field selected, click the Options button, which appears to the right of the Type field toward the bottom-right area of the window. You can also view a field's options by simply double-clicking on it in the list of fields.

6. The Options for Field window displays. This is the window in which you can specify all of a field's options, including the Auto-Enter options, Validation options, and so on. We're interested in the Auto-Enter options at the moment, so be sure to stay on that tab.

   Let's assume that most contacts in our database prefer to be contacted using their Office phone numbers. Therefore, to expedite the entry of new contacts, set up the field so that as new contacts are added, the new Preferred Phone Type field is automatically set to Office. To do so, check the Data option, and in the field located to the right of the option, enter **Office**.

7. Click OK. This closes the Options for Field window.

Let's also suppose that we want to keep track of when new contacts are added and who added them. To do so, add two additional fields.

1. Click the Field Name field, and enter **Date Created**.

2. This field's values are dates, so select the Date field type.

3. For the field comment, enter **The date that the record was added**.

4. Click the Create button to add the new field. As before, the new field appears in the list of fields, and it is selected in the list. (If not, locate the new field, and click on it.)

5. With the new field selected, click the Options button, or double-click the field.

6. The Options for Field window displays. For this field, as new records are added, we want FileMaker to automatically set the value to the current date. This time, click the Creation check box and select the Date option from the drop-down menu that appears next to it.

7. Click OK to save the Auto-Enter option that you set up.

NOTE At the bottom of the Auto-Enter window is a Prohibit Modification of Value During Data Entry check box. When this option is selected, the auto-entered value cannot be changed by the database's users. In the case of the Date Created field that you just created and the Created By field that you create in a moment, you should enable this option to prevent the values from being changed.

Finally, let's add a field to keep track of who created each new contact:

1. Click the Field Name field and enter **Created By**.

2. This field's values are names, so select the Text field type.

3. For the field comment, enter the following: **The user that added the record**.

4. Click the Create button to add the new field.

5. Double-click the newly added field.

6. The Options for Field window displays. For this field, we want FileMaker to automatically set the value to the name of the user who created the record. Click the Creation check box and select the Name option from the drop-down menu that appears next to it.

7. Click OK to save the Auto-Enter option that you set up.

NOTE As explained in Table 9.2, there are two similar options that you can use for this new field. The Creation Name option sets the field to the name of the person who created the record, and does so based on the User Name value that is set in the FileMaker Pro preferences. The other option, Creation Account Name, sets the field to the account name of the person who created the record, which is based on how the user logged in to the database. In this example, you haven't set up any user accounts yet, and you are the only person using the database at this point. Therefore, either option will do. In the future, however, you might want to add two fields: Created By Name and Created By Account Name.

TIP   When I add a new table to a database, there are six fields that I nearly always add to the table: Date Time Created, Date Time Modified, Created By Name, Modified By Name, Created By Account Name, and Modified By Account Name. I create these fields, set their Auto-Enter options accordingly, and enable the Prohibit Modification of Value During Data Entry option. These fields can prove to be immensely helpful when problems occur in the database, or when there is a need to know when a record was added or modified, who added or modified it, and so on.

At this point, you've added a few fields to the Contacts table. To commit those changes, you must close the Manage Database window. To do so, simply click the OK button located in the bottom-right corner of the window. If for some reason you do not want to save the changes that you made, click Cancel.

Once the changes to the database are saved, the Manage Database window closes, and you return to the layout that you were on when you opened the window.

 NOTE   Depending on how you have FileMaker Pro configured, you might see newly added fields automatically appear on the layout. The setting that determines this is located in the FileMaker's preferences window on the Layout tab and is titled Add Newly Defined Fields to Current Layout.

Validation Options

FileMaker's validation field options can be used to ensure that the values entered into a field meet certain criteria and to prevent you from entering incorrect or inconsistent values. For example, you might want values entered into a certain field to be unique. Or you might want values to be a certain type (a number, or date, for example). Like the Auto-Enter field options, FileMaker provides a number of different validation options. Let's take a look at them.

To explore the validation field options (see Figure 9.3), open the Manage Database window once again (File > Manage > Database). Then locate the Preferred Phone Type field that you added earlier and double-click it. The Options for Field window opens. This time, however, we want to focus on the options listed on the Validation tab.

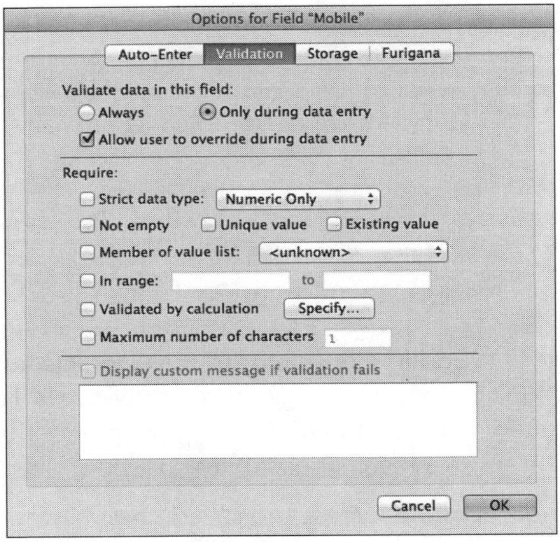

FIGURE 9.3

Field validation options.

The topmost portion of the Validation tab is used to indicate when the validation criteria should be applied and whether users should be given an opportunity to override the validation criteria. By selecting Always, the validation criteria are applied at all times, regardless of whether values are entered manually into the database or imported into the table. If records are imported and the validation is set to Always, any records that do not meet the validation criteria are not imported. By selecting Only During Data Entry, the validation criteria are ignored when records are imported and are enforced only when records are manually entered into the database.

The Allow User to Override During Data Entry option gives users the option to enter values that do not meet the validation criteria. When this option is checked and a user enters an invalid value, a dialog box displays to inform the user that the value doesn't meet the validation criteria. However, the user has the option to use the invalid value anyway. When the option is unchecked, users do not have the option and are forced to either enter a value that does meet the criteria or cancel the creation or modification of the record (see Figure 9.4).

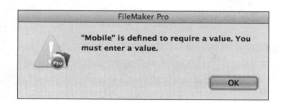

FIGURE 9.4

FileMaker's response when an invalid option is entered into a field and the Allow User to Override During Data Entry option is not checked.

The options in the middle portion of the validation window are used to specify the criteria that you want to use to validate the values being entered into the field. Table 9.3 lists and explains each of those options.

TABLE 9.3 Validation Options

Option	Description
Strict Data Type	Requires that values entered into the field are either a number (Numeric Only), a valid year (4-Digit Year Date), or a valid time (Time of Day).
Not Empty	Requires that a value be entered into the field. Use this option for fields that should always contain a value. For example, the First Name and Last Name fields in the Contacts database should probably use this option. (Records without values in those two fields aren't going to be very helpful, are they?)
Unique Value	Ensures that no two records in the database contain the same value. For example, in a database being used to track companies, you might want values in the Company Name field to be unique, which would prevent duplicates from being entered.
Existing Value	Requires that values entered into the field already exist in the field in at least one previously entered record.
Member of Value List	Is helpful in cases where there are a number of possible valid values. For example, you could create a value list that contains the abbreviations for U.S. states, and then set up a State field so that values entered into it must exist in that value list. (We discuss value lists and how to create them in Chapter 11.)
In Range	Ensures that a field's value falls within a certain numeric range. To use this option, specify the minimum and maximum valid values.

Option	Description
Validated By Calculation	We've already seen a couple of areas in FileMaker Pro where calculations can be used, and the Validated By Calculation is another one. This is perhaps the most powerful and flexible validation option available, because you can specify your criteria using any formula that you want, regardless of how complex it is. For example, suppose that you are creating a database to track orders, and that one of the fields in your Orders table is Ship Method. One of the ship methods that your business offers is Courier, but it can only be used if the order total is over $100 and it is being delivered locally (to customers in the state of Virginia). You could use the Validated By Calculation option to enforce this criteria.
Maximum Number of Characters	Restricts the amount of text that can be entered into a field.

NOTE You can use multiple validation options for the same field, and in some cases, you want to do so. For example, you might set up a State Abbreviation field so that it is not empty, that the values being entered into it are members of a value list, and that the values are only two characters long.

The bottom portion of the Validation tab contains the Display Custom Message If Validation Fails option, which gives you the ability to control the message displayed when an invalid value is entered into the field. You can use this option to display a friendlier, more helpful message, so that the user understands why the value isn't valid and gets help correcting the problem.

You can use FileMaker's validation field options to ensure that values entered into the Preferred Phone Type field are valid. To do so, follow these steps:

1. Locate the Preferred Phone Type field in the list and double-click it. The Options for Field window opens.

2. Change to the Validation tab.

3. In this case, we want the values entered to be among the values in a list (Office, Mobile, or Personal). Therefore, select the Member of Value List check box.

4. In the drop-down list that appears next to the field, select Manage Value Lists.

5. The Manage Value Lists window displays. Notice that a few value lists already have been set up in the Contacts database. However, none of them contain the values that we want to use.

6. Click the New button located at the bottom of the list. The Edit Value List window opens.

7. At the top of the window, in the Value List Name field, enter **Phone Types**.

8. Make sure that the Use Custom Values radio button is selected.

9. In the field that displays below it, enter the values **Office**, **Mobile**, and **Personal**, and place each value on its own line.

10. Click OK to close the Edit Value List window.

11. Click OK again to close the Manage Value Lists window.

12. The drop-down menu that displays next to the Member of Value List check box should now be set to the new Phone Types value list that you created. If not, select it from the list.

13. Click OK to close the Options for Field window.

With the validation options in place, users now receive a warning if they try to enter a value other than those in the value list. (In Chapter 11, you add the Preferred Phone Type field, as well as the other fields that you've created, to a layout. At that point, you can test the Auto-Enter and validation options that you configured for these new fields.)

 NOTE It is possible for you to inadvertently set up a field with validation options and forget to place the field on a layout. When a user adds a new record that doesn't meet the validation rules, they have no way to correct the problem. For example, you might set up a field defined to require a value. In these cases, FileMaker displays a message to the user indicating that the problem occurred and gives them a chance to revert the record. See Figure 9.5 for an example of the message a user might see.

FIGURE 9.5

Error message that appears when attempting to add a record that has a required field, and that field isn't available on the current layout.

Naming Fields and Tables

When naming your fields, it is important to use descriptive and meaningful names. The names that you use might make sense to you now, but will they a few months from now when you need to make changes to the database? And will they make sense to someone else who is using or modifying your database?

Every developer has her own preferred method for naming tables and fields, as well as the other things that make up a FileMaker database (including layouts and scripts). There is no "right" way to name things, and no rules that you need to stick to. That being said, here are some tips for naming tables and fields:

- Use table names that are short and plural—for example, you might name tables Products, Orders, Customers, Suppliers, and Notes.

- In cases where you need to set up a join table (a concept discussed in Chapter 20, "Expanding Your Database"), use a combination of the names of the two tables being joined with an "X" between them. For example, a join table between Students and Classes might be named Students_x_Classes. (Notice the underscores where you expect spaces to be. Avoid using spaces, both in table and field names, because they tend to cause complications with certain calculations.)

- You can name fields in much the same way that you name tables, with one exception: Use singular names. For example, in a Students table, you might see fields named First_Name, Last_Name, Middle_Initial, City, State, and Zip_Code. And while short names are good, try to avoid using abbreviations as much as possible. (This is so if another developer works on the database in the future, he won't have difficulty identifying what a field is used to store.)

Again, those are just a few suggestions for naming tables and fields. In time, you will find a method for naming things that works best for you. But also keep this in mind: FileMaker makes it easy to change the names of things in a database, whether it is a table, field, layout, or script. So if you decide to rename things later on, it won't be a problem.

 NOTE   If you are interested in learning how other developers prefer to name fields and tables, as well as some coding standards that have been suggested, visit http://filemakerstandards.org.

FileMaker is flexible with regard to the table and field names. However, if you try to use a name that FileMaker doesn't support, or one that it can use but that might prove to be troublesome later on, it lets you know. In those cases, a dialog box similar to the one in Figure 9.6 displays.

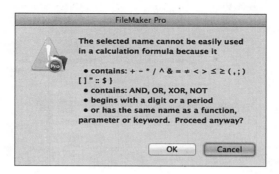

FIGURE 9.6

Warning message that displays when you specify a field name that might be problematic.

In these cases, it is probably best to change the name. Otherwise, you might run into problems later, especially when it comes to using the table and/or field in calculations.

Changing Fields

It is possible to change a field's name, as well as its type, Auto-Enter options, validation options, and so on. To make changes to a field, open the Manage Database window, just as you did when you added fields. Then locate the field in the list and click on it.

The name of the field, as well as its type and comment, appears in the area below the list of fields. You can change the name of the field, the field type, and the comments. When you are finished, click the Change button.

To make changes to a field's Auto-Enter or validation options, select the field in the list and double-click it. The Field Options window displays; this is where you can make your changes.

NOTE When changing a field's type, a window might display asking whether you really want to make the change. Whether you see the window depends on the type of field originally chosen and what you are changing it to. For example, if you change from a text field to a date field, you see a message indicating that "When changing the field type to Date or Timestamp, FileMaker will expand any partial dates to full four-digit year dates. Proceed anyway?" (see Figure 9.7). In other words, FileMaker is letting you know that it will do its best to convert values that had been entered in the original text field to dates. You can proceed with the change or cancel it.

FIGURE 9.7

Warning message that displays when you change a field's type.

Deleting Fields

If you added a field to a table, and you no longer want or need that field, you can easily delete it. To do so, open the Manage Database window, locate the field, and select it. Then click the Delete button located at the bottom of the window. FileMaker asks you to confirm the deletion of the field.

 WARNING   When it comes to deleting fields, there is no undo function. Therefore, before you delete a field, make absolutely sure that you no longer need the values in it.

 NOTE   If you attempt to delete a field being used as part of another field's calculation formula, FileMaker does not allow the field to be deleted, as shown in Figure 9.8. Similarly, if a field that you are trying to delete is being used in a script, FileMaker warns you that the field is being used in a script and gives you an option to cancel the deletion of the field.

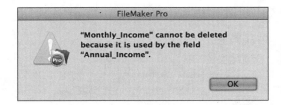

FIGURE 9.8

Error message that appears when you attempt to delete a field being used in another field's calculation formula.

Field Storage Options

In addition to Auto-Enter and validation options, FileMaker also gives you several options for how a field is stored in the database. These options are displayed on the Storage tab of the Options for Field window, shown in Figure 9.9.

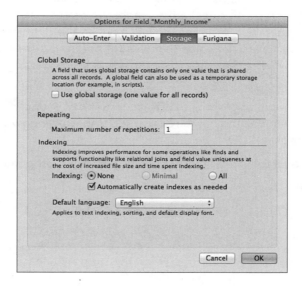

FIGURE 9.9

FileMaker's field storage options.

Global Fields

The first storage option available is called Global Storage. We refer to fields configured to use global storage as global fields.

Values stored in global fields are the same regardless of what record you are on. In addition, in databases that contain multiple tables, the values in global fields are always available, regardless of what table you are working on. Because of this characteristic, global fields are often used to store values needed throughout different areas of a database. For example, you might store a company's logo or name in a global field and then use the field on different layouts. Developers also often use global fields to temporarily store values, including those entered by users into dialog boxes (which we discuss in Chapter 13, "Automating Tasks with Scripts").

Another thing that makes global fields different is how their values are retained. For example, suppose that you are using a database stored locally on your computer, and one of the fields is set up with the Global Storage option. If you were to enter a value into the field, close the database, and reopen the database, the value in the field would be retained.

However, things get a little complicated in situations where a database is being shared (a topic that we discuss in Chapter 16, "Sharing a Database"). If you were to share that same database, the value that users see in the global field would be what it had been set to prior to the database being shared. Regardless of whether you, or any other user, changes the value, when the database is opened again, users continue to see the value that was set before the database was shared. Additionally, when a database is shared, changes made to global fields are unique to each user.

Let's add a couple of global fields to keep track of your company's name and logo. If you aren't already in the Manage Database window, open it now. Then follow these steps:

1. Click the Field Name field, and enter **Settings Company Name**.

2. Select the Text field type.

3. Click the Create button to add the new field.

4. Double-click the newly added field, and the Options for Field window displays.

5. Click on the Storage tab.

6. Check the Use Global Storage option.

7. Click OK.

Follow the same steps to create a field called Settings Company Logo. However, for this field, set the field's type to Container.

Repeating Fields

The next field storage option available is called Repeating. We call fields configured with this option *repeating fields*. Repeating fields allow you to store more than one value in a single field. For example, suppose that you want to keep track of the dates of phone conversations that you have had with your contacts. You can create a single field to keep track of all those dates.

Let's take a moment to add a repeating field. If you aren't already in the Manage Database window, open it now. Then follow these steps:

1. Click the Field Name field, and enter **Phone Call Date**.

2. Select the Date field type.

3. Click the Create button to add the new field.

4. Double-click the newly added field, and the Options for Field window displays.

5. Click on the Storage tab.

6. In the Maximum Number of Repetitions field, enter **10**.

7. Click OK.

As you can see, repeating fields are easy to set up. However, they can cause big problems later on. For example, when configuring a repeating field, you have to indicate the maximum number of repetitions that can be stored. In the previous example, you created a repeating field that can be used to keep track of up to 10 phone call dates. If you end up speaking with a contact more than 10 times, you won't have a repetition available for the additional calls. To track additional phone calls, you have to modify the field's repeating settings and also make changes to the layout that the field appears on. That's not a huge problem, but it is inconvenient. And you have to repeat that process each time the maximum number of repetitions simply isn't enough.

But a bigger problem with repeating fields is that they can be difficult to report on. If you want to create a report that lists each contact and the most recent date that you spoke with them, you have to add another field that uses a calculation function to determine the maximum call date for each contact.

 TIP Use of a repeating field often indicates that a related table is needed. In the previous example, instead of using a repeating field to keep track of the phone call dates, a related table could be set up. The advantage of the related table is that you can use it to track additional attributes of each call. For example, in addition to the date of the call, you can also track a note about the call, a follow-up date, and so on. And best of all, because of how related tables can be displayed on layouts via portals, you can keep track of as many calls as necessary. (We discuss portals in Chapter 11.) To summarize, before using a repeated field, consider using a related table instead.

Indexing Options

In FileMaker databases, indexes are used to improve the speed with which records can be found. They also facilitate setting up relationships between records and are necessary for fields that are going to be used in value lists.

Think of an index as a list of the values stored in a particular field. When FileMaker needs to determine which records have a certain value, it can refer to the field's index instead of scanning through all the records in the table.

For the most part, indexes are beneficial. They can significantly increase the speed with which finds can be performed. However, they do have a few drawbacks. One drawback is that indexes can significantly increase the size of a database. Another is that it might take longer to add, change, or delete a large number of records, because FileMaker needs to update the indexes.

 NOTE Due to the unique nature of container fields, FileMaker does not provide indexing options for them.

FileMaker's indexing options give you the ability to control when and how each field's index is created. Table 9.4 describes the three main indexing options.

TABLE 9.4 Indexing Options

Option	Description
None	With this option, FileMaker does not create an index for the field. Therefore, it cannot be used to create relationships between related tables.
Minimal	This option is available only for text fields and calculation fields that result in text values. Text fields are unique in that two types of indexes can be created for them. The first is the value index, which is created using only the first 100 characters of each line in the field. The second is the word index, which is created based on every unique word in the field. When a text field's indexing option is set to Minimal, only the value index is created.
All	For text fields and calculation fields that result in text values, this option creates both value and word indexes. For all other field types (with the exception of Container fields), this option creates a value index.

Another index-related option that FileMaker provides is to Automatically Create Indexes as Needed. When this option is selected, FileMaker creates an index for the field when one is required. For example, when a user performs a find on a field for which an index does not already exist, FileMaker creates the index. In those cases, that first find might take longer than usual as FileMaker creates the index.

NOTE When a new field is added to a table, the indexing option is automatically set to None, and the Automatically Create Indexes as Needed option is selected.

Indexing Calculated Fields

FileMaker provides an additional indexing option specifically for calculation fields. The option is displayed as Do Not Store Calculation Results—Recalculate as Needed. For calculation fields that refer to fields in related records or to summary values, this option is selected and cannot be changed. The reason is that FileMaker does not have a way to maintain an index for the field.

For calculation fields that can be indexed, the Do Not Store Calculation Results option can be checked and unchecked. When this option is selected, FileMaker recalculates the field's value every time it is needed—whether it is being displayed or searched on. As a result, performing finds on the field might be slow.

However, there are cases where a calculated field needs to be recalculated for it to return the correct value. For example, suppose that we have a database of invoices and that one of the calculation fields is used to determine the age of an invoice. The calculation formula involves taking the current date and subtracting the invoice date. If the Do Not Store Calculation Results option is unchecked, the value in the field is calculated only when a record is added. As days go by, the value would remain unchanged. By selecting the Do Not Store Calculation Results option, the value is automatically updated as needed and always reflects the age of the invoice based on the current date. (We discuss calculations in depth in Chapter 10.)

THE ABSOLUTE MINIMUM

In this chapter, you started to go beyond the basics, and you did so by making changes to the Contacts database that you created in Part I. Specifically, you learned how to modify a table by adding, changing, and deleting fields in it. Here are the key points to remember:

- FileMaker supports a number of different types of fields, and selecting the right one depends on the type of data to be stored in a field.

- Container fields are a special type of field that can be used to store nearly any type of digital file, including images, documents, movies, and more.

- A number of different Auto-Enter options are available that can be used to automatically set a field's value when a new record is added.

- You can use validation options to ensure that the values entered into a field meet certain criteria and to provide guidance to your database's users if a value entered is invalid.

- You can be flexible with the names that you give to fields and tables. However, FileMaker warns you if you use a name that might cause problems later on.

- You can use field storage options to control how values are stored in fields. For example, you can set up global storage so that a field's value is the same regardless of what record you are on.

- FileMaker also gives you the ability to control how a field is indexed. Indexes are used to improve the speed that a field can be searched on and to create relationships between related records.

WORKING WITH CALCULATIONS

In previous chapters, several references were made to "calculations." For example, you learned that one of the types of fields that you can add to a FileMaker database is a calculation field, which is a special type of field whose value is based on a formula.

In this chapter, you learn about calculations in great depth. You learn why calculations are important in FileMaker, and discover the many different ways that you can use them in your FileMaker-based solutions. We wrap up the chapter with a discussion on FileMaker plug-ins, which you can use to add even more functionality to FileMaker.

What Are Calculations?

One of FileMaker's many strengths is its capability to take a formula and evaluate it. We refer to this as *performing a calculation* based on a *calculation formula*. The calculation formula can be as simple or as complex as necessary, and can be based on values in the database, on functions built into FileMaker, on custom functions you created yourself, on functions available via FileMaker plug-ins, or any combination of the above. The result of a calculation formula can be a text value, numeric value, date, time, timestamp, container, or logical (true or false) value.

FileMaker can take the result of a calculation and either do something with it directly or take some action based on the result. In some cases, we might want FileMaker to display a calculated value to the user or include a calculated value on a report. In other cases, we might want FileMaker to evaluate the result of a calculation and determine whether some additional action should be taken, or to display or hide something from a user.

Why Calculations Are Important

In FileMaker, calculations are used in a number of ways. As mentioned earlier, one of the most common uses is calculation fields, where the value of the field is based on a formula. However, calculations can also be used in these ways:

- To specify a value to be automatically entered into a field
- To check to see whether a value that has been entered into a field is valid
- To set the value of a field during the execution of a script
- To determine whether an object on a layout should be displayed
- To change the appearance of an object on a layout based on certain conditions
- To determine whether a user has permission to perform a certain action
- To generate values to be used in a chart
- To display tooltips to users when they hover over an object on a layout
- To determine what action a script should perform next

As you can see, calculations are used throughout FileMaker and in a many different ways—and the previous list is only a partial one! Because calculations are so widely used in FileMaker, it is important that you understand what they are, how they work, and how to write your own calculation formulas.

The Specify Calculation Dialog

Regardless of how and where you are going to use a calculation in a FileMaker database, there is only one method to use to enter calculation formulas—the Specify Calculation dialog. You can see an example of it in Figure 10.1.

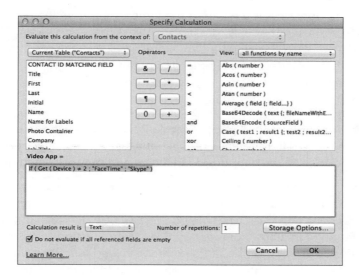

FIGURE 10.1

The Specify Calculation dialog window.

Using this Specify Calculation dialog, you can easily specify the formula that you want to use by selecting fields, operators, and functions. You can also specify a few other options, including the context in which the calculation should be performed, whether the result should be stored, and more.

Let's review the Specify Calculation dialog in detail—working from top to bottom, left to right.

If you are entering a formula to be used for a calculated field, to specify a value to be auto-entered into a field, or to validate a field's value, then the top of the dialog includes a field that you can use to specify the context in which the calculation is to be evaluated. You learn more about the concept of context in Chapter 20, "Expanding Your Database." For now, think of context as the starting point from which the calculation is evaluated.

In the top-left area of the dialog, you see the table menu, which you can use to specify the table from which you want to select fields. Below that is the field list. You can easily add a field to a formula by double-clicking on a field name.

In the top middle of the dialog are the operators that FileMaker supports. This includes common mathematical operators (add, subtract, multiply, and divide), textual operators (for concatenating text, quoting a text value, or specifying a carriage return), and parentheses so that you can specify the order in which you want parts of the formula to be evaluated.

Next to the operators is a menu of the logical operators that FileMaker supports, including equals, not equals, greater than, less than, and so on. These logical operators are used to compare two expressions, and the result of that comparison is always true or false. For example, you might use the greater than operator to determine whether an invoice is past due, like this:

```
Due_Date > Get ( CurrentDate )
```

The top-right area of the Specify Calculation dialog is used to easily locate and select the many different types of functions that FileMaker supports. By default, the list includes all the supported functions, and they are listed alphabetically.

However, you can filter the list by selecting a general category of functions using the View menu that appears above the list. The functions are grouped into categories based on what they do and what type of result they return. For example, text functions, number functions, date functions, and more. These categories, and some of the more commonly used functions, are discussed later in this chapter. Note that you can easily add a function to your formula by double-clicking the function name. Doing so adds the function to your calculation, including any parameters that the function supports.

 TIP   If you happen to know the name of a function that you want to use in your formula, and want to more easily locate it in the list of functions, click on any function name in the list, and then type the first few characters of the function that you want to use. FileMaker automatically scrolls to the first function that matches what you typed. Note that this tip also applies to the list of fields.

The middle of the Specify Calculation dialog is the area in which you specify a formula. You can manually enter a formula here, or select from the fields, operators, and functions that you want to use—or use a combination of those methods to specify a formula.

If the formula you are creating is being used for a calculated field, an additional group of options are displayed in the area toward the bottom of the window. One of those options is the calculation result type, and you use this to indicate whether FileMaker should treat the result as a text value, number, date, time, timestamp, or container. You can also indicate whether the field should be handled as a repeating field, with the default being 1 (indicating that only one value is stored in the field). And finally, you can also specify the storage options for the calculated field by clicking the Storage Options button. See the "Indexing Calculated Fields." section in Chapter 9, "Working with Fields," for a review of field storage options.

 NOTE A repeating field is designed to store multiple values. In older versions of FileMaker, particularly back when FileMaker wasn't the relational database that it is today, the use of repeating fields was common. However, they aren't used much anymore.

At the very bottom of the Specify Calculation dialog is one last option, and it has to do with whether FileMaker should even bother to evaluate the formula. The option is the Do Not Evaluate If All Referenced Fields Are Empty check box. By checking this box, you are indicating to FileMaker that in cases where the formula uses one or more fields, and those fields are empty, it should not evaluate the formula. In those cases, the result of the formula is an empty value (which we refer to in database terms as a *NULL* value).

Let's take a look at an example of why you might want to use this option. Suppose that in your contacts database, you want to add a calculated field whose value is the last name of the contact, followed by a comma and a space, and then the contact's first name. The formula might look like this:

```
Last & ", " & First
```

In cases where the first and last names are missing, and the Do Not Evaluate If All Referenced Fields Are Empty box is unchecked, the result of the formula would be a comma and a space. However, by checking the Do Not Evaluate If All Referenced Fields Are Empty box, the result is NULL.

Adding a Calculation Field

Now that you are familiar with the Specify Calculation dialog, let's add a calculated field to the Contacts database that you created in Part I, "Getting to Know FileMaker Pro." If you have not already done so, open the database and then perform the following steps:

1. Open the Manage Database window by selecting File > Manage > Database.

2. In the Field Name area, enter **First Name Initial**.

3. For the field type, select Calculation.

4. Click the Create button. The Specify Calculation dialog displays (see Figure 10.2).

5. From the list of functions, locate the Left function and double-click it. This adds the function to the formula.

6. Replace the word "text" in the formula with "First." You can manually make this change by selecting the word and typing **First**, or you can simply select the First field from the list of fields.

7. Replace "numberofCharacters" with the number "1." The formula should look like this: Left (First ; 1)

8. At the bottom of the dialog, change the calculation result from "number" to "text."

9. Click the Storage Options button. The Storage Options dialog displays (see Figure 10.3).

10. Check the Do Not Store Calculation Results option.

11. Click OK to close the Storage Options dialog.

12. Click OK again to close the Specify Calculation dialog.

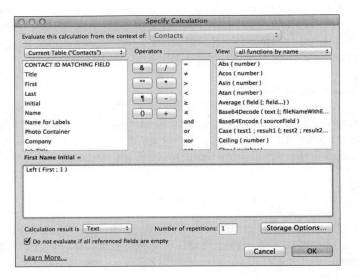

FIGURE 10.2

The Specify Calculation dialog window with the formula for the new First Name Initial calculation field.

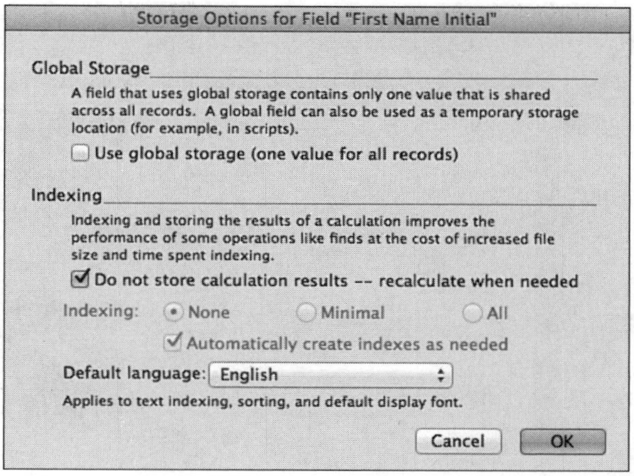

FIGURE 10.3

The Storage Options dialog for the new First Name Initial calculation field.

The new calculation field should appear in the list of fields.

Let's take a moment to add the new field to a layout, so that you can see it in action. This also serves as a preview of what we cover in Chapter 11, "Working with Layouts." Follow these steps:

1. Make sure that you are on the Desktop > Contact Details layout (see Figure 10.4).

2. Enter Layout mode. You can either select View > Layout Mode, select Layout from the menu in the bottom-left area of the window, or use a shortcut (Command+L on a Mac or Ctrl+L on Windows).

3. In the dark area of the Status Toolbar, locate the Field Picker button and click it. This opens the Field Picker floating window (see Figure 10.5).

4. Scroll to the bottom of the list of fields, and locate the new First Name Initial field.

5. Click on the field name, drag it to the area above the Title field on the layout, and release the mouse button.

6. Change back to Browse mode. You can either select View > Browse Mode, select Browse from the menu in the bottom-left area of the window, or use a shortcut (Command+B on a Mac or Ctrl+B on Windows).

7. A dialog window displays, asking whether you want to save the changes that you made to the layout (see Figure 10.6). Click the Save button.

FIGURE 10.4

The Desktop > Contact Details layout as viewed in Layout mode.

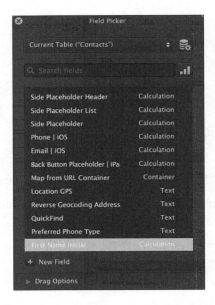

FIGURE 10.5

The Field Picker window. Use this to add the new First Name Initial calculation field to the layout.

FIGURE 10.6

The dialog window that appears when you change from Layout mode. To save your changes, click the Save button.

The field that you created and added to the layout should now appear on the layout. Click through the records, and you see that the field's value is the first initial of each contact's first name (see Figure 10.7).

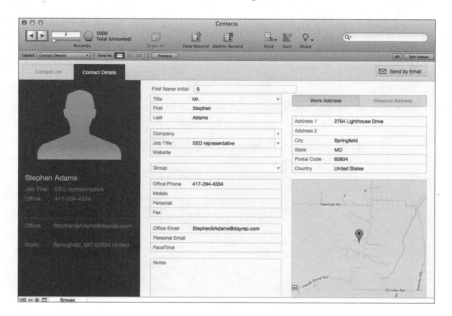

FIGURE 10.7

The updated Contact Details layout with the new First Name Initial calculation field added to it.

Let's add a second calculated field to the database. This time, we create one whose value is the first initial of the contact's first name, followed by a period and space, and then contact's last name.

1. Open the Manage Database window.

2. In the Field Name area, enter **First Initial Last Name**.

3. For the field type, select Calculation.

4. Click the Create button. The Specify Calculation dialog displays.

5. From the list of fields, select the First Name Initial field that you created earlier. Locate the field, and double-click it to add it to the formula.

6. Locate the concatenation operator (&) and click it. Your formula at this point should look like this: First Name Initial &

7. Type double quotation marks, a period, a space, and double quotation marks. Your formula should now look like this: First Name Initial & ". "

8. Add another concatenation operator (&) to the formula.

9. Locate the Last field from the field list and double-click to add it to the formula. The formula should now look like this: First Name Initial & ". " & Last (see Figure 10.8).

10. At the bottom of the dialog, change the calculation result from number to text.

11. Click OK to close the Specify Calculation dialog.

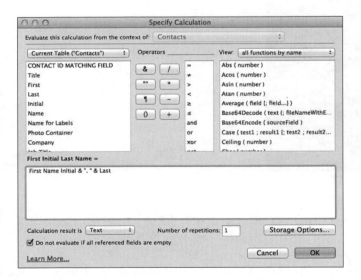

FIGURE 10.8

The Specify Calculation dialog window with the formula for the new First Initial Last Name calculation field.

The First Initial Last Name calculation field should appear in the list of fields. If you want to see this field in action, follow the same steps that you took earlier when you added the First Name Initial field to the layout. However, this time select the First Initial Last Name field.

The formula for the second field is a little more complicated than the one we used for the first field. In fact, you might have noticed that we actually used the first field in the formula for the second field. This is interesting in that it shows that you can use calculated fields in calculation formulas. Note that we could have specified the formula for the second field without using the first field, like this:

```
Left ( First ; 1 ) & ". " & Last
```

However, since we already had the field available, it made sense to use it.

 NOTE When evaluating a calculation formula, FileMaker uses the same "order of operations" rules that are used in the world of mathematics. It evaluates expressions wrapped in parentheses first. Next, it performs multiplication and division operations, going from left to right. It then performs addition and subtraction, also from left to right. And finally, any text concatenation (a term used to describe the combining of two text values) is performed last.

Types of Calculation Functions

The formula that you used to add the First Name Initial field to your Contacts database used the Left function. This is just one of the nearly 300 functions that FileMaker supports, and covering all of them would be an undertaking. This section describes the functions you will use the most often, as well as a few particularly interesting ones.

 NOTE If you are interested in learning about all the available functions, I suggest that you use the FileMaker help system. Select Help > FileMaker Pro Help (see Figure 10.9) and choose Functions Reference in the Reference area (see Figure 10.10). The Functions Reference groups functions by categories, including Aggregate functions, Container functions, Date functions, and so on.

FIGURE 10.9

The FileMaker Pro Help window. To open this open, select Help > FileMaker Pro Help.

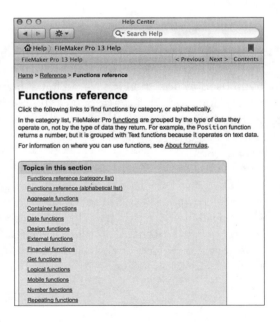

FIGURE 10.10

The FileMaker Functions Reference, as seen in the Help window. Use this handy reference tool to get detailed information on all of FileMaker's functions.

Aggregate Functions

Aggregate functions are used to calculate a statistical value, such as an average, a count, a sum, minimums and maximums, and so on. These functions can be used in values stored in multiple fields of a record, in values stored in related records, or in repeating fields.

 NOTE Don't confuse aggregate functions with the Summary Field type that you learned about in Chapter 9. Aggregate functions are used in calculations based on values in the fields of a single record, or in values from related records. Summary Fields are used to calculate aggregate values from records in the found set.

 NOTE Most of the aggregate functions ignore empty and invalid values. In other words, they only take into account numeric values. One exception is the List function, described in the following:

- **Average**—Returns the average of the values in the specified field.
- **Count**—The number of values in the specified field.
- **List**—Returns a list of the values in the specified field, with carriage returns between each one. Empty values are ignored.
- **Max / Min**—The maximum and minimum values in a specified field, respectively.
- **Sum**—The total amount of the values in a specified field.

Container Functions

Chapter 9 mentioned that container fields are possibly the most interesting type of field that FileMaker supports, and the functions related to containers are equally interesting. You can use these functions to create the content stored in containers, to change the content in them, and to analyze their contents.

- **Base64Encode / Base64Decode**—These functions can be used to Base64 encode and decode the contents of a container. Base64 encoding takes binary data and converts it to text, making it easier to exchange the data with another system, such as a Web service.
- **GetContainerAttribute**—You can use this function to get details about the contents of a container field. For example, if the container's contents are a

photo, you can use **GetContainerAttribute(Container Field; "latitude")** and **GetContainerAttribute(Container Field; "longitude")** to determine the latitude and longitude of the location in which the photo was taken. If the container contains an audio file (such as an MP3 or M4A file) you can use **GetContainerAttribute(Container Field; "artist")** to get the name of the artist that performed the song. Several attributes are available. If you want to get all the attributes applicable to the file in the container, use **GetContainerAttribute(Container Field; "all")**.

- **GetWidth / GetHeight**—Used to get the width and height, respectively, in pixels of an image stored in a container.

- **GetThumbnail**—Returns an image based on the contents of a specified container, and size based on the width and height specified. For example, to get a 300 x 100 pixel thumbnail of an image stored in a container named Container Field, you might use this formula: **GetThumbnail(Container Field; 300; 100)**.

Date Functions

Date functions can be used to calculate dates, modify date values, and transform dates into text values (such as the names of months).

 NOTE Behind the scenes, FileMaker actually stores date values as a number based on the number of days that have elapsed since 1/1/0001. As a result, doing math on dates is easy. For example, to get the date that is 30 days from the current date, you could use this formula: **Get(CurrentDate) + 30**.

- **Date**—Creates a date value based on the specified month, day, and year. For example, to create a date value for July 28, 2014, use: **Date (6; 28; 2014)**.

- **Day / Month / Year**—Returns the numeric date, month, and year for a given date, respectively. For example, to get the numeric value for the day in the date November 23, 2001, use **Day ("11/23/2001")**, which returns the value 23.

- **DayName / MonthName**—Returns the full name of the day or month, respectively, for a given date. For example, **MonthName ("11/27/1968")** returns "November."

- **WeekOfYear**—Returns the number of weeks that have elapsed since January 1 of the given date. For example, **WeekOfYear ("3/30/2014")** returns 14.

Design Functions

You can use FileMaker's design functions to get technical information about FileMaker databases. For example, you can use the **DatabaseNames** function to get a list of all of the databases currently open, or **FieldNames** to get a list of the fields on a certain layout. These functions are typically used for advanced applications.

Financial Functions

FileMaker supports four financial functions: FV (future value), NPV (net present value), PMT (payment), and PV (present value).

Get Functions

You can use FileMaker's numerous Get functions to access a wide variety of information about the FileMaker environment. For example, there are functions that can be used to determine the version of FileMaker that the user is running, the current date and time, the field that the user is in, and more.

- **Get(AccountName)**—Returns the name of the account that the user logged in to the database with.

- **Get(ActiveFieldName)**—Returns the name of the field that user is currently in.

- **Get(ApplicationVersion)**—Returns the type of FileMaker client that the user is running and the version of the software. For example, Go_iPad 13.0v2 indicates that the user is accessing the database using FileMaker Go on an iPad and is using version 13.0v2 of the app.

- **Get(CurrentDate) / Get(CurrentTime) / Get(CurrentTimestamp)**—Returns the current date, time, and timestamp, respectively.

- **Get(Device)**—Returns a number that represents the type of device that the user is accessing the database with. For example, 1 indicates that the user is on a Mac, 2 indicates that the user is using a Windows-based PC, and so on.

- **Get(InstalledFMPlugins)**—Returns information about any FileMaker plug-ins that the user has installed. You learn more about plug-ins later in this chapter.

- **Get(LayoutName)**—Returns the name of the layout the user is on.

NOTE FileMaker's Get functions are used in a number of interesting ways. For example, they are often used in scripts to determine what type of device the user is accessing the database with and the size of the dimensions of the user's screen, so that appropriate layouts are displayed. They are also used for auditing purposes, in script triggers (which we discuss in the next chapter), and more.

Logical Functions

Most of the logical functions are used to evaluate an expression to determine whether it is true or false, and return a value based on the result. Others are used to get values from other fields.

- **If**—Perhaps the most frequently used logical function, the If function evaluates an expression, and if it is true, returns one value; otherwise, it returns another value. For example, suppose that we are working in an order processing database and that we have a calculated field named Shipping Amount whose formula is **If (Order Total > 500; 0; Order Total * .05)**. With this formula, orders over $500 are shipped at no charge. For all other orders, the shipping is calculated by multiplying the order amount by 5%.

- **Case**—This function is similar to the If function, except that it supports multiple tests and results. For example, suppose that the previous Shipping Amount example is actually a bit more complicated: Orders under $250 are charged $15 in shipping; orders between $250 and $499 are $7.50; and orders $500 and over are shipped at no charge. In this example, we can use the following formula: **Case (Order_Total < 250; 15; Order_Total ≥ 250 and Order_Total < 500; 7.5; 0)**.

- **ExecuteSQL**—You can use the ExecuteSQL function to get the results of a SQL SELECT statement. You can specify the SELECT statement with dynamic parameters, as well as the delimiters to use for the fields and rows. Note that only SELECT statements are supported. You cannot use ExecuteSQL to modify data, or to make changes to the structure of the database itself.

- **IsEmpty**—This function can be used to determine whether a given field is empty. If so, it returns True. Otherwise, it returns false.

- **Let**—The Let function is typically used to break complex formulas into smaller, more manageable pieces. To do so, you can specify multiple variables whose values persist for the duration of the calculation. You can then reference those variables to return a result. For example, we can use a Let statement to create the First Initial Last Name calculated field, like this: **Let ([initial = Left (First ; 1)]; initial & ". " & Last)**.

NOTE Using the Let function is one way to manage complicated calculation formulas. However, you might find that managing some of your more complicated formulas is easier if you add whitespace and comments to them. In some cases, adding whitespace (including spaces, tabs, and carriage returns) to a formula makes it easier to read—and FileMaker ignores that whitespace when it evaluates the formula.

You can add comments to your formulas in two ways. For single-line comments, you can add two forward slashes, like this: **// This is my comment.** For multiline comments, you start the comment with a forward slash and an asterisk, and you close the comment with an asterisk and forward slash. For example:

```
/*
This is a multi-line comment.
FileMaker will ignore this when it evaluates the
formula.
*/
```

Mobile Functions

FileMaker supports two functions that apply exclusively to users running FileMaker Go on iOS devices. Those functions are **Location** and **LocationValues**. The Location function can be used to determine the latitude and longitude of the device. The LocationValues function is similar, except that it also returns the altitude of the device. Both functions can take an optional timeout parameter, which can be used to specify the maximum number of seconds within which the values are to be returned.

Number Functions

The number functions are used to perform mathematical operations and to generate numeric values. Most common mathematical functions are supported, including

- **Abs**—Returns the absolute value of a given number
- **Ceiling**—Takes a given number and rounds it to the next highest integer
- **Floor**—Takes a given number and rounds it down to the next lowest integer
- **Mod**—Returns the remainder after a number is divided by another
- **Round**—Rounds a number to a specified number of decimal places
- **Sqrt**—Returns the square root of a specified number
- **Random**—Generates a random number between 0 and 1

Text Functions

FileMaker supports a number of functions that can be used to manipulate and evaluate text values. We used the Left function earlier in this chapter to get the first initial of a contact's first name. There are similar functions for extracting words from a value, capitalizing values, and more. There are also several functions that can be used to work with text values that are actually return-delimited lists.

- **Exact**—Compares two text values and determines whether they are exactly the same, including the use of upper- and lowercase letters.

- **GetAsDate**—Converts a text value into a FileMaker date—for example, **GetAsDate ("11/23/2001")**.

- **GetAsNumber**—Converts a text value into a numeric value and ignores any non-numeric characters in the process. For example, **GetAsNumber("Suite 151")** returns 151.

- **GetAsTime**—Similar to the GetAsDate formula, except that this function converts a text value to a FileMaker time value.

- **GetValue**—Obtains a specific value from a return-delimited list of values. For example, suppose that you have a Shipping Methods field with this value: Standard+Two-Day+Overnight (where + is a carriage return). To get the second value from the list, you would use: **GetValue ("Shipping Methods"; 2)**

- **Left / Right**—Return a specified number of characters from the left or from the right of a text value. For example, **Left ("FileMaker"; 4)** returns "File" while **Right ("FileMaker"; 5)** returns "Maker."

- **Middle**—Similar to Left and Right, except it extracts characters starting at any point within a text value. For example, **Middle("FileMaker"; 5; 4)** returns "Make."

- **LeftWords / RightWords / MiddleWords**—Similar to the Left, Right, and Middle functions described earlier. However, these functions work at the word level. For example, **LeftWords ("FileMaker 13 Absolute Beginner's Guide"; 2)** returns "FileMaker 13" while **RightWords ("FileMaker 13 Absolute Beginner's Guide"; 3)** returns "Absolute Beginner's Guide." To determine when one word starts and another begins, FileMaker looks at special characters, including spaces, tabs, carriage returns, and most common punctuation marks.

- **LeftValues / RightValues / MiddleValues**—Also similar to the Left, Right, and Middle functions described earlier. However, these functions are used to extract values from return-delimited lists.

- **Upper / Lower**—Returns the text value with all letters in uppercase or lowercase.

- **Proper**—Returns the text value with the first letter of each word in uppercase and all others in lowercase. For example, **Proper ("fileMaker")** returns "Filemaker."

- **Length**—Calculates the number of characters in a text value. Note that spaces, numbers, and special characters (including other "whitespace" characters such as tabs and carriage returns) are counted.

- **PatternCount**—Determines the number of times that a value appears in another value. For example, **PatternCount ("This is a test." ; "is")** returns 2. Note that PatternCount is not case-sensitive. Therefore, **PatternCount ("This is a test." ; "IS")** and **PatternCount ("This IS a test." ; "Is")** also return 2.

- **Position**—Determines the position of one value in another value. For example, **Position ("This IS a test." ; "Is"; 1; 1)** returns 3, indicating that the first occurrence of "is" in the sentence is at the third character. The third parameter of the function is used to specify where the search should begin, based on the number of characters from the beginning of the value. The fourth parameter is used to specify the occurrence of the value. For example, **Position ("This IS a test." ; "Is"; 1; 2)** returns 6, because the second occurrence of "is" begins at the sixth character.

- **Replace**—Replaces characters in a text value with another value. For example, **Replace("FileMaker"; 1; 4; "Money")** returns "MoneyMaker."

- **Substitute**—Similar to Replace in that it can also be used to replace characters in a text value with another value. However, with Substitute, you specify a value to replace instead of the starting position and number of characters. For example, **Substitute("FileMaker"; "File"; "Money")** also returns "MoneyMaker."

- **Trim**—Removes any leading or trailing spaces from a text value.

- **ValueCount**—Returns the number of values in a return-delimited list. For example, **ValueCount ("Standard+Two-Day+Overnight")** returns 3.

- **WordCount**— Returns the number of words in a given text value.

Text Formatting Functions

Using FileMaker's text formatting functions, you can change the appearance of text, including the color, font, size, and style of the text.

- **RGB**—Use this function to specify a color when using the other color-related text formatting functions. The function returns a number that represents the color based on its red, green, and blue values. For example, **RGB (255; 0; 0)** specifies red, **RGB (0; 255; 0)** represents green, **RGB (0; 0; 255)** represents blue, **RGB (0; 0; 0)** represents black, and **RGB (255; 255; 255)** represents white.

- **TextColor**—Use this function to change the color of a text value. For example, **TextColor("File"; RGB(0;0;255)) & TextColor("Maker"; RGB(0;0;0))** returns the word "FileMaker" with "File" in blue and "Maker" in black.

- **TextColorRemove**—Use this function to remove either all colors or a specific color from a text value.

- **TextFont**—Use this function to change a text value's font. For example, **TextFont("FileMaker";"Courier")** results in a text value "FileMaker" formatted in Courier.

- **TextFontRemove**—Use this function to remove either all fonts or a specific font from a text value.

- **TextSize**—Use this function to change the size of a text value. For example, **TextSize("File"; 12) & TextSize("Maker"; 18)** results in a text value of FileMaker, where "File" is 12 points and "Maker" is 18 points.

- **TextSizeRemove**—Use this function to remove either all text sizes, or a specific text size, from a text value.

- **TextStyleAdd**—Use this function to apply one or more styles to a text value. Supported styles are Plain, Bold, Italic, Underline, HighlightYellow, Condense, Extend, Strikethrough, SmallCaps, Superscript, Subscript, Uppercase, Lowercase, Titlecase, WordUnderline, and DoubleUnderline. You can apply multiple styles simultaneously by joining them with a "+" symbol. For example, **TextStyleAdd ("FileMaker"; Bold+Underline)** results in "FileMaker" in bold and underlined.

- **TextStyleRemove**—Use this function to remove one or more styles from a text value. Like **TextStyleAdd**, you can choose to remove multiple styles simultaneously by joining them with a "+" symbol.

Time Functions

FileMaker supports four time-related functions. **Hour**, **Minute**, and **Seconds** can be used to extract hour, minute, and seconds portions of a specified time value. The **Time** function can be used to generate a FileMaker time value. For example, Time (12; 40; 33) returns a time value of 12:40:33.

TimeStamp Function

There is only one timestamp-related function, and it is appropriately named **TimeStamp**. You can use this function to combine a date and time value into a single timestamp value. For example, **Timestamp(Date(03;15;2014); Time(13;33;55))** returns a timestamp value of 3/15/2014 1:33:55 PM.

Trigonometric Functions

As you might expect, FileMaker also supports a number of trigonometric functions, including **Acos** (arccosine), **Asin** (arcsine), **Atan** (arc tangent), **Cos** (cosine), **Degrees**, the **Pi** constant, **Radians**, **Sin** (sine), and **Tan** (tangent).

Custom Functions

As mentioned earlier, FileMaker supports nearly 300 built-in functions, and as you can see from the previous lists, a wide variety of functions are available. However, if you need a function that isn't available, you can create your own function and add it to your FileMaker solution. FileMaker refers to these as *custom functions*.

Custom functions work much like FileMaker's standard functions. They have a name, can take parameters, and return a result. You create a custom function in much the same way that you create a calculation, by specifying a formula to be applied when the function is called. However, one big difference between a custom function and a standard FileMaker function is that custom functions can call themselves. In other words, you can create a custom function whose formula actually includes the function itself. We call this *recursion*.

 TIP   In addition to being able to write your own custom functions, libraries of free custom functions are available online that you can select from. One of the oldest and most complete libraries is Brian Dunning's FileMaker Pro Custom Functions library, available at http://www.briandunning.com/filemaker-custom-functions/.

You might be wondering what the catch is with custom functions. There is a catch, and it is that you cannot add custom functions to a database using the standard version of FileMaker Pro. Instead, you need to use FileMaker Pro Advanced to add custom functions to a database. Users of standard FileMaker Pro can use custom functions. However, they cannot add their own custom functions.

FileMaker Plug-Ins

In addition to custom functions, you can also extend FileMaker through the use of FileMaker plug-ins. Plug-ins are a special type of software that you can purchase from third-party developers. There are plug-ins that serve a wide range of purposes, including generating barcodes, sending and receiving email, manipulating images, and more. To get an idea of the type of plug-ins available, visit FileMaker's Made for FileMaker page at http://solutions.filemaker.com/made-for-filemaker/.

One of the interesting things about plug-ins is that they actually extend FileMaker by making additional calculation functions available. When a plug-in is installed, you see that plug-in's function listed in the functions area of the Specify Calculation dialog, and you will find them grouped in the External Functions category.

THE ABSOLUTE MINIMUM

In this chapter you learned a great deal about calculations and their importance in the FileMaker world. We covered a lot of ground, but here are the key points to remember:

- Calculations are used throughout FileMaker databases, including calculation fields to validate values, enforce security, and more.

- FileMaker provides nearly 300 built-in functions that you can use in your calculation formulas.

- The functions that FileMaker supports include those can return text values, numbers, dates and times, and even the contents of container fields.

- If you need a special function that FileMaker doesn't provide, you can add a custom function. However, you need FileMaker Pro Advanced to do so.

- FileMaker also supports plug-ins, which further extend FileMaker's capabilities.

11

WORKING WITH LAYOUTS

Chapter 10, "Working with Calculations," gave you a preview of what we cover in this chapter: layouts. As you saw briefly, you control what appears on the screen of a FileMaker database through the use of layouts.

In the example in Chapter 10, you simply added a field to an existing layout. In this chapter, you learn much more about layouts. You learn how to create and modify them, how to add objects to them, how to change their appearance, how to select from the various types of layouts that FileMaker supports, and more. This sets the stage for Chapter 12, "Creating Reports and Charts," where you learn about generating reports and creating data-driven charts.

What Are Layouts?

In FileMaker databases, layouts provide the interface with which you work and view your data. Layouts are used to present data to users onscreen, as well as to generate other types of output (such as reports, labels, letters, and envelopes). Layouts are a critical component of a FileMaker database. Without them, you would be limited with regard to getting data into your database, and you would have no way to view or work with your data once it was in the database.

In Part I, "Getting to Know FileMaker Pro," you created a Contacts database using a FileMaker Starter Solution. One of the nice things about the Starter Solutions is that they create databases that include both the structure of the database (the tables and fields used to store the data) and professionally designed layouts, so you can immediately start working with the database. Whether you have realized it or not, you have been using layouts throughout the course of this book.

Exploring Layout Mode

As you learned in Chapter 3, "Exploring FileMaker Pro," FileMaker provides four modes for working with databases: Browse, Find, Layout, and Preview. As you probably guessed, you use Layout mode to work on layouts.

You can enter Layout mode in several different ways:

- Select View > Layout Mode.
- Use the Command+L (Mac) or Ctrl+L (Windows) keyboard shortcut.
- If you are in Browse mode, you can click the Edit Layout button in the Status Toolbar.
- Select Layout from the mode menu (located in the bottom left-hand corner of the screen).

If you haven't already done so, open your Contacts database, navigate to the Desktop > Contact Details layout, and enter Layout mode (see Figure 11.1).

Just as you have seen with the other modes, when you change to Layout mode, the command menu and Status Toolbar change to provide access to commands and tools relevant to this mode. We explore these commands and tools in just a moment. But first, let's examine the window itself to get an overall sense of how layouts work.

FIGURE 11.1

The Contact Details layout as seen in Layout mode.

As you can see, the layout area contains several different items, including text, field placeholders, and more. These items are of various sizes and colors. If you look closely, you might notice that the "things" on the layout correspond with things that you see when you view the layout in Browse mode. If you want, toggle back and forth between Layout mode and Browse mode to see how the items that appear in Layout mode appear when viewed in Browse mode. We talk more about these layout objects in a moment.

Adding Layouts

To fully explore and understand how layouts work, let's create a new layout that you can experiment with. To do so, first enter Layout mode, and then

1. Click the New Layout/Report icon in the window. You can also select Layouts > New Layout/Report, or use the Command+N (Mac) or Ctrl+N (Windows) keyboard shortcut.

2. The New Layout/Report dialog appears (see Figure 11.2). Using this dialog, FileMaker assists you in creating your new layout based on your needs.

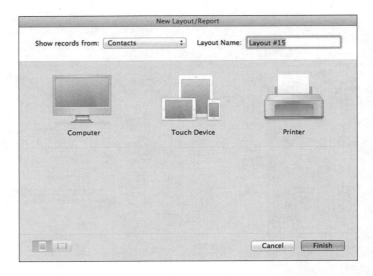

FIGURE 11.2

The New Layout/Report window.

3. At the top of the window, select Contacts from the Show Records From menu. Your Contacts database consists of a single table. If it contained multiple tables, you would be able to select the table that you want to base this new layout on by selecting it from the list.

4. In the top-right corner of the window, you can specify a name. Note that FileMaker provides a default name for you based on the number of layouts that have been created in the database—for example, Layout #15. To give the layout a more descriptive name, simply highlight the name that FileMaker has come up with and enter your own name. Let's name this new layout "Test."

5. Next, you need to indicate what type of device you intend for this layout to be used on. The options include Computer, Touch Device, or Printer. Take a moment to select each of these options, and notice what happens when you do. You should see that, based on the device that you have selected, FileMaker provides additional options (layout types) for you to choose from (see Table 11.1). For example, if you select Touch Device, you are asked to specify the touch device that you plan to use (iPad/iPad Mini, iPhone 3.5-inch, iPhone 4-inch, or a custom mobile device). If you select Printer as the device, the layout types change, with four common output types given as choices (labels, vertical labels, envelopes, or a report). When you have finished exploring these options, select Computer as the device, and then select Form as the layout type.

TABLE 11.1 Understanding Layout Types

Layout Type	Supported Devices	Description
Form	Computer and mobile devices	The Form layout type is used to view one record at a time and is commonly used for data entry purposes. They are also useful when performing finds, because a larger number of fields are available to enter criteria into.
List	Computer and mobile devices	The List layout type is used to view multiple records at one time. They are useful when you want to see a group of records at the same time, without having to click through each one individually. I like to use List view layouts to display a list of records to the user, and provide the user with an easy way to select a record from the list to see it in detail (using a Form type of layout).
Table	Computer and mobile devices	The Table layout type is used to display a list of records in a spreadsheet-like style. Each record in the found set is represented as a row, and each field is a column. This type of layout is helpful when you want to work with multiple records at one time, and when you want the flexibility of making changes to the layout "on the fly." For example, you can reorder and resize a table's columns as necessary, without ever leaving browse mode.
Report	Computer, mobile devices, and printer	Layouts based on the Report type are much like those based on List view. Multiple records are displayed, each on a separate line, with columns for each of the fields being displayed. However, when you select this layout type, FileMaker provides additional options for setting up subtotals and grand totals. It also displays additional screens during the Layout creation process, so that you can sort, group, and summarize records.
Labels	Printer	As the name implies, this type of layout is used to create layouts that will be used to print mailing labels. A number of standard label sizes are supported, including most of the more popular Avery labels. You can also create labels using custom sizes.

Layout Type	Supported Devices	Description
Vertical labels	Printer	The Vertical Labels option is used in special cases, where the labels that you want to generate need to be printed vertically to accommodate Asian and full-width characters.
Envelope	Printer	This option is used to create a layout that is ideal for printing standard Number 10 envelopes.

NOTE   If you select a mobile device for your new layout, an additional (and easily overlooked) option becomes available. In the bottom-left corner of the screen are icons that you can choose from to indicate whether you intend for the layout to be used when the device is in portrait or landscape orientation.

Understanding Layout Parts

A new layout has been created for you, and there isn't much to it yet. Let's explore what FileMaker has done to the new layout.

Take a look at the outermost edge of the layout. You might see the layout rulers, which are designed to help you position objects on the layout. (If you do not see the ruler, select View > Rulers, and the rulers should appear.) Note that the rulers are not actually a part of the layout itself, just a tool to help you design your layout.

Along the left-hand side of the layout, and just inside the vertical ruler, you should see three vertically positioned labels: Header, Body, and Footer. These labels indicate where the layout's parts begin and end. Also, in the window itself, you see corresponding dark gray vertical lines across the layout, which also indicate where the layout parts begin and end.

There are several different types of layout parts, and depending on the type of layout you choose to create, FileMaker automatically adds the appropriate layout parts. We chose to create a Form layout type, so FileMaker created the layout with Header, Body, and Footer parts. Had you created another type of layout, such as a Report, FileMaker might have also created parts for the Sub-Summary, Trailing Grand Summary, and so on.

The importance of different layout parts should become clearer in Chapter 12, when we create reporting layouts that include some of these other types of layout parts. For now, just keep in mind that a layout consists of one or more parts, and that the parts determine when and how objects appear on a layout.

 NOTE The layout part labels are actually buttons. You can double-click on a label to access the Part Definition dialog window (see Figure 11.3) and make changes to a layout part. You can also right-click on a layout part's button to access a contextual menu from which you can quickly change a part's style or fill color.

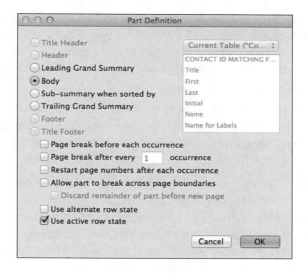

FIGURE 11.3

The Part Definition dialog.

 NOTE Normally, the layout part labels are displayed vertically. However, you can also choose to view them horizontally. To do so, in the bottom-left corner of the window, click the fifth button from the left. Click the button again to display them vertically.

Resizing Layout Parts

If you position your mouse over the vertical line that separates two layout parts, the pointer changes, indicating that you can click and drag up or down to resize a layout part. For example, you can give the header area more room by positioning the cursor between the header and body parts, clicking and holding down the mouse button, and dragging down.

Setting Layout Widths

If you expand your window a little, you can also see that the layout has a hard right edge, represented by a dark gray vertical line. This is the point at which the objects on the layout stop, and a light gray space appears off to the right. Just as you can resize a layout's parts, you can resize a layout's width by positioning the cursor on the vertical line, clicking and holding down the mouse button, and dragging left or right.

To help you to more easily and correctly set the width of a layout, FileMaker provides screen stencils. Each stencil represents the dimensions of common screen sizes of the devices used by FileMaker users. There are stencils for various resolutions of desktop machines, as well as different types of iPhones and iPads.

To view a stencil, click the down arrow located next to the stencil icon in the toolbar, and select one of the options from the drop-down menu (see Figure 11.4). You then see orange horizontal and vertical lines appear on the layout, which represent the dimensions of the screen and device that you selected. With a stencil displayed, you can more easily adjust the width of the layout, as well as the heights of the layout parts, to ensure that the layout appears properly on a certain device.

TIP   You can view multiple stencils at one time. Simply select one stencil and then another stencil from the menu. You can also toggle all your selected stencils on and off by clicking the stencil button itself in the toolbar.

NOTE   In cases where a layout's size is longer than what a device can display, the user has to scroll horizontally and/or vertically to see the entire layout.

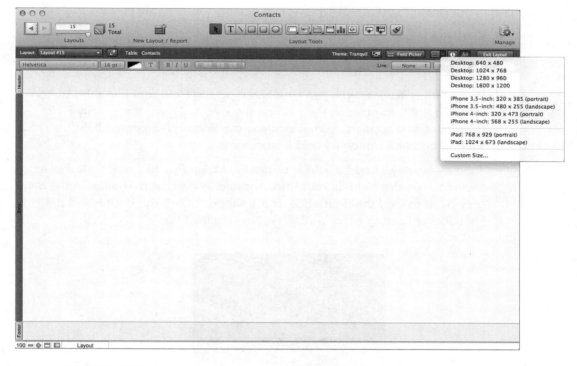

FIGURE 11.4

The stencils menu.

Adding Objects to Layouts

At this point, the new layout is still empty. If you switch to Browse mode you see that nothing is actually displayed on the layout. So this layout isn't very helpful, at least not yet.

What the layout is missing are the objects. As you see in the next few sections, you can add many different types of objects to a layout.

Adding Fields

The most common type of layout object is the Field object, which, not surprisingly, is used to display and provide access to the contents of a field.

There are several ways to add a field to a layout:

- From the Insert menu, select Field. The Specify Field dialog window appears, from which you can find and select the field that you want to add. Note that you can optionally choose to add a label for the field.

- In the Status Toolbar, you can click and drag the Field tool (the third button from the right) to position the field on the layout. Again, the Specify Field dialog window appears, from which you can find and select the field that you want to add and optionally add a label for it.

- The easiest way to add a field is to use FileMaker Pro 13's new Field Picker tool. You see the Field Picker button located in the Status Toolbar in the dark gray band toward the right edge of the window. Click the button and the Field Picker floating window displays (see Figure 11.5).

FIGURE 11.5

The Field Picker floating window.

The Field Picker is a powerful layout tool. With it, you can easily locate and add a single field (or multiple fields) to a layout. You can also choose whether the field(s) should have a label, and if so, where the label should be placed relative to the field. When adding multiple fields at the same time, you can indicate how the fields should be positioned relative to each other. You can also search for fields by name (which comes in handy when you are working with tables that have many fields in them). You can sort the list of fields by creation order, name, type, and so on. And you can also add new fields on the fly directly from the Field Picker.

Let's use the Field Picker to add a field to the new layout.

1. If you haven't already done so, open the Field Picker window. Again, you find the button for this located in the bottom right area of the Status Toolbar.

2. Let's start by adding the first name field to the layout. Locate the First field in the list and click on it to select it.

3. With the First field selected, click and drag out to the layout. Notice that as you drag, a rectangle appears indicating the size and location of the layout (see Figure 11.6). Position the field in the Body layout part, and then release the mouse to place the field.

You should see that a field object, along with a field label, has been added to the layout. The field object itself has the name of the field (in this case, "First") in it to indicate which field the object represents.

FIGURE 11.6

The new layout with First name field layout object added to it.

Now let's switch to Browse mode and see our progress (see Figure 11.7).

NOTE   If you have made changes to a layout, when you switch to Browse mode, a dialog window displays and asks whether you want to save the changes that you made. Click Save to save your changes. If, however, you do not want to save your changes, click Don't Save, and your changes are discarded. (Clicking Cancel returns you to Layout mode with your changes still in place.) Also, you can click the Save Layout Changes Automatically check box so that, going forward, changes will be saved without asking you first.

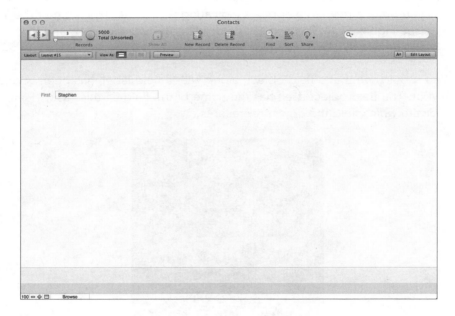

FIGURE 11.7

The new layout with First name field layout object added to it, as seen in Browse mode.

Take a moment to click between a few of the records, and you see that the newly added field layout object accurately displays the contents of the First Name field in the various records.

Now, let's add a few more fields to the layout:

1. Again, open the Field Picker window.

2. This time, let's add the last name field (Last), Company, and Job Title. To select multiple fields at the same time, locate a field, and then click the Command key (Mac) or Control key (Windows) while selecting it.

3. With those three fields selected, click and drag on any of the fields. Just as before, as you drag, a rectangle appears. However, this time the rectangle indicates the size and location of the three fields that are about to be added to the layout.

4. Position the fields in the Body layout part, below the First Name field, and then release the mouse button to place the field.

 NOTE Notice that as you drag the field objects to the layout, blue lines appear on the screen to help you position the objects relative to the First field object. You see similar behavior when you add other types of objects to the layout.

With the additional fields on the layout, let's switch back to Browse mode and see the progress. As before, you should see that the new field objects accurately display the contents of the records.

Specifying the Tab Order

When a user tabs between fields on a layout, FileMaker determines what the next and previous fields are based on what is known as the *tab order*. By default, FileMaker sets the tab order based on the position of the fields, starting from left to right, and then working from the top of the layout to the bottom. Unfortunately, that's not always the order in which you want the fields to be entered.

FileMaker does provide a tool that you can use to customize the tab order. To access it, enter Layout mode and select Layouts > Set Tab Order. The Set Tab Order dialog opens (see Figure 11.8). With it open, you can clear the existing tab order and then click the arrow button next to each field. The tab order is set based on the order in which you click the buttons. You can also click directly into the arrows to manually enter its tab order. FileMaker automatically adjusts the other fields in the tab order.

FIGURE 11.8

The Set Tab Order dialog.

Also note that you can choose not to include fields in the tab order. To enter those fields, the user needs to click directly into them.

Selecting and Modifying Objects

You have now seen how easy it is to add field objects to a layout. We explore the other object types in a moment. Before we do that, let's spend a few minutes learning how you can select and modify objects already on a layout.

To select a specific, single object on a layout, enter Layout mode and click on the object. Select one of the field objects on your layout. Notice that the selected object displays with a blue border around it and several dots positioned around it. You can click on those dots to resize the object. (Try making the First name field object longer by clicking on one of the dots on the right edge of the object and then dragging to the right.)

 NOTE When selecting a field object, the field's label object is not automatically selected. That's because FileMaker treats the label as if it is a separate object. The label is a text object, which you learn about later (see the "Adding Basic Objects" section later in this chapter).

Now, let's select multiple objects. To do so, enter Layout mode, then click somewhere on the surface of the layout itself (anywhere other than an object), and then drag. Notice that as you drag, a rectangle appears, which indicates your selection area. As you continue to drag, the rectangle grows, and objects that it touches are selected. Again, selected objects appear to have a blue border around them. However, unlike selecting a single object, when multiple objects are selected, the dots that appear around the selected objects appear to the entire group of objects. You can click on the dots to resize the entire group of selected objects.

 NOTE When selecting multiple objects using this click and drag method, an object is selected as soon as the selection rectangle touches any part of the object. In other words, you do not have to completely surround the object with the rectangle to select it.

There will be times when you want to select multiple objects, and the objects aren't positioned near each other. For example, suppose that you want to select both the First and Company field objects and their labels. To do so, you would Shift-click on the layout objects and add them individually. Also, you can Shift-click an object that has already been selected to remove it from the selected group of objects.

You learned that you can select one of the dots around a selected object to resize it. However, there are a number of other things that you can do to selected objects to modify them. For example, suppose that you want to change the fill colors of the field objects. To do so, follow these steps:

1. Use the click and drag method described previously to select the four fields.

2. Locate the Fill button in the rightmost area of the formatting bar. (If the Formatting Bar isn't visible, you can display it by selecting View > Formatting Bar.)

3. Click on the Fill button, and hold down the mouse button. A color selection pop-up window displays.

4. Select a color from the pop-up window.

Notice that the fields are now displayed with the fill color that you selected.

Similarly, you could make changes to an object's font, font size, text color, style (bold, italics, underline), alignment, and border line color and width by using the other tools in the formatting bar.

 NOTE In the previous examples, we modified multiple objects; however, you can also make changes to individual objects.

 NOTE The options available via the formatting bar are also available to you via the Format menu. Also, you can right-click on a selected object to easily change attributes such as fill color, pen color, pen width, and so on.

Take a few minutes to experiment with modifying the various attributes of the field objects that you have added to the layout. Also, switch to Browse mode to see how those changes impact the layout.

You can also easily reposition an object (or objects) on a layout. To do so, highlight the object and then click on the selected object and drag it to another location.

Using the Layout Inspector

Using the formatting bar, you can change some of the more common attributes of layout objects. However, FileMaker also gives you the ability change several additional attributes, some of which are specific to the type of object that you have selected. To view and change these other attributes, you use FileMaker's Inspector tool. There are several ways to open the Inspector window:

- Click the Inspector button in the layout bar. The button looks like a lowercase "i" surrounded by a circle.

- Select View > Inspector from the menu bar.

- Use the Command+I or Ctrl+I keyboard shortcut.

The Inspector window displays and floats above the layout itself. By default, the window is positioned toward the right edge of your screen (see Figure 11.9). However, you can easily reposition it by clicking on the window's header area (where the word "Inspector" appears) and dragging it to another location.

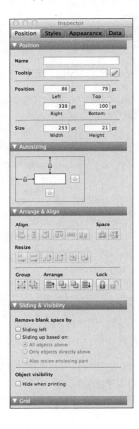

FIGURE 11.9

The Inspector window opened to the Position tab.

 NOTE   If you want to work with multiple Inspector windows open at the same time (perhaps with each one open to a different tab), you can do so by selecting View > New Inspector.

The Inspector window provides a tabbed interface to many object attributes. The tabs available include Position, Styles, Appearance, and Data. We review each tab in turn in the following sections.

The Position Tab

The Position tab provides information about the object's position on the layout as well as several other related attributes. The tab itself is further divided into five sections.

Position Options

In this area, you can see and adjust an object's position and size. You saw earlier how you can manually reposition and resize objects. Using the position and size fields of the Inspector window, you can reposition and resize objects with a fine level of control.

 NOTE By default, all the size and position information for an object is given as points. However, you can adjust the unit of measure to inches or centimeters as well. To do so, simply click on the current unit of measure (pt, in, cm) that is displayed to the right of any of the position or size values.

 NOTE Two additional fields, which don't have anything to do with an object's position or size, are also listed in the Position area. The Name field can be used to give an object a name, which can be useful when referring to the object in scripts. (You learn more about this in Chapter 13, "Automating Tasks with Scripts.") The other field is the Tooltip field, which can be used to provide users with a tooltip that appears when they hover over the object in Browse and Find mode.

Autosizing Options

Using FileMaker's autosizing options, you can dynamically resize layout objects based on the size of the window, which might differ based on how the user has resized the window and/or their device's screen and orientation. The Autosizing area gives you the option to anchor an object to the top, right, left, and bottom of the screen. By anchoring an object, the distance that the object appears relative to the edge of the window remains constant if the window is resized. Objects added to a layout are automatically anchored to the top-left corner of the window.

You can mix and match the anchors to achieve a variety of results. For example, you can anchor an object to the bottom-right corner, so that as the window resizes, the object automatically is repositioned to that corner. Also, by setting two opposing anchors (such as the top and bottom anchors, or left and right anchors), the object stretches to fill the available space. By anchoring an object to all four corners of the window, the object stretches both horizontally and vertically.

 NOTE It is also possible to configure an object so that no anchors are set, in which case the object repositions relative to the center of the window.

Arrange & Align Options

Often, you want to position an object relative to another object on the layout. For example, you might want a group of fields to be positioned so that they share the same left edge or so that their labels share the same right edge. You could manually reposition the objects or use the position and size fields mentioned earlier to align the objects. However, several of the tools in the Arrange & Align area of the Inspector make it much easier to achieve that goal.

To align objects, you must first select them. Then select one of the align options in the Inspector window. There are buttons to align the objects to the left, center, right, top, middle, or bottom. The objects align based on the position of the leftmost, rightmost, highest, or lowest object selected.

Similarly, you see buttons that assist you in spacing two or more objects. For example, you might want to vertically space a set of fields so that they make the best use of the available space.

There are also buttons available that make it easy for you to resize a group of objects relative to one another. For example, with a group of fields selected, you could choose to resize all of those fields based on the smallest width, the largest width, the smallest height, the largest height, or some combination of width and height.

You see a few other buttons listed in this area of the inspector whose functions also apply to a group of two or more objects. The Group button can be used to logically group two or more objects so that until they have been ungrouped they acts as if they are one object on the layout.

As objects are added to a layout, they are not only given left/right and top/bottom coordinates, but also a front/back (or *stacking*) coordinates. In other words, newly added layout objects are placed on layers above the existing objects on the layouts. If you position two objects so that they share the same space on the layout, the object that is "to the back" appears behind the object that is "to the front." With the Arrange buttons (front, forward, backward, and back) you can change an object's position in the stack, so that it appears in front of or behind other objects.

Finally, you also see the Lock and Unlock buttons listed in this section. If you want to prevent objects from being modified as you work on other areas of the layout, you can select the objects and lock them. Once locked, the objects cannot be modified until they have been unlocked.

Sliding & Visibility Options

The most important thing to know about the options in the Sliding & Visibility section is that they apply only to the layout when it is being viewed in Preview mode or is being used to print or generate a PDF document from the layout. The first set of options, which are listed under Remove Blank Space By, are used to slide objects to the left or upwards when blank space is available. These options are typically used when the size of the object being printed varies. When designing your layout, you want to be sure that you've given the object enough room so that when it is large, it prints correctly. However, when the object's content doesn't need the full amount of room that you allotted to it, you can recover the extra space using the Sliding Left and Sliding Up options.

The other option in this section, Hide When Printing, can be used to display objects normally when the layout is being viewed in Browse mode, but prevent objects from being printed (or displayed in Preview mode). For example, you might include a button on a layout, or perhaps some instructional text, which should really only be visible to users in Browse mode. Using the Hide When Printing option, you could suppress those objects from appearing on the printed output.

Grid Options

The final section of the Inspector window's Position tab provides easy access to another layout-related tool known as the Grid. When the Grid is enabled, major and minor grid lines appear on the layout in Layout mode to help you more easily position, align, and size objects. The options in this section make it easy for you to toggle the grid on and off, to indicate whether you want objects to snap to the grid lines, and to control the spacing of the major grid lines and the number of minor grid lines that appear between them.

The Styles Tab

Unlike the other tabs that make up the Inspector, the Styles tab does not use tabs to break its functionality into logical sections (see Figure 11.10). Instead, this tab provides easy access to many of FileMaker's themes-related capabilities. Themes are professionally designed groups of styles (fonts, colors, and so on) that, when applied to a layout (and to a database in general), provide users with an interface to the database that is both consistent and pleasing to the eye. While there are several different themes to choose from, each layout is based on one and only one theme at a given time. It is possible, however, to change a layout's theme and to adjust the individual styles that make up the theme, and to apply ad hoc styling to objects on a layout.

FIGURE 11.10

The Inspector window opened to the Styles tab.

Before we explore the options available on the Styles tab, let's learn a little more about layout themes. First, to determine what theme a layout is using, you need to look no further than the top of the Styles tab itself. The theme is listed there, along with a button that can be used to save changes to an existing theme, create your own theme, and so on.

To change a layout's theme, select Layouts > Change Theme. The Change Theme window displays, which lists all the layouts available and displays a preview of what each one looks like. Related themes are grouped together, and the themes whose names end in "Touch" are designed specifically for use with layouts that are going to be used on touch devices such as iPads and iPhones.

Take a moment to change your layout's theme. Again, select Layouts > Change Theme, and choose an alternative layout. Notice how the appearance of the field objects changes with the various themes. Depending on what theme you choose, attributes of the objects, such as the fonts, colors, and so on change. In some cases, the layout parts (header, body, and footer) change as well. (When you are finished exploring the themes, change the theme back to Tranquil.)

Now that you have an understanding of how themes work, let's explore the Styles tab of the Inspector. Remember that a theme is a collection of various styles, each of which applies to a specific type of object. Click on one of the field objects and then take a look at the Inspector, and you see what style is being applied to the object. Then click on one of the field labels, and you see that a different style has been applied to it.

Many FileMaker themes provide optional styles for each object type. Again, click on one of the field objects, and notice that the list of available themes for the object consists of two styles: Default and Minimal Edit Box. Click on Minimal Edit Box, and notice how the field's appearance changes. Then do the same thing with one of your field labels. The important thing to remember is that each theme has default styles for every type of layout object, but many themes provide you with optional styles that you can choose from.

Earlier in this chapter, you manually changed the appearance of some of the layout objects. Let's do that again. Click on one of the field objects, and change its appearance using the formatting bar. Perhaps change the field's font, color, or background color. Now take a look at the Inspector window, and notice how next to the style that the object is using there is a button with a red down arrow in it. This indicates that while this is the style being applied to the object, this specific object's appearance differs from the style in one or more ways. If you want to set the object's appearance back to that of the style, you can click on the button and select Revert Changes to Style. However, another option is to save the appearance of the object as a new style, which is added to the theme. To do so, click on the button and choose Save As New Style. Another option, Save Changes to Current Style, updates the existing style. When choosing this option, any objects that reference that style take on the style's updated attributes.

As you can see, Themes and Styles make it easy for you to apply a consistent look and feel to your database. However, you should keep a few other things in mind:

- When adding or modifying styles on a layout, the layout itself takes on its own customized version of the theme. In other words, the changes to the styles only apply to and are available on the layout that you are on when you make those changes.

- You can, however, apply changes to styles and new styles so that they apply to all layouts in the current database using that layout's theme. To do so, after changing the styles, select the button that appears next to the style's name (which also appears with a red down arrow in it, just as a modified style does) and select Save Changes to Theme.

- Another option is Save As New Theme. Using this option, you can add your own themes to the current database, and then choose them as the theme for other layouts.

- While changes made to a theme apply only to the current database, it is possible to import your custom themes from other FileMaker databases. To do so, you can easily import them by selecting Layouts > Change Theme, and then clicking the Import Themes button in the bottom-left corner of the window.

- FileMaker provides a handy way for you to get an overview of and manage a database's themes. Simply select File > Manage > Themes, and the Manage Themes window appears (see Figure 11.11). From this window, you can import themes from other databases, rename, duplicate, and delete themes, and more.

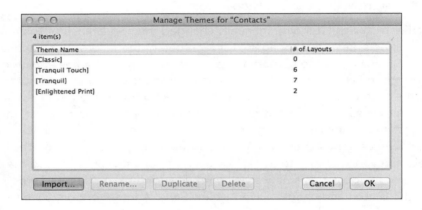

FIGURE 11.11

The Manage Themes window.

The Appearance Tab

At first glance, the options available under the Appearance tab of the Inspector appear similar to those of the Styles tab. In fact, they are somewhat similar. However, where the Styles tab focuses exclusively on an object's style, the Appearance tab provides easy access to more granular attributes of an object, including its fill color, border, padding, and more (see Figure 11.12).

FIGURE 11.12

The Inspector window opened to the Appearance tab.

Let's start by examining the top section of the Appearance tab. Like the Styles tab, the theme that the current layout is based on is listed first, followed by the style that has been applied to the selected object. Next, the object's type is listed, and below that a menu of the various states in which that object can be styled is provided. By selecting one of the states, you can choose to apply alternative styles and attributes to an object based on its state. For example, you can indicate how an object can be styled when it is in its normal state, when the mouse is positioned over it (hover), when the object is being clicked on (pressed), and when an object is active (in focus).

Graphic Options

The Graphic section of the Appearance tab provides options for indicating how you want an object to be filled. For example, you can choose to fill an object with a solid color, a gradient, and even an image, or you can choose for an object to have no fill at all. The section also gives you options for styling an object's border, including its line type, width, corner radius, and more.

Advanced Graphic Options

This section can be used to set up an object with both outer and inner shadows, and to specify padding for the object's contents. Using the padding options, you can set the whitespace that appears between the object border and its content, and you can set the padding for the top, right, bottom, and left sides independently. If the text in a field appears to bump up against the side of the field, you can use these padding options to add white space and make the field's contents more readable.

Text Options

Next up are the object's text attributes. In this section, you can change the font face, size, color, and other styles (bold, italic, underline, and more). You can also set the attributes of the object's text baseline should you want to display them.

Paragraph Options

Using an object's paragraph options, you can set the alignment of its text, the vertical orientation of its text (top, center, or bottom), line spacing, and even its indents. These attributes are particularly helpful when styling a text field that will be used to enter multiple lines of text.

Tab Options

Finally, with the tab options, you can add and specify the attributes of tabs within a field object or a long running text object. Again, these options are helpful when you are styling a field that will potentially hold a lot of text.

The Data Tab

The final tab of the Inspector is the Data tab, shown in Figure 11.13, and with one exception, it is used to set the attributes of a field object.

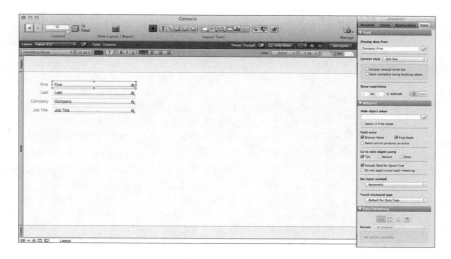

FIGURE 11.13

The Inspector window opened to the Data tab.

The Field Options

The topmost section of the Data tab is used to specify which field in the database is to be associated with the field object. When you place a field object on a layout, you indicate what field that object is associated with. However, you can change the field that the object is associated with by clicking the icon next to the field's name and selecting an alternative field.

Next is the field's control style. The way that a field appears on a layout is certainly important, but you also want to consider how the field will function when a user works with it. You want to make it as easy as possible to enter values into a field, and you also want to do as much as possible to ensure that the values being entered are accurate. To help you achieve those goals, FileMaker provides support for different field control styles. You can use control styles to limit the values that are entered into a field, or to present a list of values that are acceptable. For example, you can set up a field as a radio button set, from which Yes or No values can be selected. Table 11.2 shows the six control styles that FileMaker supports.

TABLE 11.2   Field Control Styles

Style	Description
Edit box	This is the default field control style for fields added to a layout using the Field tool. Fields set up as edit boxes are ideal for manual entry of text values. Edit boxes can be configured so that if a large amount of text is entered into them, a vertical scrollbar appears. You can also configure these types of fields so that as values are entered they autocomplete using values previously entered into the field on other records.
Drop-down list	When you are working with a field that has been set up as a drop-down list, you have the option of either manually entering a value into the field (just as you would with a field set up as an edit box), or selecting a value from a list of values. FileMaker refers to these types of lists as value lists, and we discuss them in detail in a few moments. With drop-down lists, you can specify when you want the value list to appear. You can either have the list appear as soon as you click into the field, or when an arrow is clicked. To set this option, use the Include arrow to show and hide the list in the Inspector window.
Pop-up menu	Like drop-down lists, pop-up menus are designed to provide a list of values that you can use to select a field's value. However, unlike drop-down lists, pop-up menus do not give you the opportunity to manually enter a value into the field. Also, the way in which the value list appears is a little different. First, to view the list of values, you must click on the field itself. Second, the list expands vertically and runs the entire length of the screen if necessary to display the list. (Even then, if the list of values is long, you might need to scroll through the list to find the value you want.) Therefore, pop-up menus are best used in cases where the list of values is relatively small.
Check box set	Check box sets also make use of value lists. However, each value is presented as a check box, which you can toggle on or off. This type of control style is ideal for fields where multiple values are possible. For example, suppose that you are working on a database used to track clothing products, where each product might be available in sizes ranging from Small, Medium, to Large. You might set up a Sizes Available field as a check box set, with the possible sizes as its value list. Then for each product you could click to select the sizes that the product is available in.
Radio button set	Radio button sets are like check box sets, and it is easy to confuse the two. The key difference is that, while check box sets are designed to give you the option of selecting multiple values, radio buttons are designed for cases where you want to select one, and only one, value. In fact, when you select a value in a radio button set, any value that you previously selected is automatically deselected. A good example of a field that makes good use of a radio button set is one where the values are either Yes or No.

Drop-down calendar For fields that are dates, the drop-down calendar control style is ideal. When these types of fields are entered, a small calendar appears, from which a date can be selected. The calendar also includes buttons that you can use to easily flip the calendar betweens months and years. You can specify when you want the calendar to appear. You can either have it appear as soon as you click into the field, or when a calendar icon is clicked. To set this option, use the Include icon to show and hide calendars in the Inspector window.

There are two ways to configure a field's control style:

- You can add a field to a layout (as we did earlier), and then specify its control style using the Control Style field on the Data tab of the Inspector window.

- You can add a field by selecting from the Field/Control tool in the Status Toolbar, which gives you the opportunity to select a control style before the field is added to the layout. (To use the Field/Control tool, click on its button in the Status Toolbar, and select one of the field control styles. Then click into the layout, and drag to position and size the field.)

 TIP   I am often asked how, when using fields set up as pop-up menus or radio buttons, you can clear the selected value. To do so, click on the field and then click either the Delete or Backspace key.

 NOTE   While control styles are designed to make the values entered into a field more accurate, you should not solely rely on them to do so. For example, you might set up a field as a pop-up menu or radio button and assume that the user will only select one value from the list. Clearly, that is what you are assuming the user will do. However, it is possible to select multiple values by Shift-clicking. Therefore, if you want to ensure that the values being entered are valid, you will also want to use the field validation options that you learned about in Chapter 9, "Working with Fields."

Behavior Options

The Behavior section of the Data tab is used to specify how a field should behave on the layout in certain conditions. First is the Hide Object When option, which you can use to specify conditions in which the object should simply not be displayed. You can specify those conditions using any valid calculation formula, which you learned about in Chapter 10. You can also indicate whether the formula should be applied when the layout is being viewed in Find mode. This option is somewhat like the Hide When Printing option you saw in the Sliding & Visibility section of the Position tab but provides a much higher degree of control. (Also, while the majority of the options available on the Data tab apply specifically to field objects, the Hide Object When option can be applied to the other object types as well.)

Next are the field entry options, which you can use to indicate under what conditions a field can be entered (Browse mode or Find mode). For example, you might want to set up a field so that it can be entered in Browse mode but not in Find mode because performing finds on the field is simply too slow.

The Go To Next Object Using options are used to specify what keys a user can press to move from the selected field to the next field. By default, the only key that does this is the Tab key, and some newer users of FileMaker sometimes find this difficult to get used to. With this option, you can specify that pressing the Return or Enter keys should also take the user to the next field, which might help those users transition to using your database.

In Chapter 6, "Finding Records," you learned about FileMaker's Quick Find function, which gives the user the ability to perform a find by entering a value in the Quick Find field in the toolbar, and FileMaker then searches across the fields on the layout to locate records that contain that value. In some cases, you might want to exclude a field from being included in Quick Finds, and you can do so by unchecking the Include Field for Quick Find check box.

By default, FileMaker spell checks values entered into fields automatically and underlines words whose spelling is questionable. This is an option that you can disable at the database level by selecting File > File Options and unchecking the Indicate Questionable Words with Special Underline check box. However, you can also disable this feature on a field-by-field basis using the Do Not Apply Visual Spell-Checking option.

For layouts that you plan to use on touch devices (with FileMaker Go), you have the option of using special keyboards to assist users in entering field values based on the nature of the fields. For example, if the field is being used to store an email address, you might choose to select the Email keyboard, which presents the user with a special keyboard designed specifically for easy entry of email addresses. You find other keyboards listed to assist in entering numeric values, phone numbers, URLs, and more. (Again, these special keyboards only apply to and are only presented to FileMaker Go users.)

Data Formatting Options

And finally, the last section of the Data tab provides you with options that you can use to specify how you want the values to be formatted for display purposes. You can format four types of values: Numbers, Dates, Times, and Graphics. The options available differ for each type of value, and they are comprehensive. For example, you might choose to format a numeric value as currency, in which case you can specify the number of decimal places to display, the currency symbol, and more. For dates, you can choose from a variety of common date formats, or specify a custom format. Time values are similar in that most common formatting options are provided, and you can indicate the level of precision that you want the time displayed in.

The formatting options for graphics are a little different than those of the other data types. There are four general options for graphics, and they are used to indicate how the graphic should appear in the allotted space. The first option, Reduce Image to Fit, scales down the image (if necessary) so that you can see it in its entirety. Crop to Frame does not scale the image at all but instead shows whatever portion of the image it can in the field's space. Enlarge Image to Fit only scales an image up if necessary so that it fills the field's height and width and crops anything that doesn't quite fit. The most flexible option is Reduce or Enlarge Image to Fit, which evaluates the size of the graphic and the size of the field, and then scales the graphic up or down depending on how those sizes differ. (If you are unsure which option to use, Reduce or Enlarge Image to Fit is a safe bet.)

Images can also be aligned within their fields, so that they align to the left, right, middle, top, center, or bottom of the field. By default, images are set to align to the middle center of the field.

As you learned in Chapter 9, container fields can be used to store a variety of different types of fields, from images to sounds to movies and more. The last two options on the Data tab can be used to optimize a field object so that it displays the contents of a container field in the best possible way. By default, container fields are optimized images.

However, if the field is going to be used primarily to store content that you want the user to be able to interact with in the field itself, without first having to export the field's contents, then you might want to optimize the field for Interactive Content. When this option is selected, containers that contain PDFs, sound files, or movies are displayed in such a way that interacting with them is as easy as possible (see Figure 11.14). For example, if the container contains a PDF document, then scrollbars and options to zoom the document and select and copy from it are displayed. Audio and video files are displayed with controls that can be used to play and pause the content. So the optimization option that you want to select depends on what type of content you are expecting the field to contain.

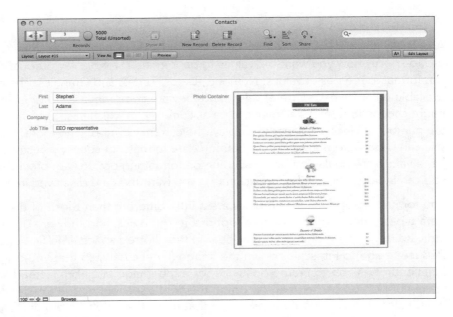

FIGURE 11.14

A container field optimized for interactive content.

Understanding Value Lists

In Chapter 9 you learned about the various ways that you can set up a field so that its value is validated. One of those options is Member of Value List. We also referred to this value list concept earlier in this chapter, when we discussed the various control styles that can be applied to a field object. (Drop-down lists, pop-up menus, check box sets, and radio button sets all use value lists.)

So what are value lists, exactly? Think of them as lists whose values can either be set up manually or automatically (based on values stored in fields). Let's take a look at these two types of value lists and the tools that FileMaker provides for managing them.

The easiest way to set up and maintain value lists is through the Manage Value Lists tool, which you can open by selecting File > Manage > Value Lists. The Manage Value Lists dialog window appears and lists any value lists that have already been set up (see Figure 11.15). In your Contacts database, you see that six value lists are already in place. The dialog window shows each list's name, source, and values.

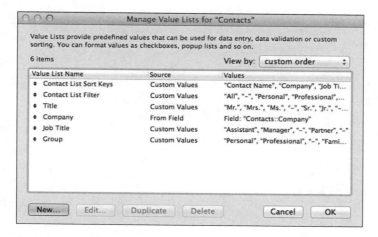

FIGURE 11.15

The Manage Value Lists dialog window.

Let's examine one of the existing value lists. Double-click the Title value list, and the Edit Value List window displays, as shown in Figure 11.16. At the top of the window is a field where the name of the value list can be specified. The source for this value list is custom values, which simply means that the list consists of values that have been manually entered into the list. Click into the Use Custom Values area of the window, and you see that the list is simply a return-delimited list of text values. If you want, you can type into the field to add a few of your own values. Also note that some lines of the list are simply a dash ("-"), which FileMaker displays as a separator between the preceding and subsequent values.

When you have finished adding your own values to the list, click OK and then click OK again to save your changes and exit the Manage Value Lists dialog window. Then change to the Desktop > Contact Details layout, and click into the Title field. You see that the changes that you made to the value list are represented in the pop-up menu for the Title field. (Also note that at the bottom of the list is an option to Edit the list, which is another way to quickly edit this type of value list.)

The Title value list is an example of a value list based on custom values. However, there might be times when the values that you want to provide in a field, or as part of a field's validation options, aren't as straightforward and instead need to be based on values stored in the database itself. In that case, you want to set up a dynamic value list whose source is based on values From Field.

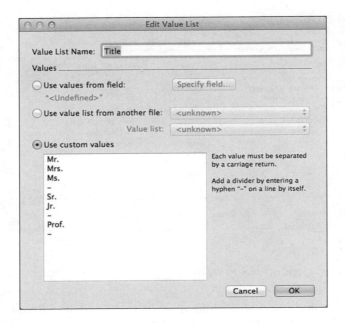

FIGURE 11.16

The Edit Value List window with the Title value list displayed.

Open the Manage Value Lists tool again, and this time, double-click on the Company list. Notice that this list's values are set up to come from the Company field in the Contacts table (see Figure 11.17). So, as the values in that field change, the value list's values change as well. Let's take a look at this value list in action.

Click OK and then click OK again to exit the Manage Value Lists dialog window. On the Desktop > Contact Details layout, click into the Company field and change its value to My New Company. Then click outside the fields to commit the change. Now click on the down arrow in the Company field to bring up the list of companies and scroll down until you see My New Company. FileMaker has automatically updated the value list with the new company name. Next, click back into the Company field, change the value to Acme Industries, and then commit your changes. If you click on the down arrow in the Company field again, you see that Acme Industries is now included in the list and My New Company has been removed. So FileMaker is automatically removing unnecessary values from the list as well.

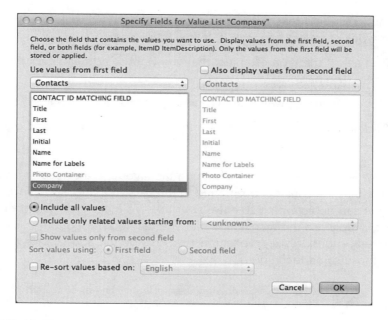

FIGURE 11.17

The Edit Value List window with the Company value list displayed.

You can also set up value lists so that their values are driven by multiple fields (where the value displayed in the list comes from one field while the actual value being stored is from another field). Another option is to generate a value list based on values stored in another FileMaker database, or from a different database altogether (that has been set up as an external datasource).

We've only scratched the surface of what value lists can do and how they can be configured. However, you now know enough about them to use them to validate field values and to make good use of the drop-down list, pop-up menu, check box set, and radio button set field control styles.

Adding Basic Objects

At the beginning of this chapter, you added a few field objects to the layout, and throughout the chapter you learned about the many different ways that you can change the size, position, and appearance of objects. Now we explore a few of the other basic types of objects that you can add to layouts.

As mentioned before, when you are in Layout mode, the Status Toolbar changes to display tools that help you design a layout. The second group of icons in the toolbar represents some of the more basic types of objects that can be added to a layout, including text, lines, rectangles, rounded rectangles, and ovals. To add these types of object to a layout, follow these steps:

1. First select the type of object that you want to add and click on its icon in the Status Toolbar.

2. Move the cursor, which should now appear as a cross-hair, to the layout itself.

3. Click in the position that you want the object to appear, and drag to size the object.

The new layout object then appears on the layout. In the case of a text object, you see that the cursor is positioned in the text area and is flashing, indicating that you can begin typing to enter your text. To make changes to these types of object, simply use the techniques that you learned throughout this chapter. You can select, group, resize, reposition, and change the appearance of these objects using those same techniques.

 NOTE   To change the contents of an existing text object, simply double-click it. The flashing text cursor will display within the text, so that you can make any changes.

Adding Graphics

One type of layout object that isn't represented as an icon in the Status Toolbar is a graphic object. However, you might want to add a graphic, such as a company logo, directly to a layout without placing it into a container field. To add a graphic to a layout, follow these steps:

1. Enter Layout mode.

2. Select Insert > Picture.

3. Navigate to the folder in which the graphic is stored, locate it, and click Insert. (Note that you probably do not want to use the Store Only a Reference to the File option, as doing so might cause the graphic to not appear when other users are viewing the layout.)

Once the graphic has been added to the layout, you can resize it, reposition it, and so on, just like any other type of object. However, before resizing a graphic, one option that you might want to make use of is the Maintain Original Proportions option, which is located toward the bottom of the Data tab in the Inspector window. When this option is selected, the graphic resizes without its dimensions being distorted.

Adding Advanced Objects

So far, you have learned about some of the more basic layout objects, including field objects, shapes, and graphics. We now focus on some of the more advanced types of objects, including buttons, tab controls, slide controls, popovers, and Web viewers. (We cover other advanced layout objects in future chapters; we discuss charts in Chapter 12 and portals in Chapter 20, "Expanding Your Database.")

Buttons

The button layout object can be used to automate tasks performed in the database. These tasks can be simple (such as pasting the contents of the clipboard into a field, navigating to another layout, changing from Browse to Preview mode, and so on) or complex (involving potentially multiple steps).

Let's add a button to the layout that you have been working on throughout this chapter. To add the button, follow these steps:

1. Locate the Button tool in the Status Toolbar and click it.

2. Move your cursor to the layout itself, and position the crosshair so that it is in the header area toward the right of the window.

3. Click and drag to draw the button on the layout.

4. The Button Setup dialog window displays. You see a list of options presented in the left portion of the window. Scroll down and select Go to Layout from the list.

5. The right portion of the window displays options based on the option that you selected. In this case, you can specify what layout you want to navigate to. Select Layout, and then choose the Desktop > Contacts layout from the list. Then click OK.

6. Click OK again to close the Button Setup window.

7. The button displays on the layout, with the flashing text cursor within it, indicating that you can enter text to appear on the button. Type **List View** and then click anywhere on the layout to save the changes.

Let's test the new button. Enter Browse mode, and click on it. You are automatically taken to the Desktop > Contacts layout.

You can add as many buttons to a layout as you want, and you can use them to automate a number of common tasks. You can also use buttons to run scripts, which you learn about in Chapter 13, "Automating Tasks with Scripts."

NOTE   While the button layout object is truly a type of layout object, any object type can serve as a button. To set up an object so that it acts as button, simply right-click on it, and select Button Setup. To stop an object from behaving as a button, select it, and then select Arrange > Ungroup. A dialog box appears and asks you to confirm that you want to delete the button definition. Click OK, and the object behaves as it normally would.

Tab Controls

Next, we explore the tab control layout object. Tab controls are a great way to add objects to a layout when space is limited and/or when you want to group and present objects logically (see Figure 11.18).

Let's add a tab control to your layout now. To do so, follow these steps:

1. Locate the Tab Control tool in the Status Toolbar and click it.

2. Move your cursor to the layout itself, and position the crosshair so that it is in the header area toward the right of the window.

3. Click and drag to draw the tab control on the layout. Make it around 400 pixels wide and 200 pixels high.

4. The Tab Control Setup dialog window displays with the cursor positioned in the Tab Name field. Type a name for the first tab. Enter **Basic Info** for the name, and then click the Create button. The tab is added to the list of tabs in the control.

5. Add a second tab to the control. This time, name it Notes.

6. Add one additional tab. This time, name it Web. Then click OK.

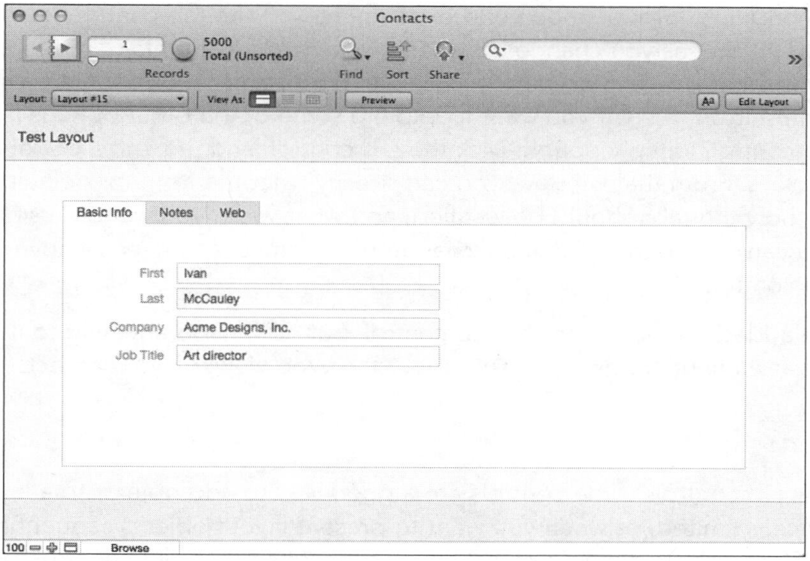

FIGURE 11.18

A tab control layout object.

The tab control is added to the layout. Note that you can resize it, reposition it, and change its attribute just like the other layout objects you have learned about.

Enter Browse mode, and click on the tabs in the tab control. You see that as you select a tab, the highlight tab changes. However, because you have not added anything to the tabs yet, there really isn't much to look at. So let's fix that.

1. Select Layout mode.

2. Select the four field objects that you added to the layout earlier in the chapter. Or if you want, add a few additional field objects to the layout.

3. Click and drag the fields so that they are repositioned on the Basic Info tab of the tab control.

4. Click on the Notes tab of the tab control, so that it is the active tab.

5. Use the Field Picker to add the Notes field to the layout, and position it on the Notes tab.

Go back into Browse mode and experiment with the tab control again. This time you see that as you change between the tabs, the contents of the tabs display. If you want, you can go back into Layout mode and reposition and resize the tab control itself. Also, if you want to explore some of the other options available with tab controls, simply double-click the tab control, and the Tab Control Setup dialog displays. From that window, you can specify what the front (or default) tab should be, how the tabs should be justified, and what width you want to use for the tabs. You can also reorder the tabs, change their names, and even remove tabs from the control.

We added a Web tab to the tab control, but didn't add anything to it. We do that in a few minutes when we learn about the Web viewer layout object.

Slide Controls

Like tab controls, slide controls are a good way to add objects to a layout when space is limited, or when you want to present layout objects sequentially. Figure 11.19 shows an example of a slide control. Let's add a slide control to your layout now.

1. Select the Slide Control tool in the Status Toolbar. Note that this tool shares space with the Tab Control tool, so to get to it, you must first click on the Tab Control tool and hold down the mouse button. A pop-up menu displays, from which you can select the slide control layout object.

2. Just as you have with the other layout objects, position your mouse somewhere in the layout itself, click and drag to draw the slide control.

3. The Slide Control Setup dialog displays. Let's use the default settings of the slide control and focus on adding content to the slides. So you can close the dialog window, or simply click outside it.

4. Notice that the slide control appears on the window, and just like we saw with the tab control, its slides have nothing on them yet.

5. On the first slide, add one of the basic objects—perhaps a circle.

6. On the second slide, add another object, such as a square. (To get to the second slide, click on the second dot that appears below the slide control.)

7. Add an object to the third slide as well.

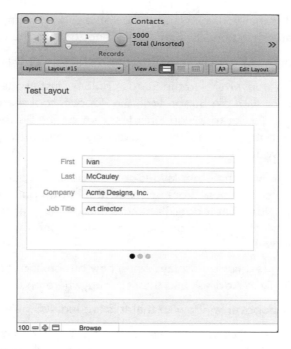

FIGURE 11.19

A slide control layout object.

Now enter Browse mode, and click on the dots below the slide control to navigate between them. Notice that the contents of each slide appear to "slide" left and right. This example isn't impressive (simply because we don't have good content to work with), but you can the potential use of this layout object. You could use it to walk the user through a series of steps, to display photos, and so on.

Should you want to make changes to the slide control, simply go back into Layout mode and double-click the control to bring up the Slide Control Setup window again. From there you can increase or decrease the number of slides, change the point size of the navigation dots, or hide them completely. You can also choose to enable or disable swipe gestures, which allows FileMaker Go users to swipe left and right between the slides.

Popovers

The next advanced layout object that we cover is the popover. Popovers are interesting because they are actually a combination of a button and an additional area of layout real estate that appears when the button is clicked. Popovers are ideal when you have some additional information that you want to display to a user, additional fields that you want them to be able to work with, or as a way to gain access to related functionality without needing to leave the current layout.

To add a popover to the layout, follow these steps:

1. Select the Popover tool in the Status Toolbar. Just as the Slide Control tool shared space with the Button tool, the Popover tool shares space with the Button tool. To get to it, you must first click on the Button tool and hold down the mouse button. A pop-up menu displays, from which you can select the popover layout object.

2. As you have with the other layout objects, position your mouse somewhere in the layout itself, click and drag to draw the button portion of the popover on the layout. Note that it doesn't need to be very big, as this is just the button itself. The button displays on the layout, along with the popover window it is associated with.

3. The flashing text cursor displays in the new button, indicating that you can enter text into it. Type **Address** and then click anywhere on the layout to continue.

4. Resize the popover window so that it is around 400 pixels wide.

5. Using the Field Picker, locate and select the Work Address-related fields (Work Address 1, Work Address 2, and so on), and drag them on to the layout, positioning them on the popover window.

Now enter Browse mode. Notice that the popover window disappears. To view it, click on the Address button that you just added to the layout. The popover window displays along with the fields we added to it (see Figure 11.20). To close the popover window, click anywhere outside the window.

A few additional popover-related options can be accessed by entering Layout mode, clicking on the button associated with the popover, and then double-clicking on the header area of the popover window. The Popover Setup dialog displays, from which you can change the name that appears at the top of the window or choose to hide the title altogether. You also see that you can indicate where you want the window to appear relative to the button. (FileMaker does its best to display the window in the preferred location, but its capability to do so depends on the user's device, screen size, and so on.) You can also see options for specifying script triggers that fire when the popover window opens, closes, and so on. We discuss script triggers in Chapter 13.

The popover window is interesting in that you can place just about any other layout object type on it. For example, you can set up a popover whose contents included a slide control, a tab control, and so on. However, you cannot nest popovers inside other popovers.

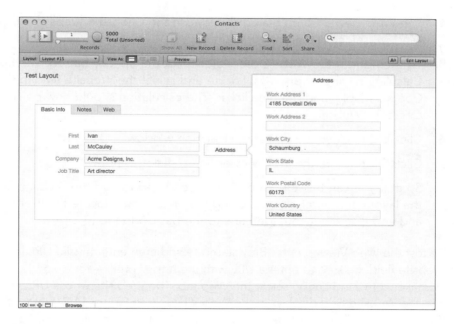

FIGURE 11.20

A popover object.

Web Viewers

The last advanced layout object type that we are going to discuss is the Web Viewer. Think of a Web Viewer as a small Web browser embedded into your layout. You can specify the URL of the Web page that you want to display and specify whether the user should be able to interact with the Web viewer's contents and more.

Earlier in the chapter, we added a tab control to the layout, and one of the tabs on it was named Web. We're going to use that tab in this example. To add a Web Viewer to the layout, follow these steps:

1. Click on the Web tab of the tab control that we added earlier, so that it is the active tab.

2. Locate the Web Viewer tool in the Status Toolbar.

3. Position your mouse toward the top-left corner of the Web tab, and then click and drag to draw the Web viewer so that it takes up as much of the tab's space as possible.

4. The Web Viewer Setup dialog displays. In the Choose a Website area of the window, select Custom Web Address.

5. To the right of the Web Address area, click the Specify button. The Specify Calculation window displays. Locate and select the Website field in the Contacts table, and double-click it. The calculation should now be set to Contacts::Website.

6. Click OK to close the Specify Calculation window.

7. Click OK to close the Web Viewer Setup dialog window.

8. So that you can test the Web Viewer, you need to add the Website field to the layout and enter a value. Using the Field Picker, locate the Website field and add it to the layout (perhaps to the Basic Info tab).

To test the Web Viewer, enter Browse mode and then enter a valid URL into the Website field. Be sure to enter a URL with the http:// prefix—for example, http:// filemaker.com. And finally, select the Web tab. The Web site whose URL you entered into the Website field displays in the Web Viewer (see Figure 11.21). Note that the Web viewer is fully interactive, so you can scroll in it, click on links, and so on.

FIGURE 11.21

An example of a Web viewer layout object.

This example used a single field to act as the URL that the Web viewer displayed. However, you could also use one of the other options that the Web Viewer Setup dialog presents, such as Google Maps, MapQuest, Google Web search, and so on. When using those options, FileMaker assists you in mapping fields to the values that the Web sites need to properly render the Web page. For example, you could use the Google Maps option, and map the address to the various work-related fields in the Contacts database.

Just as we've seen with other layout objects, you can resize and reposition Web viewers. Also, using the Autosizing options that we learned about earlier, you can set up a Web viewer so that it resizes automatically to take advantage of available space in the window.

 NOTE   FileMaker's Web viewers also support Data URLs. This is a special type of URL that can be used to set the contents of the Web viewer to something other than a Web site. For example, you could set the Web viewer's contents to be that of a dynamically generated HTML page based on values in the database itself, such as a report. For more information about Data URLs, visit http://help.filemaker.com/ and search for TechNote 6455 ("Web Viewer Enhancements in FileMaker Pro 9"). This is an older TechNote, but its information about Data URLs applies to FileMaker Pro 13.

Changing Layout Options

Throughout this chapter, you have been working with and learning about layout objects, and you've learned how make changes to those objects. However, it is also possible to make changes to the layout itself. For example, you can change a layout's name, change the table that the layout is based on, and more. You do this through the Layout Options, which are available via the Layout Setup window.

There are several ways to access Layout Options:

- Click the pencil icon located next to the layout's name in the layout bar.
- Select Layouts > Layout Setup.
- Select File > Manage Layouts, select the layout that you want to work with, and then click Edit. (You learn more about managing layouts in the next section.)

Like many of the other windows that you see in FileMaker Pro, the Layout Setup window groups its functionality into various tabs (see Figure 11.22).

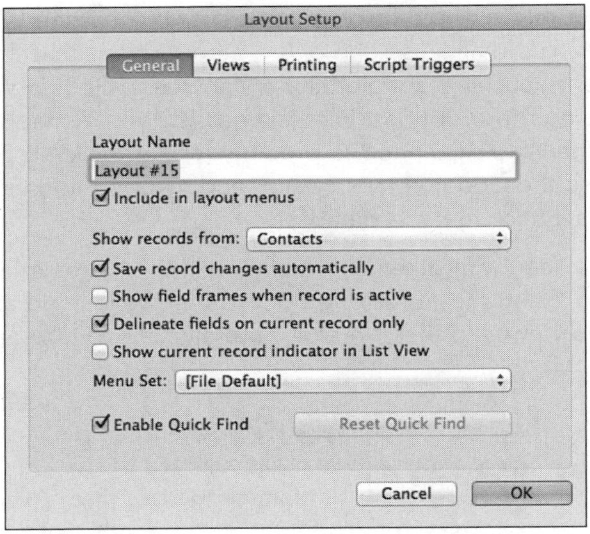

FIGURE 11.22

The Layout Setup window.

The General tab provides access to the layout's name, and you can also indicate whether you want the layout to appear in the pop-up list of layouts. (This is a nice option as there might be some layouts that you do not want users to be able to navigate to manually.) You can also use options on this tab to indicate whether changes made to records should be saved automatically or should require that the user indicate whether the changes should be saved via a dialog box. There is also an option to enable or disable the Quick Find function on the layout. (When disabled, the Quick Find field still appears in the Status Toolbar, but users cannot click into it.)

From the Views tab, you can indicate what views (Form, List, or Table) the layout can be viewed in, as well as the default view. For example, if you designed a layout intended to be viewed as a list, you can disable Form and Table views.

The Printing tab gives you the ability to specify the number of columns that the layout should print in, as well as the page margins that should be used.

And finally, the Script Triggers tab gives you the option to set up scripts that run when layout-based events occur. For example, you can indicate that a certain script should run when the layout is entered. You learn more about scripts and script triggers in Chapter 13.

Managing Layouts

FileMaker also provides a tool that makes it easier to get an overview of and manage all the layouts in your database. To access this tool, select File > Manage > Layouts, and the Manage Layouts window displays. Using this window, you can change the layout order, group layouts into folders, duplicate layouts, delete layouts, and more.

The Manage Layouts window works much like the FileMaker other tools that you've explored. To work with a layout, select it, and then you can delete it, duplicate it, and so on by selecting one of the buttons displayed at the bottom of the window. You can click and drag to change the order of the layouts. Additionally, you can use click the "New" button to add a new layout folder. Layout folders can be used to group related layouts into folders, making them easier to locate.

Layout Tips and Tricks

In this chapter, you learned a lot about layouts and layout objects. Here are a few additional tips and tricks for working with layouts.

Undoing Layout Changes

Starting with FileMaker Pro 13, you can now make changes to a layout, enter Browse or Preview mode, and then return to Layout mode to undo the changes that you made. You can undo changes that have been made to a layout going as far back as you want. However, as soon as you change to another layout or close the file, the history of your changes is lost and you can no longer undo changes. To undo changes, select Edit > Undo, or use the Command+Z or Ctrl+Z shortcuts.

Icons on Layout Objects

As you worked through the examples in the chapter, you may have noticed icons, such as the letter T or a magnifying glass, that display on some of the layout objects. Those icons indicate that an object has an attribute set that might not be immediately apparent to you. For example, the "T" indicates that the object has a tooltip assigned to it. The magnifying glass that appears on a field indicates that it will be included in the event that a Quick Find is performed. A small blue rectangle indicates that the object acts as a button. You might also see objects (and the layout itself) that have a small scroll-like icon on them, which indicates that the object (or layout) has one or more script triggers assigned to it.

Duplicating Layouts

In many cases, especially in large and complex FileMaker solutions, you might find it more convenient to duplicate and modify an existing layout rather than start from scratch. You can duplicate a layout by selecting Layouts > Duplicate Layout, or from the Manage Layouts tool (File > Manage > Layouts). If the layout that you need to create is going to be used to display records from another table, you can change the duplicated layout so that it references the other table. To do so, choose Layouts > Layout Setup, and then choose the other table from the Show Records From drop-down menu.

THE ABSOLUTE MINIMUM

In this chapter, you learned how to create, update, and manage layouts, and about the various types of objects that can be placed on layouts. Here are the key points to remember:

- When creating a new layout, it is important to consider what table the layout should be based on, as well as the type of device that you intend the layout to be used on and the layout's purpose.

- FileMaker provides a number of professionally designed themes that you can choose from to make your layouts, and your databases in general, look nice and appear consistent.

- A number of different types of objects can be placed on a layout, from fields to buttons to tab controls and more.

- Using the Layout Inspector, you can change the position, appearance, behavior, and more of one or more objects on a layout.

- Value lists can be used to validate values entered into fields, as well as to present the user with a list of options for fields being displayed as drop-down lists, pop-up menus, check box sets, and radio button sets. The values in value lists can be manually entered or can be dynamically controlled based on values in fields.

CREATING REPORTS AND CHARTS

In Chapter 11, "Working with Layouts," you learned that in FileMaker databases, the layouts provide the interface with which you work with and view data. You learned how to create a basic form layout and add layout objects to it. That type of layout is useful for working with data—performing finds, adding, updating, and deleting records, and so on. However, it doesn't help you analyze the data. Using that type of layout, you cannot summarize data, look for trends, and so on.

In this chapter, you learn how to create other types of layouts that help with those types of tasks. You learn how to create the most common type of report, known as a *sub-summary report*. You also learn how to create layouts that can be used to generate other types of output, including labels and envelopes. You also explore FileMaker's charting function, which can be useful when you need to visually analyze your data.

Planning Your Report

To help ensure that the report you are going to create truly meets your needs, it is always a good idea to take a few minutes to think about what the goal of the report is. What fields should be displayed? Should the records be grouped and summarized, and if so, how? Are grand totals needed? Do you want the records to be displayed in a particular order?

In some cases, you might be replicating a report or spreadsheet that is already being used and generated outside FileMaker. In those cases, you have a model to refer to. Regardless, before creating the report in FileMaker, take a moment to think about what you are trying to accomplish. Doing so makes the process of creating the report layout much easier.

Understanding Sub-Summary Reports

In this chapter, our goal is to create two reports using the Contacts database that you have been using throughout the book.

The first report is a list of contacts grouped by state. For each contact, we want the first and last names to be displayed, as well as the company that the person works for and a job title. For each state grouping, we want to see a summary indicating the total number of contacts in the state. Also, at the end of the report, we want to see the total number of contacts in all the states. In FileMaker terms, this type of report is known as a sub-summary report.

The second report is similar to the first. It, too, groups contacts by state. However, for this report, we also want the contacts in the same company to be grouped together, with the number of contacts that work in each company displayed. In other words, the second report requires that we have multiple levels of groupings, first by state, and then by company name.

Creating Report Layouts

Let's start by creating the layout for the first report. If you do not already have your Contacts database open, do so now. Then follow these steps:

1. Go to Desktop > Contacts layout and make sure that your found set includes all records.

2. Enter Layout mode.

3. Click the New Layout/Report button in the Status Toolbar. The New Layout/Report window appears, as shown in Figure 12.1.

4. Give the layout a name. Call it Contacts Directory.

5. The type of layout that you want to create is Report, which is available for all devices. Choose Computer > Report, and then click Continue.

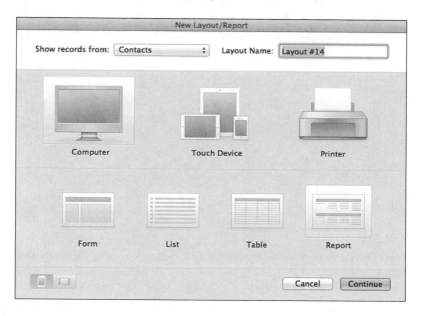

FIGURE 12.1

The New Layout/Report window with Computer selected as the device and Report as the report type.

TIP Although the Report layout type is an option for all three device types, the layout is created in a slightly different way depending on the device that you select. In particular, the width of the layout varies depending on the device. Therefore, if you plan to view the report on a computer or mobile device, select the appropriate device. If you intend to print the report, select Printer as the device.

6. Unlike the Form layout that you created in Chapter 11, when creating a Report layout, FileMaker guides you using a multistep process. After choosing to create a Report layout, the next step in the process is to indicate whether you want subtotals and grand totals to be included in the report. For this report, you want the contacts to be grouped by state as well as a total count of the number of contacts included in the report. Therefore, you want to include both subtotals and grand totals (see Figure 12.2). Be sure that both check boxes are checked, and then click Next.

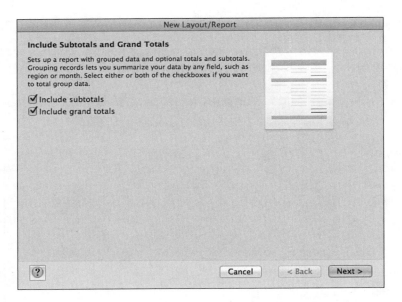

FIGURE 12.2

The New Layout/Report window with the options for including subtotals and grand totals displayed.

7. Select the fields that you want to appear on the report. The Specify Fields dialog, shown in Figure 12.3, is similar to other dialog windows you have used throughout the book to select one or more fields. You select fields using the list to the left, and they then appear in the list to the right. For this report, select First, Last, Company, Job Title, and Work State. Then click Next to continue to the "Specify Fields" step.

8. Indicate the field (or fields) by which you want the records to be grouped. The list of fields on the left includes only the fields that you selected for inclusion on the report. You want to group contacts based on the state that they work in, so select Work State and click the Move button to add it to the Report Categories list. Notice that the Work State field is added to the list of Report Categories, and a check box appears to the left of the field name in the list (see Figure 12.4). The check box can be used to indicate whether you want the field to appear as a column in the report. By default, the field is included as a column, and the small preview icon showing a page of the report indicates this. However, in this case, we want to display the state name above each group of contacts. Therefore, including the state name as a column is redundant. So be sure to uncheck the check box. Click Next to continue to the "Sort Records" step.

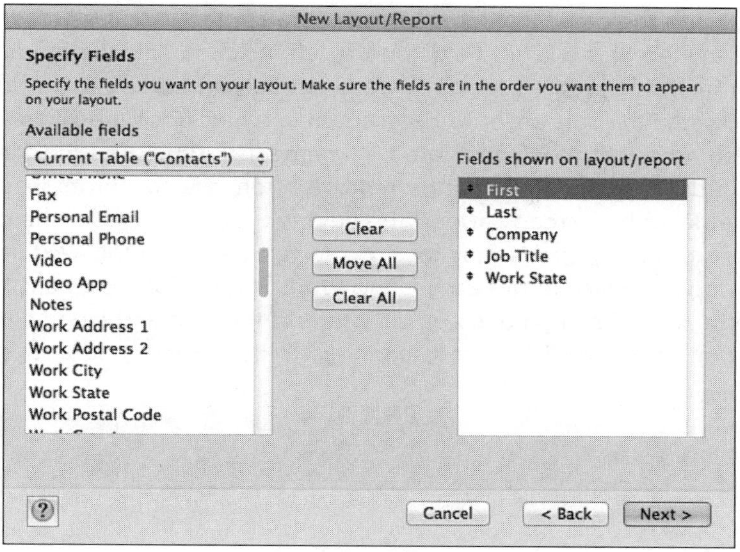

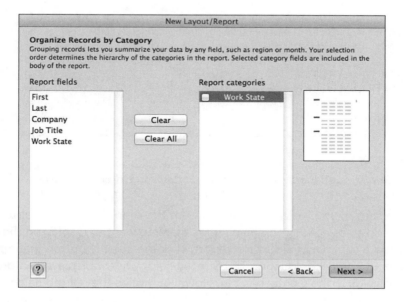

FIGURE 12.3

The New Layout/Report window, with the Specify Fields dialog displayed.

FIGURE 12.4

The New Layout/Report window with the Organize Records by Category dialog displayed.

9. Indicate the order in which you want the contacts to appear on the report. As in step 8, the list of fields on the left includes only the fields you selected for inclusion on the report. However, notice that the list on the right, which indicates the sort order to be used, already includes the Work State field. Also note that the Work State field name includes a small lock icon next to it, indicating that it cannot be removed from the sort order (see Figure 12.5). FileMaker has already added the field for you because for the contacts to be grouped properly they must be sorted based on the field used to do the grouping (which in this case is the Work State field). You want the contacts to be sorted by name, so be sure to add the Last and First fields to the Sort order list. Then click Next to continue to the "Specify Subtotals" step.

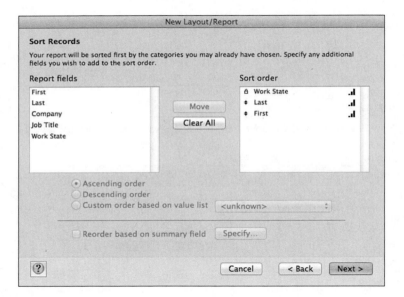

FIGURE 12.5

The New Layout/Report window with the Sort Records dialog displayed.

10. In step 6, you indicated that you want the report to include subtotals. You now need to select any summary fields that you want to display on the report. To add a summary field to the report, click the Specify button that appears below the Summary field label. The Specify field window displays and provides a list of fields in the Contacts table. However, notice that all the fields are grayed out, indicating that they are not applicable for selection. This is because none of the existing fields in the table are summary field types.

FileMaker makes it easy to add a summary field. Simply click the Add button that appears below the list of fields. The Options for Summary Field window displays. For the Summary Field Name, enter **Contact Count**. For the report, we want a count of all contacts in each state. Therefore select Count Of for the summary type. Then select CONTACT ID MATCHING FIELD as the field to be counted (see Figure 12.6). Finally, click OK to add the new summary field to the table. The new field now appears in the list of fields and is automatically selected for you. Click OK to continue.

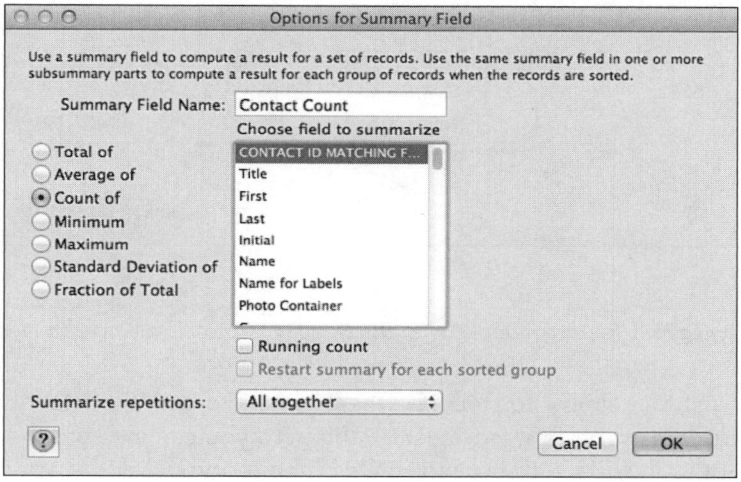

FIGURE 12.6

The Options for Summary Field window, which can be used to add summary fields to the database during the creation of a sub-summary report layout.

The new Contact Count field is now ready to be added to the list of subtotals. However, before adding it, set the Subtotal Placement menu to Below Record Group so that the count only appears at the end of each group of contacts (see Figure 12.7). Then click the Add Subtotal button to add the field to the list of subtotals, and click Next to continue to the "Specify Grand Totals" step.

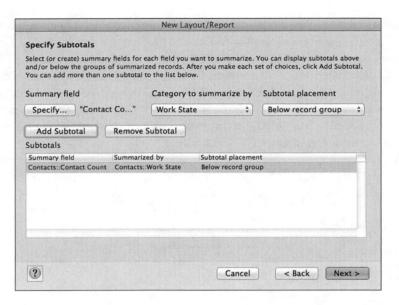

FIGURE 12.7

The New Layout/Report window, with the Specify Subtotals dialog displayed.

11. This step is similar to step 10, where you indicated the fields that you want to include as subtotals. However, in this step you can indicate the fields that you want to include in the grand totals of the report. Click the Specify button that appears below the Summary field label, and as before, the Specify field window appears. Scroll to the bottom of the list to select the Contact Count field that we added earlier, and then click OK. Click the Add Grand Total button to add the field to the list of grand totals (see Figure 12.8), and click Next to continue to the "Header and Footer Information" step.

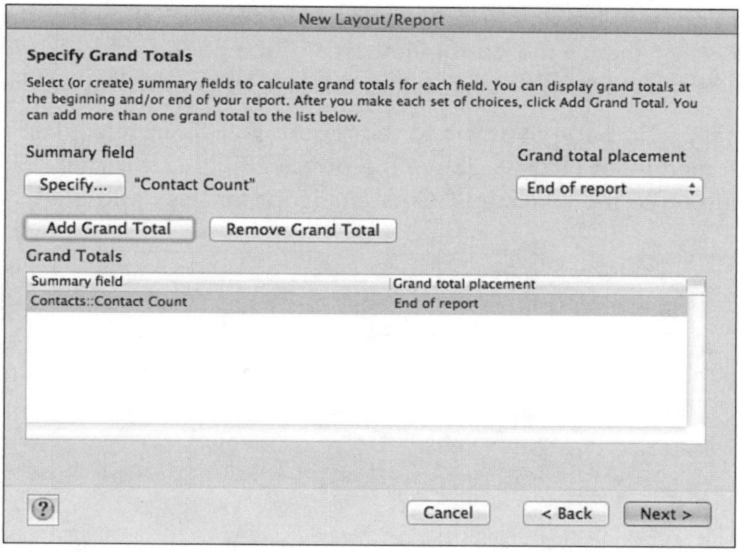

FIGURE 12.8

The New Layout/Report window with the Specify Grand Totals dialog displayed.

12. Often, you want some additional information displayed on the report—information that isn't necessarily available from the database itself. For example, you will likely want the report to include a title, page numbers, and perhaps the date on which the report was generated. Adding that type of information is easy.

In this step, the current window is divided into two areas, both of which are similar. The top portion is used to indicate any information that you want to appear in the header area of the report, and the bottom is used to indicate what you want to appear in the footer area. You can choose to have information appear to the left, center, or right of the header and footer areas.

For this report, let's choose to display a report title in the top left area of the header. To do so, select Large Custom Text from the menu that appears above the Top Left label. The Custom Text dialog window displays in which you can enter the text that you want to display. Enter **Contacts Directory** and then click OK. The window will refresh to reflect that you have specified Large Custom Text for the top-left header area of the report, as shown in Figure 12.9.

It might also be nice to indicate the date on which the report was generated. Let's add that to the bottom-left area of the page footer. To do so, select Current Date from the menu that displays above the Bottom Left label.

Finally, add page numbers to the report. This time, select Page Number from the menu that displays above the Bottom Right label. Then click Next to continue on to the final step ("Create a Script for this Report").

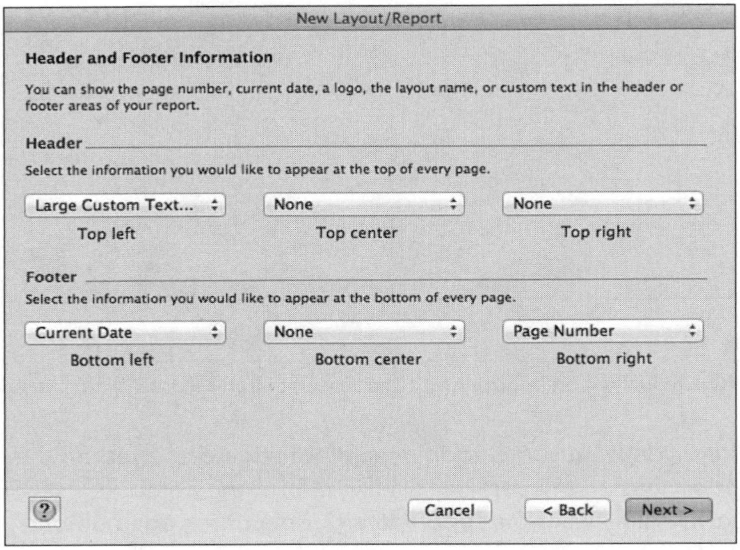

FIGURE 12.9

The New Layout/Report window with the Header and Footer Information dialog displayed.

13. The final step in the report creation process involves creating a script for the report. You learn more about scripts (and how to create them) in Chapter 13, "Automating Tasks with Scripts." However, using the option presented in this step, you can have FileMaker automatically create a simple script that can be used whenever you want to run the report. It changes to the new report's layout, sorts the records, and displays the report in Preview mode.

Let's use the feature. To do so, simply select the Create a Script radio button (see Figure 12.10). Notice that the name used for the script is automatically set to match the name of the layout that you are creating. Another option available is Run Script Automatically. By selecting this check box, FileMaker also adds a script trigger to the new report layout. You also learn about script triggers in the next chapter. But for this report, do not select the check box. Instead, click the Finish button to complete the process of creating the report.

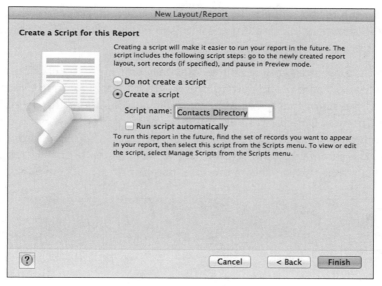

FIGURE 12.10

The New Layout/Report window with the Create a Script for this Report dialog displayed.

The new layout is created, and you can see it in Layout mode (see Figure 12.11). Take a moment to investigate the layout. Note that FileMaker created the layout with the various layout parts that are needed, including the header, a leading sub-summary part that appears above the body part, the body part itself, a trailing sub-summary part, a trailing grand summary part, and the footer. It has also added the report's title to the header area and symbols for the current date and page number to the footer. In summary, FileMaker takes all your specifications for the report and creates a layout based on them.

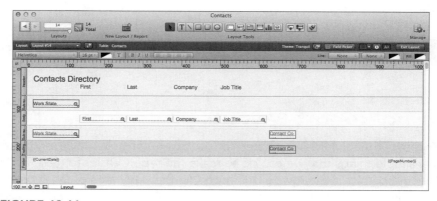

FIGURE 12.11

The new report layout as created by FileMaker and seen in Layout mode.

To view the report, change to Browse mode. The report might look a little odd, with the summary information missing (see Figure 12.12). That's because the records aren't sorted properly.

To sort the records, you can either manually sort them (by clicking the Sort button in the Status Toolbar and sorting on the Work State, Last, and First fields), or you can run the script that FileMaker created (available under the Scripts menu and titled Contacts Directory). Once the records are sorted, the leading and trailing sub-summary areas of the report appear. Be sure to scroll up and down the report to see the summaries, and scroll to the bottom of the report to see the trailing grand summary (which shows the total number of contacts in all states).

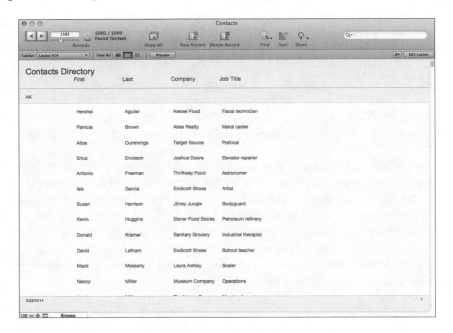

FIGURE 12.12

The new report layout as seen in Browse mode.

Improving Report Layouts

The layout that FileMaker created for you is a great start. However, there are a few simple things that we can do to make the report easier to read. For example, it would be nice if the rows of the report (in the body area of the report) alternated in color. It might also help to make the Work State field in the leading sub-summary area more prominent. There are also a few things that we can do to the trailing sub-summary and grand summary parts to draw attention to them as well. And finally, it appears that some of the columns (especially Company and Job Title) aren't wide enough, and as a result some of the values in them aren't fully displayed. So we might want to make them a little wider.

 NOTE Keep in mind that even though FileMaker created this layout for you, it is just like any other layout in that you can enter Layout mode to make changes to it.

Let's start by making the colors of the body part alternate. To do so, go into Layout mode and double-click the body layout part button. The Part Definition dialog displays. One of the options available is Use Alternate Row State. Select the check box for that option, and then click OK to close the window. Go back to Browse mode, and you can see that the background color of the rows now alternates between white and light gray (see Figure 12.13). That makes the individual rows a little easier to read.

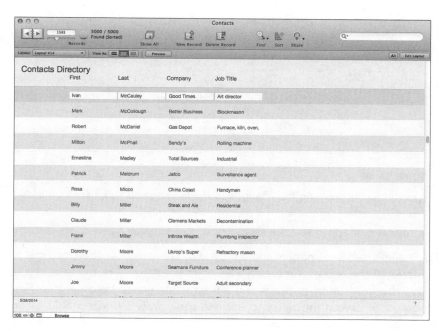

FIGURE 12.13

The report layout showing the change to the Alternate Row State option in use.

Now let's make the Work State field in the leading sub-summary area more prominent. Again, go into Layout mode. Select the Work State field in the leading sub-summary layout part, and increase its size from 12pt to 18pt (see Figure 12.14). If you want, you can also experiment with changing the field's color, or even changing the background color of the layout part itself (using some of the techniques that you learned about in the previous chapter).

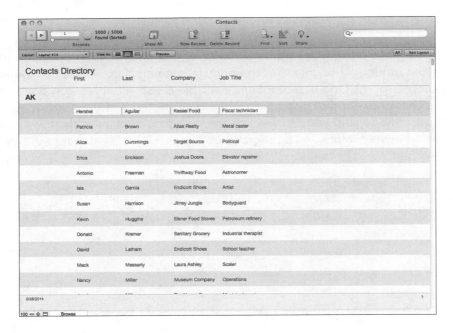

FIGURE 12.14

The report layout showing the changes to the leading sub-summary area of the layout.

The report is starting to take shape now. Let's make a few more improvements.

The trailing sub-summary is still a little difficult to see. It seems to get lost among the rows of the report. One easy way to make it stand out is to add a ruled line above the fields in layout part and a little white space below it (see Figure 12.15). To do so, in Layout mode using the line tool, draw a horizontal line above the Work State and Contact Count fields. Then, to add some white space to the layout part, simply resize the part itself. Click on the line that appears between the trailing sub-summary part and the trailing grand summary part, and drag down. Then go back into Browse mode to review your changes.

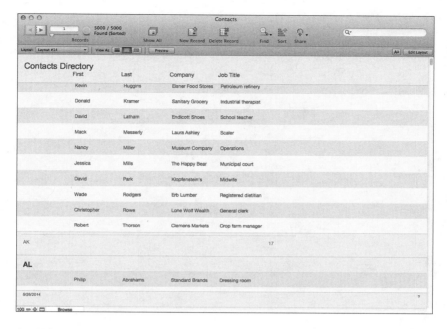

FIGURE 12.15

The report layout showing the changes to the trailing sub-summary area of the layout.

Let's move on to the trailing grand summary. The layout part only includes the Contact Count field, so it is little wonder that it is easy to overlook. There are a few easy things that we can do to improve this area as well. First, enter Layout mode and using the text tool add the text Total Contacts to the left of the field. Then using the rectangle field, draw a rectangle around the new text and the field. After drawing the rectangle, be sure to place it at the bottom of the "stack" (so that it appears behind the text and field objects). To do so, select the rectangle, and select Arrange > Send to Back. You might also want to add some white space to this layout part as well, by making the layout part bigger and positioning the objects in it so that they are aligned toward its middle. Switch to Browse mode, and then scroll to the bottom of the report to see your changes. Now the grand summary looks much better (see Figure 12.16).

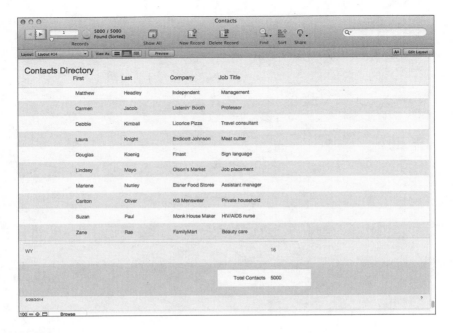

FIGURE 12.16

The report layout showing the changes to the trailing grand summary area of the layout.

One final change that we need to make is to resize the Company and Job Title fields. As mentioned earlier, they are too narrow to properly display many of the longer values in those fields. To make the two fields wider, go into Layout mode. Then before resizing the fields, move the Job Title field to the right, which frees up space for the Company field. Be sure to move the field's column header text as well, which appears in the Header layout part. Then make the Job Title field and the Company field wider. Return to Browse mode, and you can see that the longer company names and job titles are now visible on the report (see Figure 12.17).

By making these simple changes to the layout, the report now looks much better. The important thing to remember is that even though FileMaker originally created the report layout for you, it is really just like any other layout. You can make as many changes to it as you want.

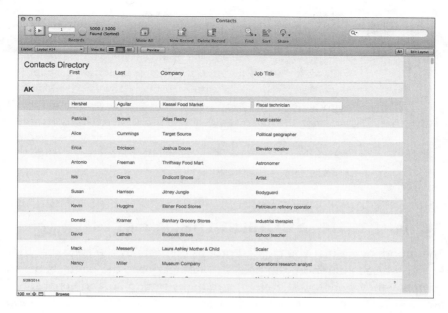

FIGURE 12.17

The report layout showing the resized and repositioned Company and Job Title fields. Note that the values in those fields now display properly.

Changing Found Sets

As you've been working on the report layout, you have been using all the records in the Contacts table. You can, however, also view the report based on a subset of the data. Let's give this a try.

1. First change to the Desktop > Contact Details layout.

2. Enter Find mode, and perform a find for "teacher" using the Job Title field. You should find approximately 70 records.

3. Select Contacts Directory from the Script menu to run the report.

You are now viewing a report of all contacts whose job titles includes the word "teacher," grouped by state, with the number of contacts in each state. The total number of contacts whose titles include "teacher" is displayed at the end of the report. You can also perform other types of finds—for example, a find for contacts in one or more states—and then run the report.

NOTE The layout itself simply provides instructions for how the report will be displayed. The records displayed in the report are entirely up to you and the found set that you are working with when you run the report. This is an important concept to understand, as it also illustrates just how powerful FileMaker's reporting function is. You can create a single layout, and then by adjusting the found set, generate many different reports from it. In the next section, you also see that by simply changing the sort order of the records, you can also dynamically change the appearance of the report itself.

Adding Multiple Sub-summary Parts

The report layout that you created groups contacts by the state that they work in. For the second report, the goal is to further group the contacts based on the company they work for. Therefore, it requires setting up additional sub-summary layout parts. To create the second report, you modify the layout that you created for the first report.

Before you begin, make sure that you are working with all the records in the Contacts table. Select Records > Show All Records.

To create the new report, follow these steps:

1. Enter Layout mode.

2. Switch to the Contacts Directory layout.

3. From the Layouts menu, select Part Setup. You see a list of the parts that make up the layout.

4. Click on the Sub-summary by Work State (Leading) part.

5. Click the Create button.

6. Select the Sub-summary When Sorted By option, and then select Company from the list of fields.

7. Click OK. Another dialog window appears, asking whether you want the new layout part to appear above or below the records that it summarizes. Select Print Above, and the dialog window closes. You should see the new layout part listed in the Part Setup window.

8. Now let's add a similar trailing sub-summary part. Click on the Body part in the list of parts.

9. Click the Create button.

10. Select the Sub-summary When Sorted By option, and select Company from the list of fields.

11. Click OK. Another dialog window appears. This time, select Print Below and the dialog window closes.

The list of layout parts should include the two new parts that you added. If necessary, change the order of the layout parts so that they are nested properly. You want the Sub-summary by Work State (Leading) first, followed by Sub-summary by Company (Leading), Body, Sub-summary by Company (Trailing), and Sub-summary by Work State (Trailing), as shown in Figure 12.18. Note that some layout parts, including the Header, Footer, and Trailing Grand Summary, are locked so that their position in the layout cannot be inadvertently adjusted.

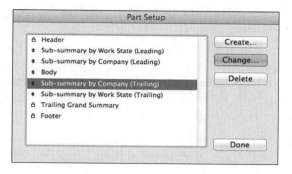

FIGURE 12.18

The Part Setup dialog, showing the newly added leading and trailing sub-summary parts for the Company field.

12. Click Done to close the Part Setup window.

You now see the new leading and trailing sub-summary layout parts. However, no layout objects are in them yet. In the leading sub-summary part, add a field layout object and use Company as the field. You might want to style the field a little so that it stands out. For example, you might want to make it bold and 14 pt. In the trailing sub-summary part, add a field layout object, and this time use Contact Count as the field. You might want to style this layout part in a manner similar to the trailing sub-summary part for the Work State.

To view your changes, enter Browse mode. To see the new sub-summary parts that you have added, you need to sort the records properly. Click the Sort button in the Status Toolbar, and then sort the records by the Work State, Company, Last, and First fields.

You should now see that the report includes two levels of grouping. Contacts are first grouped by the state that they work in followed by the company that they work for. While many of the companies include only one contact per state, several have two or more contacts listed.

Importance of the Sort Order

You've seen a few examples of how the sort order determines whether a given sub-summary layout part appears on the report. For a sub-summary part to appear, the records in the found set have to be sorted by the field that the layout part is based on. And now that we have two sub-summary levels (one based on the Work State, the other on Company), the records have to be sorted first by Work State and secondarily by Company for the layout parts to appear. But what happens if you only sort the records based on one, and not both, of those fields? Let's take a look.

Click the Sort button in the Status Toolbar and then sort the records by the Company, Last, and First fields. In other words, this time sort without including the Work State field. Notice that the report automatically adjusts and includes only one level of grouping. What you are seeing is a report that groups contacts by the company they work for, regardless of what state they are in.

Now sort the records by the Work State, Last, and First fields, and this time omit the Company field. Again, the report automatically adjusts, showing contacts grouped by the state that they work in, regardless of what company they work for. (In other words, you are back to seeing the report that you originally created.)

The point is that when you have a report layout that includes multiple sub-summary layout parts, you can significantly change the appearance of the report by simply changing the sort order. As such, you can create a single report layout that can serve many different purposes. Combine this functionality with the ability to report based on various found sets, and again you can see just how powerful FileMaker's reporting capabilities truly are.

Removing Body Parts

You've seen how you can use the reports that you created to summarize the data in the found set. However, in those examples, you displayed the details of that data. In other words, your reports included not only the summary information, but the detailed contact information as well. But what if you really only want the summary information without all the detailed contact information? Let's take a moment to create a report that does that.

To create this final report, follow these steps:

1. Enter Layout mode.

2. Change to the Contacts Directory layout.

3. From the Layouts menu, select Duplicate Layout. A new layout is created, based on the original layout, and named Contacts Directory Copy.

4. From the Layouts menu, select Part Setup.

5. Click on the Sub-summary by Work State (Leading) part, and click the Delete button. Confirm the deletion. Do the same thing for the Sub-summary by Company (Leading) part.

6. Delete the body part.

Enter Browse mode, and then sort the records by Work State, Company, or both. The report now includes only the summarized data. None of the details about the contacts are displayed.

The important thing to note is that you can create sub-summary reports that do not include body layout parts. As such, you can create reports that include only summarized information, which, in many cases, might be all that you need.

Previewing and Printing Reports

The report layouts that you created are designed to be viewed on a computer. Remember that when we first created the report layout, we selected Computer as the device and then selected Report as the layout type. Therefore, FileMaker created the layout using a width and theme that takes advantage of the size of your computer's screen or monitor. This layout is not intended to be printed.

To see what the layout would look like if it were to be printed, switch to Preview mode. You will likely see that the Job Title column either doesn't appear at all or if it does appear it is cut off at the page's right edge (see Figure 12.19). Also, the page number does not appear, as it is located on the layout in a position well beyond the right edge of the printable page.

Note that you can click the Page Setup button in the Status Toolbar to adjust the orientation of the page from portrait to landscape mode and see what impact that has on the printed page.

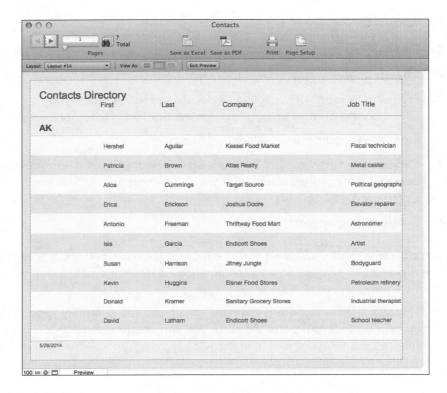

FIGURE 12.19

The report layout as seen in Preview mode. Note how the rightmost content of the report is either not displayed at all or is truncated.

NOTE   Another way to see what will and what will not fit on a printed page is to enable the View > Page Margins options.

To create layouts that are more easily printed, always start by selecting Printer as the device. In doing so, you see that FileMaker makes minor changes to the layout that it creates to help ensure that the layout prints properly.

Regardless, there will be times when you need to manually adjust the size of the layout and layout objects, and reposition objects so that everything fits properly. Using Preview mode (and the Page Margins option mentioned previously), you can adjust the layout as needed.

When you are ready to print your report, either select File > Print, or if you are in Preview mode, click the Print button in the Status Toolbar. The Print dialog box displays, and the options provided depend in large part on the type of printer you use (see Figure 12.20).

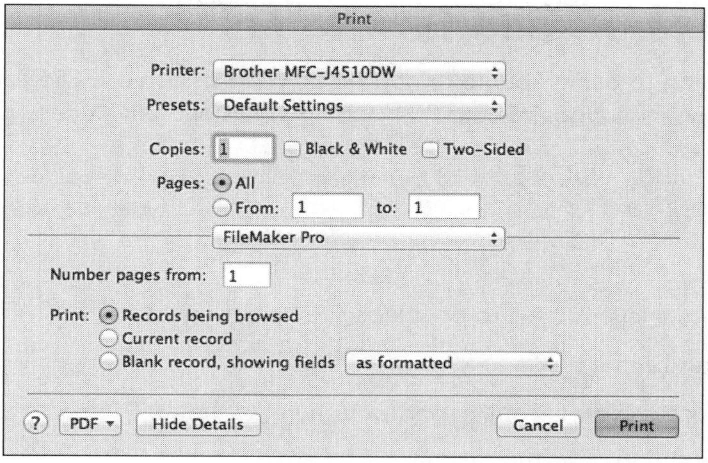

FIGURE 12.20

The Print dialog box with the FileMaker-specific print options displayed.

Following are some FileMaker-specific options that you should be aware of as well:

- **Number pages from**—This option allows you to indicate the starting page number that FileMaker should use. This option can come in handy when the report that you are generating from FileMaker is going to be included as just one part of a larger document. Don't confuse this option with the Print Pages From option that might be available to you depending on your printer. That option isn't used to change the page numbering. Instead, it changes what pages are actually printed.

- **Print**—This option lets you specify what records should be printed. You typically want to use the Records Being Browsed option, which prints the report based on all the records in your found set. However, the Current Record option can also be handy, especially when you only want to print based on the specific record that you are viewing. (For example, if you were viewing a table of invoices, you might only want to print an invoice for the current record instead of the entire found set.) The final option, Blank Record, Showing Fields, gives you the ability to print the layout as if it were a form with no real data included. You can specify how you want the blank fields to be printed (as formatted on the layout with boxes (borders) or with underlines.

Printing Labels and Envelopes

In addition to being able to print reports, you can also use FileMaker to print other common types of output, including labels and envelopes.

 NOTE The Labels and Envelopes layout types are only available when you are creating a new layout and select Printer as the device.

To create a layout used to print labels, follow these steps:

1. Enter Layout mode.

2. Click the New Layout/Report button in the Status Toolbar.

3. Select Printer as the device.

4. Select Labels as the layout type.

5. Click Continue.

6. If you are going to be printing the labels using a standard label type (from a manufacturer such as Avery or Dymo), click on the menu that appears next to Use Measurements For and select the correct label type. Note that many of the alternative label manufacturers often refer to the Avery label number that their product corresponds with. If the labels you are using are not a standard type, you can use the Custom Measurements options to specify their size, page margins, and so on.

7. Click Next to continue.

8. The Specify Label Contents step appears. You can add a field to the label by finding it in the list of available fields and either double-clicking it or selecting it and clicking the Add Field button. Notice that as you add a field, a placeholder is added to the Label Contents area of the window, and the placeholder is the name of the field surrounded by two less than and two greater than signs.

9. As you add fields to the label, you can add spacing, line breaks, and even static text to the label as well. To do so, simply click into the Labels Contents field. For example, you want to add a space between the First and Last name columns, a carriage return at the end of each line, a comma between the City and State fields, and so on.

10. When you have finished adding fields to the label, click Finish.

    The new Labels layout is created for you. Enter Preview mode to see what the labels would look like if you were to print them. You should see them displayed in a way similar to Figure 12.21.

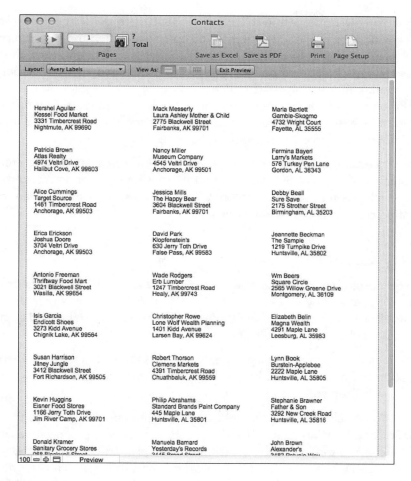

FIGURE 12.21

An example of a Labels layout type as seen in Preview mode.

NOTE FileMaker refers to the placeholders used in both label and envelope layout types as Merge Fields. You can also use Merge Fields on other types of layouts. To do so, create a text layout object, position your cursor to where you want the placeholder to appear, select Insert > Merge Field, and select the field that you want to create the placeholder for. Unlike field layout objects, merge fields cannot be entered into. They are primarily intended to be used on layouts that are going to be printed.

When you are done, return to Layout mode. Notice that when FileMaker created the layout, it took all the fields that you specified during the creation process, as well as any spacing and carriage returns that you added, and used them to create a text layout object. It is possible for you to make changes to the label's content and format after the layout is created. To do so, double-click on the text object, and then make your changes. You can apply text formatting options (change the font face, the point size, and so on), and using the Merge Field function just described, you can add and remove fields as well.

The process for creating Envelope layouts is similar to that used to create Label layouts. The only real difference is that there is no step for selecting the size of the envelopes that you want to print. FileMaker assumes that you are going to be printing on standard-size envelopes.

Creating Charts

In addition to being able to generate powerful and flexible reports that can provide summaries of your data, FileMaker also provides tools for creating visually compelling charts that can also be used to analyze your data. And best of all, you can create charts in a matter of minutes.

Let's look at an example. First, open your Contacts database, and change to the Desktop > Contact Details layout. Be sure that you have all the records in your found set. Then sort the records by Work State.

Next, right-click into the state field, and from the contextual menu that appears, select Chart by Work State. The Chart Setup window appears with a preview of the chart to the left of the screen and various chart options on the right (see Figure 12.22). The chart itself is a columnar chart with states represented by the x-axis and the number of contacts in each state represented along the y-axis.

The options to the right of the chart allow you to easily customize the chart. Let's explore some of the more commonly used options.

Starting from the top, you can change the title of the chart. It is currently set to "Work State Count," but you can use another name if you want, or click the ellipsis next to the title field to specify the chart name using either a value in a field, or a value that is the result of some calculation. Feel free to change the name if you want.

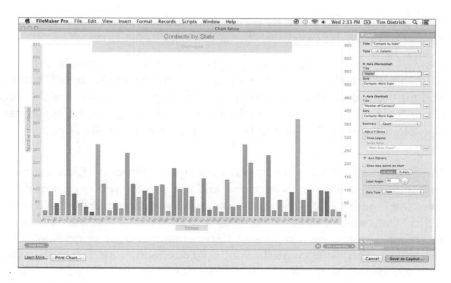

FIGURE 12.22

The Chart Setup window.

Next up is the chart type. Click on the pop-up menu, and you see that FileMaker supports a variety of different chart types—from the columnar chart you are viewing now to bar charts, pie charts, and more. Again, feel free to change the chart type so that you can see how FileMaker responds. Also note that as you change the chart type, the options available change to show only those options that are applicable. When you are done experimenting, be sure to switch back to the Column chart type (to make it a little easier to follow along with the rest of this section).

The next set of options is used to customize the appearance of the x-axis. First is the title field, and like the chart title, you either enter static text into the field, or choose to have the axis's name based on another field or a calculation. Let's change the title of the x-axis from "Work State" to "States." For the data used by the x-axis, you see that the state names (values from the Work State field) are used.

The y-axis has similar options. Notice that the title for the axis is set to "Work State Count." Let's change that to "Number of Contacts." Like the x-axis, the y-axis is also based on the Work State field, but you also see that the values being charted are the counts from each state. This is similar to the Contact Count summary field created earlier in the chapter when creating the sub-summary reports, except that in this case FileMaker creates the counts on-demand. In some cases, you might want to create a columnar chart whose y-axis includes multiple series of data, and you would do so by clicking the Add A Y Series button in this section. For our example, let's stick with the single data series.

Next are a few additional options for the axis. You can choose to show data points on the chart itself, to change the angle at which the labels appear, and more. And for the y-axis, there are also options for displaying things like the major and minor "ticks," to set minimum and maximum values, and more. Again, feel free to explore these options to see how using them impacts the appearance of your chart.

The next set of chart options involves the style of the chart. Click on the arrow next to Styles to expand the options, and you see the wide range of options available (see Figure 12.23). There are options for everything from the Chart Style (Solid - Flat, Shaded - Flat, Solid - 3D, and Shaded - 3D) to the color scheme used and more. You can even choose to display major and minor gridlines and specify their colors. You can change the font, font size, and more. Depending on whether you have chosen to display a legend for your chart, you can also stylize that as well.

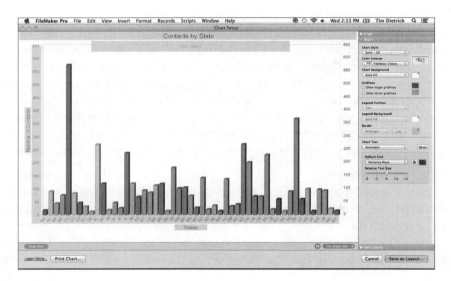

FIGURE 12.23

The Chart Setup window with the Styles option displayed. FileMaker supports a number of different chart types and a wide range of color schemes that can be used to customize charts.

The next set of options involves the source of the data used in the chart. For basic charts, the currently selected options are what you want to use. You want the chart to be based on the data of the current found set, and you want to use summarized groups of records. However, for more advanced charts, you can also choose to use delimited data from the current record only, or data from related records.

When you have finished experimenting with the chart, you can do a few things with it. First, you can choose to print the chart, which you can do by clicking the Print Chart button located in the bottom-left corner of the window. This is a good option if you are in a hurry to generate a printed version of the chart and think that you will not need to modify the chart in the future.

The other option is much more interesting and much more useful. In the bottom-right corner of the window is the Save as Layout button. Click it, and then either provide a name for the layout or use the one that is suggested. In doing so, FileMaker automatically creates a new layout for you and places a chart layout object on it. Enter Layout mode and you see that this is indeed the case. If you want to make changes to the chart, you can double-click on the chart layout object, and the Chart Setup window reappears.

Now here is where charts get interesting. So far, you've been looking at the chart based on all records in the found set. However, that isn't a requirement. You can also easily generate a chart based on a subset of records.

First, change back to the Desktop > Contact Details layout. Next, enter Find mode, and perform a find for the word "teacher" in the Job Title field. You should end up with around 70 records in your found set. Now, switch back to the chart layout that you created a few minutes ago. (It may be listed under the Charts layout folder.) Note that the chart appears in much the same way that it did earlier, but the values being charted are clearly different. What you are seeing is a chart showing, for each state, the number of contacts whose job titles include the word "teacher." In other words, you are charting a subset of your data.

So, much like the sub-summary reports explored earlier in the chapter, it is possible to create a single chart layout and then manipulate the found set to generate a variety of different charts.

 TIP When viewing a chart on a layout in Browse mode, you can click on the chart and copy it. You can then paste the chart into another application, such as a page layout or word processing application.

THE ABSOLUTE MINIMUM

In this chapter, you learned a lot about how to use layouts to use the data in a FileMaker database. Here are the key points to remember:

- FileMaker makes it easy to create layouts that generate sub-summary reports, which are the most common type of report.

- Before creating a report, you should take a few moments to think about what goals you are trying to achieve with it. What fields do you want to include? Do you want to summarize the data?

- With a single report layout, you can add multiple sub-summary layout parts. You can then easily change the appearance of the report by simply changing the sort order of the records in the found set.

- FileMaker also provides support for layouts that can be used to generate other common types of output, including labels and envelopes.

- Using FileMaker charting functionality, you can easily generate a chart on-the-fly and then save the chart to a new layout.

- FileMaker supports a wide variety of chart types, including columnar charts, bar charts, pie charts, and many more. Using the various chart options, you can customize charts to meet your needs.

13

AUTOMATING TASKS WITH SCRIPTS

One of the benefits of using a database is that it can be used to automate repetitive or complex tasks. For example, in Chapter 12, "Creating Reports and Charts," you learned how to create layouts that can be used to generate reports. Creating the layout is the first step in generating a report, but to use the layout you have to take additional steps to get the report you want. You have to navigate to the report layout, find the records that you want to include in the report, and sort the records properly. With FileMaker, you can "script" those steps so that, rather than performing each step manually, you can run a script and have FileMaker perform them for you.

In this chapter, you learn about FileMaker scripts. You learn to create scripts that perform basic tasks, and then you learn to create more advanced scripts that interact with users. You learn how to design scripts so that they can gracefully handle errors that might occur when they are running. You also learn how to manage scripts and the various ways in which scripts can be run.

What Is a Script?

In FileMaker, a *script* is a set of instructions that perform a specific function or action. We refer to the individual instructions as *script steps*, and as you see in a moment, FileMaker supports a wide range of script steps. The function or action that a script performs can be as basic or as complex as you need. For example, a basic script might simply navigate the user to a specific layout. A more advanced script might interact with a user, asking him to provide criteria for a report, and then navigate to the report layout, perform a find using the criteria that was provided, sort the records, and even enter Preview mode.

The Manage Scripts Window

To work with scripts in FileMaker, you use the Manage Scripts window (see Figure 13.1), which you can access by either selecting the Manage Scripts command from the Scripts menu, or by using a shortcut (Command+S on a Mac, Ctrl+Shift+S on Windows). Open the Manage Scripts window now.

As you can see, your database already includes several scripts. These scripts were automatically added to your database because it was created using a Starter Solution. Had you created the database from scratch, no scripts would be present, and the Manage Scripts window would be empty. The list includes both individual scripts, as well as a few folders into which some of the scripts have been grouped. You learn how to create your own folders in a few moments.

At the top of the Manage Scripts window are a drop-down menu and a search field. The drop-down menu includes a list of the folders into which the scripts have been grouped, and selecting a folder name filters the list so that only the scripts in the selected folder are displayed. Selecting the Show All option restores the list so that all scripts are displayed. The search field can be used to quickly locate a script based on its name (see Figure 13.2). For example, you can type "contact" into the field, and the list will then consist only of those scripts whose names include "contact." These options make locating a script as quick and easy as possible, and they are particularly helpful in complex databases that contain many scripts.

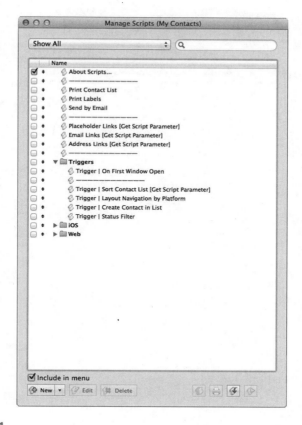

FIGURE 13.1

The Manage Scripts window, which serves as the primary interface to managing and working with FileMaker scripts.

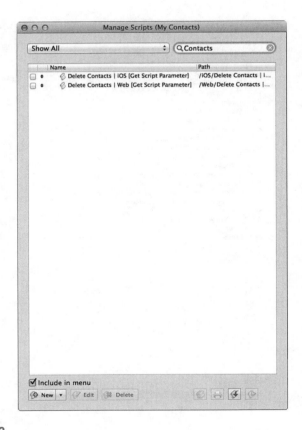

FIGURE 13.2

The Manage Scripts window showing a filtered list of scripts based on the word "Contacts."

The leftmost column of the scripts list includes a check box, and you can see that only one of the scripts (About Scripts) is checked. The check box indicates that the script can be accessed directly from the Scripts menu. Click on the Scripts menu, and you see About Scripts listed. Click the check box next to Print Contact List and then click on the Scripts menu again. You should now see that the Print Contact List script is listed, as shown in Figure 13.3.

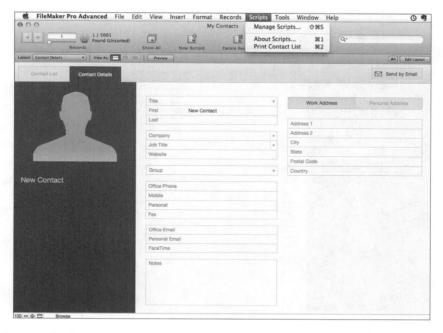

FIGURE 13.3

The Scripts menu, with Print Contact List listed as an option.

You can easily include or exclude scripts from the Scripts menu by toggling the check box. Adding scripts to the Scripts menu is one of the ways that you can make scripts available to users. To run a script, all the user needs to do is select it from the Scripts menu. You learn about other ways that scripts can be run in a few moments.

You can add as many, or as few, scripts to the Scripts menu as you want. However, there may be some scripts that you do not want to include in the list, especially those that are only applicable when a user is on a certain layout, or scripts that perform a function dependent on the current found set.

When adding scripts to the Scripts menu, FileMaker automatically assigns those scripts a shortcut. The shortcut is either Command on a Mac or Ctrl in Windows followed by a number that represents the script's position in the list of scripts. For example, in your database the shortcut Command+1 (or Ctrl+1) represents the About Scripts script, because it is the first checked script in the list. If you add Print Contact List to the list, it is assigned the shortcut Command+2 (or Ctrl+2). The tenth checked script assigns shortcut Command+0 (or Ctrl+0), and any additional scripts appear in the Scripts menu but are not assigned shortcuts. In other words, FileMaker assigns only up to 10 shortcuts to the scripts included in the Scripts menu (see Figure 13.4).

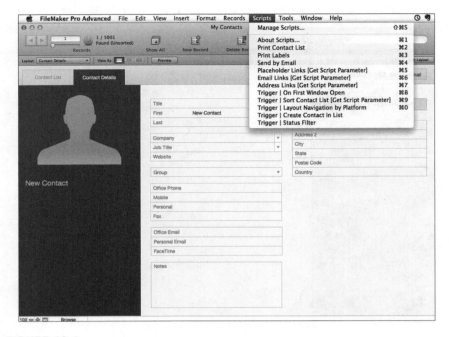

FIGURE 13.4

The Scripts menu, with more than 10 scripts listed as options. Notice that only the first 10 scripts have been assigned keyboard shortcuts.

TIP   To change the shortcut assigned to a script, reposition the script in the Manage Scripts window. To do so, simply click on a name and drag it up or down in the list.

TIP   To make the list of scripts in the Script menu easier to read, you can add ruled lines to separate related scripts. To add a ruled line, you can create a script whose name is simply a dash (-), position it in the list so that it appears between the scripts that you want to separate, and then enable the check box for the script so that it is included in the Scripts list. FileMaker adds a ruled line to the Scripts menu in place of the "-" script. These scripts are not assigned shortcuts, as they are really just placeholders for the ruled lines. Figure 13.5 shows the Scripts menu with ruled lines.

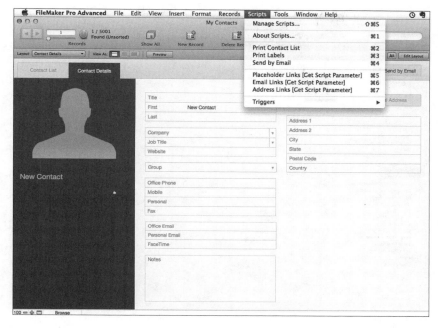

FIGURE 13.5

The Scripts menu, with ruled lines (separators) between groups of related scripts.

Creating Scripts

Now that you are familiar with the Manage Scripts window, let's use it to create a script. In this example, you create a script that automates the process of generating the Contacts Directory report that you created in Chapter 12.

Start by clicking the New button, which is located in the bottom-left corner of the window. The Edit Script window opens. Figure 13.6 shows how the window appears when you start to add a new script. The script has been named New Script and has no script steps. Also note the list of available script steps, displayed in the left column of the window.

Before proceeding, let's take a moment to explore with the Edit Script window. At the top of the Edit Script window is a field that can be used to specify a script's name. FileMaker automatically assigns the script the name New Script. Change the script name to Contacts Directory Report.

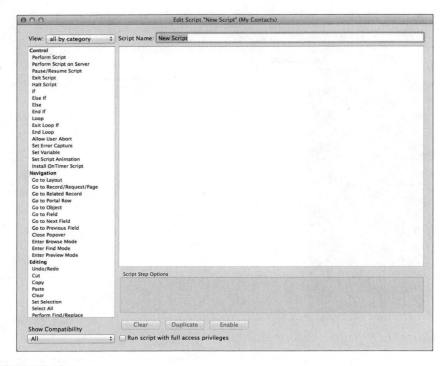

FIGURE 13.6

A blank Edit Script window

The left column of the window lists all the script steps that you can use in a script. Many of the script steps, such as Enter Browse Mode and Sort Records and so on, have names that might seem familiar to you because they represent the FileMaker commands that you are familiar with. The script steps are grouped by functional categories to make them easier to locate. For example, you see script steps grouped in categories such as Navigation (which include steps that can be used to move the user around the database), Records (steps that involve working with records), and more. Above the list of script steps is a View drop-down menu that you can use to quickly filter the list of script steps by category, or you can select the All By Name option to view the steps in alphabetical order by name.

At this point, you have a new script, but it doesn't have any script steps assigned to it. To add a step to a script, locate it in the list of script steps and then double-click it. For the example script, let's start by adding a step to navigate the user to the Contacts Directory layout (see Figure 13.7). We use the Go To Layout script step to do that.

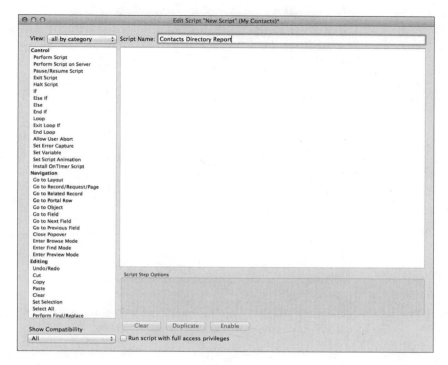

FIGURE 13.7

The Edit Script window showing the Contacts Directory Report script. The script has been renamed, but does not yet include any script steps.

Locate the Go To Layout step, which is in the Navigation category, and double-click it. You see that the step is added to the right column of the window. Also notice that a small area of the window appears at the bottom of the right column, titled Script Step Options. Many script steps have options that can be set, and this is the area in which you can configure those settings. In this case, the script step has a single option titled Specify, and it is used to indicate what layout to navigate the user to. Click on the Specify field and select Layout. The Specify Layout window opens, as shown in Figure 13.8.

Use the window to locate the Contacts Directory layout that you created in Chapter 12. Then double-click the layout name. The Specify Layout window closes, and you see that the Go To Layout script step now specifies that the Contacts Directory layout will be navigated to when the script runs (as shown in Figure 13.9).

FIGURE 13.8

The Specify Layout window, which is used to specify the layout that will be navigated to when the Go To Layout script step is reached.

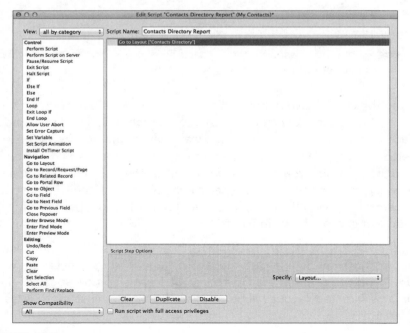

FIGURE 13.9

The Edit Script window showing the Contacts Directory Report script with a single Go To Layout script step.

Now let's run the script to see what it does. First, close the Edit Script window. You can do so by either clicking on the close window button in the window's title bar, or by using the Command+W or Ctrl+W shortcut. A dialog window displays and asks whether you want to save the changes that you have made to script. Click Save to save your changes.

 TIP   When working on a script in the Edit Script window, you can periodically save the changes that you have made to the script by using the Command+S or Ctrl+S shortcut.

Your new script, Contacts Directory Report, now appears in the Manage Scripts window at the bottom of the script list. To run the script, first select it, and then click on the Perform icon, which is located in the bottom right-hand corner of the window. The script runs, and FileMaker automatically navigates to the Contacts Directory layout.

At this point, the script works, but it doesn't do much. As you learned in Chapter 12, for the Contacts Directory report to display properly, you also need to sort the records. Let's enhance the script so that it sorts the records.

First, reopen the Manage Scripts window by selecting Scripts > Manage Scripts. Then locate the Contacts Directory Report script in the list, and double-click it. The Edit Script window opens. Next, locate the Sort Records script step, which is located in the Found Sets category.

 TIP   Another method for quickly locating a script step is to click on a step in the script step list and type the first couple of characters of the script step that you are looking for. FileMaker scrolls to the first script step whose name starts with those characters.

Once you have located the Sort Records script step, double-click it to add it to the script. Notice that the Sort Records script step has two options. The first, Perform without Dialog, can be used to sort the records without asking the user to review the sort option. For the moment, let's leave this option unchecked.

 TIP   When adding a step to a script, FileMaker automatically places the new step below the set that is currently selected in the right-hand side of the editing window. If no script step is selected, then the new step is positioned at the end of the script.

The second option, Specify Sort Order, is used to specify the order in which you want the records to be sorted. Click the check box next to this option, and the Sort Records window opens. The window should look familiar to you. It is the same Sort Records window that you learned about in Chapter 7, "Sorting Records." Use the window to specify that records should be sorted by Work State, and subsorted by the Last and First fields, as shown in Figure 13.10.

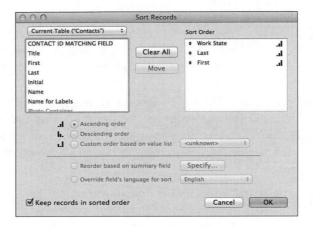

FIGURE 13.10

The Sort Records window, which appears when you configure the Sort Records script step. In this example, records are sorted by Work State and subsorted by the Last and First fields.

When you are finished, click OK to close the Sort Records window. Now, let's run the updated script. Close the Edit Script window, and FileMaker again asks whether you want to save the changes that you made to the script. Click the Save button to save the changes. Finally, as before, locate the Contacts Directory Report script in the Manage Scripts window and click the Perform icon to run the script. Notice that the script behaves much like it did when you ran it earlier. However, this time you see the Sort Records dialog window open, with the sort criteria that you specified preset for you. Click the Sort button to sort the records, and you should see that the records are sorted properly.

The script is starting to take shape. Let's make a few additional changes make it even more useful.

Reopen the Manage Scripts window by selecting Scripts > Manage Scripts. Then locate the Contacts Directory Report script in the list and double-click it. The Edit Script window reopens.

The first change that you want to make is to the Sort Records script step. Remember that when you added it to the script, you did not select the Perform Without Dialog option. That is why the Sort Records window appeared when the script ran. For the Contacts Directory report, it is safe to assume that the user will want the records sorted using the criteria that you specified, so let's suppress that Sort Records window. To do so, select the Perform Without Dialog option.

To change the Sort Records script step, locate it in the right column of the Edit Script window, and click on it. The script step options appear at the bottom of the column. Check the Perform Without Dialog option. Again, this prevents the Sort Records window from appearing. Now, FileMaker automatically sorts the records as you specified, without asking the user for input.

Another nice enhancement to the script is to automatically put the user into Preview mode, so that he can see what the report would look like if he were to print it or save it as a PDF document. FileMaker provides the Enter Preview Mode script step for just this purpose.

To add the Enter Preview Mode script step, locate it in the script step list and double-click it. This script step has a Pause option. Click the Pause option check box. When FileMaker reaches this step of the script, it enters Preview mode and then pauses until the user indicates that he wants to continue. Figure 13.11 shows the updated script, with the additional script steps added.

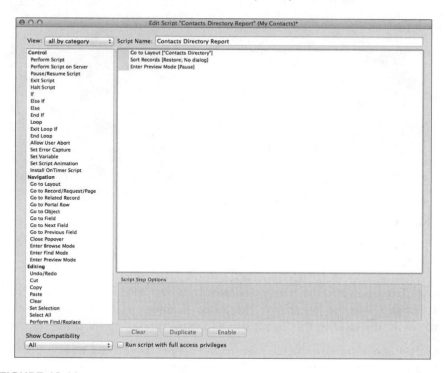

FIGURE 13.11

The Edit Script window, showing the Contacts Directory Report script and three script steps.

Let's run the script again to see the impact of the changes that have been made. As you did before, close the Edit Script window, save your changes, and then run the script. This time, the script runs without displaying the Sort Records window, and it places you into Preview mode. Notice that when it reaches the Enter Preview Mode script step, the script pauses. A message, located in the bottom-right area of the Status Toolbar, indicates that the Script Is Paused, and Continue and Cancel buttons are located next to the message (see Figure 13.12). Your script is actually still running, and FileMaker is waiting for you to click either Continue or Cancel before proceeding.

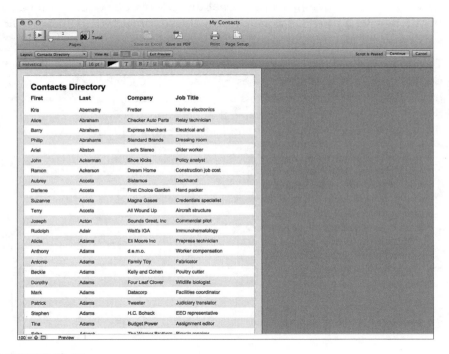

FIGURE 13.12

The Contacts Directory layout displayed in Preview mode with the Contacts Directory Report script paused.

Click Continue and the script resumes. However, because the Enter Preview Mode script step was the last step in the script, nothing much happens. It would be nice to return the user to the layout she was on when she ran the script.

Let's make another enhancement to the script. As you did before, reopen the Manage Scripts window, locate the Contacts Directory Report script in the list, and double-click it so that the Edit Script window opens. Then locate the Go To Layout script step in the list and add it to the script. However, this time leave the Specify script step option set to Original Layout. When the Go To Layout script step is set to Original Layout, FileMaker navigates back to the layout that the user was originally on when the script was run.

Save the change that you have made to the script, then switch to the Desktop > Contacts layout and enter Browse mode. As before, FileMaker navigates to the Contacts Directory layout, sorts the records, enters Preview mode, and then pauses. However, this time, when you click Continue, FileMaker sends you back to the Desktop > Contacts layout. The only problem is that you are left in Preview mode.

Let's make one final change to the script, so that when the script completes, the user is returned to Browse mode. As before, open the Contacts Directory Report script for editing. Then locate the Enter Browse Mode script step and add it to the script. Be sure to leave the Pause script step option unchecked (see Figure 13.13). Then save the change that you made and run the script again. This time, when you continue the script (by clicking Continue), you return to the Desktop > Contacts layout and are placed in Browse mode.

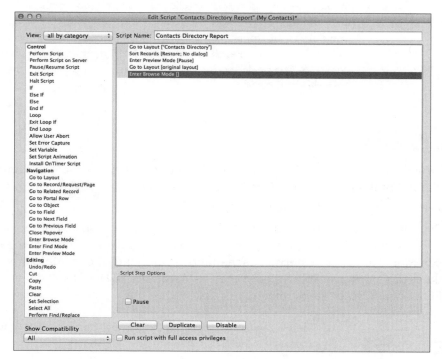

FIGURE 13.13

The Edit Script window, showing the Contacts Directory Report script with several script steps. This version of the script returns the user to the layout that they were originally on and also returns them to Browse mode.

Run the script one more time, and when FileMaker reaches the Enter Preview Mode script step and pauses, click Cancel. Notice that FileMaker simply halts the script. None of the remaining script steps are executed.

 TIP FileMaker provides an Allow User Abort script step, and when its option is set to Off, the user is not given the option to cancel a paused script. The Cancel button is not presented, and the user's only option is to Continue.

As you can see from this example, creating FileMaker scripts is often an iterative process. Getting a script "just right" often takes several rounds of changes and enhancements. But thankfully, FileMaker makes this easy, allowing you to make as many changes to a script as is necessary.

 TIP In some cases, you might want to adjust the order of the steps in a script, or move multiple steps at one time. FileMaker makes this possible. You can click on a script step, and then drag it to the desired position in the script. You can Shift-click to select multiple script steps and then drag those as well. You can also select script steps and then copy and paste them in the desired location. And finally, to remove script steps, you can select them and click Delete.

Script Steps

When you created the Contacts Directory Report script, you were introduced to a handful of the more common script steps that FileMaker provides. In this section, you learn about several additional script steps.

By default, FileMaker displays the list of available script steps by grouping them into categories (Control, Navigation, and so on). We discuss some of the more commonly used script steps in each of those categories. For a complete list of the script steps available, refer to the FileMaker Pro 13 Help function and see the Reference > Script steps reference.

 TIP Below the list of script steps is a Show Compatibility drop-down menu, with options for All (the default value), Macintosh, Windows, Server, iOS, Custom Web Publishing, and FileMaker WebDirect. By selecting an option from the menu, FileMaker grays out any script steps not supported by the selected platform or FileMaker technology.

Control Script Steps

The script steps in the Control category are helpful when you want FileMaker to perform actions based on certain conditions. For example, in the Contacts Directory Report script, we assume that the user's found set of records isn't empty. Using the Control script steps, you can check for this condition so that, if no records are in the found set, the script doesn't display an empty report.

Let's modify the Contacts Directory Report script so that it does just that. Open the script for editing, just as you did earlier. Then locate the If script step and double-click it to add it to the script. Notice that FileMaker actually adds the End If script step as well. It does this because all If script steps must have corresponding End If steps.

Next, click and drag both the If and End If steps to the top of the script (as shown in Figure 13.14), so that they are the first steps FileMaker performs when the script runs.

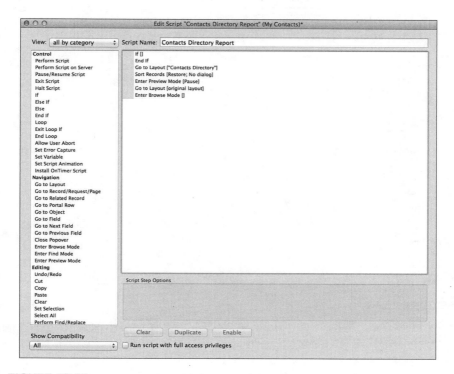

FIGURE 13.14

The Edit Script window showing the Contacts Directory Report script with the newly added If and End If script steps.

When FileMaker performs the If script step, it evaluates the condition specified, and if that condition is true, it performs any script steps between the If step and the End If step. To specify that condition, you assign a calculation formula to the If step. To do that, click on the If step and then click the Specify button in the step's options. The Specify Calculation window, which you are now familiar with, appears.

The goal is to have FileMaker cancel the script if no records are in the found set. Therefore, the calculation formula that you want to specify is simply: Get (FoundCount) = 0. Enter that formula into the Specify Calculation window and then click OK. Notice that the calculation is now displayed as part of the If script step, as shown in Figure 13.15.

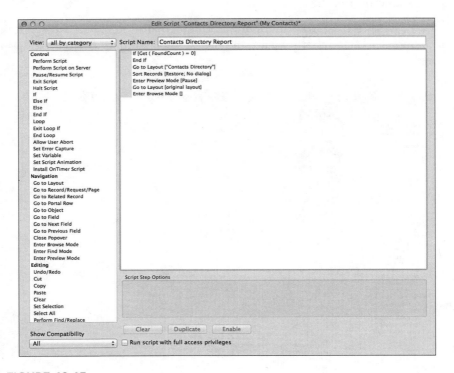

FIGURE 13.15

The Edit Script window showing the Contacts Directory Report script with the If script step configured with a calculation formula.

You now need to indicate what script step (or steps) should be performed when the calculation formula is true. There are two Control script steps that you can use to do that: Exit Script and Halt Script. Those two script steps are similar. When FileMaker encounters the Exit Script step, it exits the current script. However, if that script was actually called by another script as a subscript (which we discuss later), then FileMaker returns to the calling script and continues processing it. When FileMaker encounters the Halt Script step, it not only exits the current script but it stops completely—even if that script was called as a subscript. The Contacts Directory Report script isn't called by another script, so you can use either Exit Script and Halt Script. Select one of those steps and add it to your script, and be careful to position it so that it is between the If and End If script steps (see Figure 13.16).

 TIP Another difference between the Exit Script and Halt Script steps is that Exit Script includes an option for specifying a Script Result. In cases where a script has been called as a subscript of another script, it might be helpful for the subscript to return a value to the calling script, and the Script Result option can be used to do that. The calling script can then use the Get (ScriptResult) function to access the result that subscript returned.

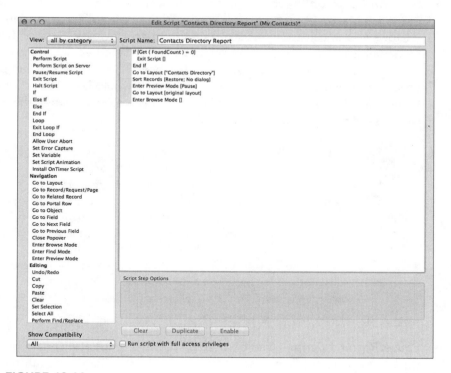

FIGURE 13.16

The Edit Script window, showing the Contacts Directory Report script with an Exit Script script step added. This step is performed when the calculation formula in the If script step evaluates to True.

Save the changes that you made to the script and run it. If your found set includes records, the script performs as it did earlier. (To test the script when no records are present, you can first select Records > Show All Records and then select Records > Show Omitted Only.)

The changes that you made to the Contacts Directory Report script use three of FileMaker's Control script steps: If, End If, and either Exit Script or Halt Script. However, several additional important and useful Control script steps are available, including

- **Perform Script**—Used to call another script, in which case the second script becomes known as a *subscript*. Subscripts make it possible for you to develop scripts in a modular fashion, so that a series of steps common to multiple processes can be set up in a single script, and that script can be called by other scripts whose purposes are more specific.

- **Perform Script on Server**—This powerful script step was introduced as part of the FileMaker 13 platform. It is similar to the Perform Script step in that it allows you to call another script as a subscript. However, Perform Script on Server is different in that the subscript being called actually runs on a FileMaker server. As a result, the speed with which the subscript can be processed is typically much greater than what it would be if the script were running locally. Perform Script on Server is only applicable when the FileMaker database is being hosted using FileMaker Server.

WARNING The Perform Script on Server script step is a powerful script, and if not used properly, it can cause a lot of problems. When FileMaker Server receives a request to run a script from the Perform Script on Server step, it acts as though the user who ran the script has logged in to the database again, and done so locally on the server itself. As such, the script will run in a context that might be different from what the user who initiated the script was in—meaning it is possible that the subscript will run based on a different layout, found set, sort order, and so on. Therefore, when using Perform Script on Server, do so with great caution.

- **Pause/Resume Script**—Can be used to pause a script at a certain point, and then either wait indefinitely for the user to click the Continue button before proceeding, or proceed automatically after a specified number of seconds. This step can be useful when you want to display a layout (such as a splash screen) for a few seconds before continuing.

- **Loop, End Loop, and Exit Loop If**—*Looping* is a common concept among many programming languages, and FileMaker supports it using these script steps. A *loop* is one or more steps repeated until a certain condition occurs. For example, you can create a script that loops over the found set of records and makes a change to each one.

> **TIP** When using loops, be sure to include a condition that will eventually be true and allow FileMaker to break out of the loop; otherwise, FileMaker might get stuck in that loop—a condition known as an *infinite loop*. To break from a loop, you can use the Exit Loop If script step (with a calculation formula), the Go to Record/Request/Page step (with the Previous/Next and Exit After options), or the Go to Portal Row step.

- **Allow User Abort**—By default, a user can abort a script by pressing Command+period or Ctrl+period. However, you can prevent the user from aborting a script by adding the Allow User Abort step and setting it to Off. This is helpful in cases where you want to be sure that a script runs to completion.

> **WARNING** When the Allow User Abort script step is set to Off, it is still possible that a script might not run to completion. For example, a user might force quit FileMaker, or, if the user is running FileMaker Go, she might take some action that prevents the script from completing (such as switching to another application, answering a phone call, and so on).

- **Set Error Capture**—One of the nice things about editing FileMaker scripts is that, because you simply select script steps from a list, it is difficult to create errors that have errors in them. However, it is still possible for FileMaker to encounter an error condition when it is processing a script. The Set Error Capture script step makes it possible for you to look for errors as they occur and take action to resolve them. You learn how to handle errors later in this chapter.

- **Set Variable**—Variables are another concept common in most programming languages, and the Set Variable script step brings them to FileMaker. Like fields, variables can be used to hold data. However unlike fields, variables are not part of a table, and they can be created as needed. Variables are often used to hold temporary values, such as loop counters.

TIP FileMaker supports two types of variables: local and global. Local variables exist for the duration of a script, while global variables persist until the database is closed or the user logs out. To indicate that a variable is to be a local variable, you give it a name that starts with a single dollar sign. Global variables are created by naming them with two dollar signs.

- **Set Script Animation**—This is a new script step introduced in FileMaker 13. It can be used to enable or disable the animations used when a user changes between slide control panels.

- **Install OnTimer Script**—This step can be used to schedule another script to run at a certain interval. Once the specified amount of time has passed, and when FileMaker is idle (meaning that no other script is running), FileMaker runs the specified script. It repeats this process, running the specified script at each interval, until the window that was active when the Install OnTimer Script step was run is closed, or until a script runs that includes the Install OnTimer Script step with no script and/or interval specified.

TIP You can use the Install OnTimer Script step to set up an OnTimer script for each open window. However, a single window can only ever have one active OnTimer Script. When calling the Install OnTimer Script step a second time, that step replaces any previously OnTimer Script that was set.

Navigation Script Steps

As you might expect, the Navigation script steps are used to move around a FileMaker database. There are steps that can be used to move between layouts, records, and even within specified objects on a layout.

For the most part, the Navigation script steps are self-explanatory, and their names clearly indicate their purpose. However, a few Navigation steps have interesting options and are possibly a little confusing. We review them here.

- **Go to Record/Request/Page**—The behavior of this script step differs depending on what mode the user is in when FileMaker encounters it. When in Browse mode, the step navigates between records in the found set. When in Find mode, it navigates between the Find requests that have been set up. When in Preview mode, it navigates between the pages of the document being previewed. The script step can be used to go to the first, last, previous, or next record, request, or page. When using the script step to navigate to the previous or next record, request, or page, you can also indicate that, in cases where the step is being called as part of the loop, when the first or last record has been reached, FileMaker should break out of the loop.

- **Go to Related Record**—This powerful script step can be used to navigate a user from a certain record to one or more related records—and can do so by optionally going to another layout and even opening another window. For example, suppose that your Contacts database included a second table named Communication whose records were used to store information about the communication that you have had with a contact. Each record might represent a phone call, email, or letter sent to a contact. Using a script that includes the Go To Related Record script step, you can automatically open another window, navigate to a layout based on the Communication table, and find only those records related to the contact that you were on when the script ran—or to the Communication records related to all the Contact records in the found set when the script ran.

- **Go to Object**—In Chapter 11, "Working with Layouts," you learned that layouts are made of the objects that you place on them, such as fields, portals, web viewers, and so on. Using the Go To Object script step, you can have a FileMaker script act as if it were clicking on, or into, a layout object. To do so, you use the script step's option to indicate the name of the object that you want it to navigate to. (To give a layout object a name, go to the layout, enter Layout Mode, click on the object, and use the Inspector window's Position > Name field.)

Editing Script Steps

Most of the Editing script steps correspond to the commands available to you under the Edit menu, such as copy, paste, and so on. However, two Editing script steps do not have corresponding commands. These are

- **Set Selection**—With the script step, you can have FileMaker simulate the process of selecting part of a field's value. You specify the field that you want to work with and both the starting and ending position. You can then use the other Editing script steps to cut, copy, paste/replace, or clear the selected text.

- **Perform Find/Replace**—This script step has a number of options that make it possible to find and optionally replace values within a field, and to do so either on the record currently being viewed, or across the current found set. For example, you can use this step to locate all occurrences of a misspelled word and replace it with the correct value.

Field Script Steps

The script steps listed in the Fields category are used to set, update, and extract data to and from a database at the field level. Many of these script steps have equivalent commands available via the Insert menu that you are already familiar with, such as Insert Picture, Insert From Index, and so on. Therefore, we discuss only the script steps not available as menu commands.

- **Set Field**—This is a straightforward script step in that it simply allows you to specify the field that you want to set and the value to set it to. As you have seen in many other areas of FileMaker, you can use a calculation formula to specify the field's value.

- **Set Field by Name**—This step is identical to the Set Field script step, except that instead of selecting a field to set, you can specify its name using a calculation formula.

 TIP Often, when copying scripts from one database to another, you find that some script steps "break" because the tables, fields, layouts, and so on, that they reference either aren't set up in the database that the script is being copied to or have been set up in such a way that FileMaker cannot properly resolve the references. Scripts that use the Set Field by Name step, as well as the Go to Layout step (with the Layout Name by Calculation option), tend to be easier to reuse.

- **Set Next Serial Value**—In Chapter 9, "Working with Fields," you learned that one of the Auto-Enter Options for a field is Serial Number. When new records are created, FileMaker automatically assigns the next serial number to the record and then increments the next value so that the next record gets the next correct value. You can manually adjust a field's next value setting, but with the Set Next Serial Value script step, you can have FileMaker make an adjustment for you.

- **Insert Text**—Use this script step to have FileMaker paste static text into a text field. The step includes three options: Select Entire Contents is checked by default and causes the value of the field to be completely replaced. When that option is unchecked, the specified text is appended to any existing text in the field. You can use the Go to Target Field option to specify the field into which you want the text to be pasted. If you do not specify a field, FileMaker pastes the text into the currently active field. And finally, the Specify option provides a dialog box into which you can enter the text that you want to paste.

- **Insert Calculated Result**—This script step is similar to the Insert Text script step, except that instead of static text being pasted into a field, the result of a calculation field is pasted.

- **Insert from Device**—This script step can be used only in databases running in FileMaker Go on mobile devices. It provides you with a way to specify the source of content to be entered into a container field. For example, you can indicate that the content is to be obtained using the device's music library, photo library, camera, video camera, or microphone. You can also indicate that the source is a barcode, in which case the user is asked to scan the barcode using the device's camera. Another option is to capture a signature.

- **Insert from URL**—With this script step, you can set a field's value to content that has been obtained from a URL. The content can be text or, when used to set the value of a container, a file (such as a PDF file, an image, and so on). Insert from URL supports several protocols, including http, https, httppost, httpspost, ftp, ftps, and file. You can use a calculation formula to indicate what URL the content should be pulled from.

   TIP When using script steps that involve inserting values into a field, keep in mind that the field you are trying to insert into must be on the layout that is being viewed when the script runs. Otherwise, the script step will fail. Note that you can hide the field by moving it beyond the right edge of the viewable layout. As long as a field is on the layout, the Insert script steps will be able to refer to it.

- **Replace Field Contents**—This script step is equivalent to the command of the same name listed under the Records menu. You can use it to replace the value in a field across a found set of records, and the replacement value can be either the value of the field in the current record or the result of a calculation.

- **Relookup Field Contents**—Like Replace Field Contents, this script step is also equivalent to the command of the same name listed under the Records menu. For fields that have been configured to auto-enter using a looked-up value, this step will re-lookup their related values and do so across the current found set of records.

- **Export Field Contents**—This step exports the contents of a specified field. Unlike the Export Records command located under File menu, the script step only exports the value from the current record. While this script step is typically used to export the contents of container fields, it can also be used to export the contents of text fields as well (in which case FileMaker creates a text file). The step provides two options. The first allows you to specify the target field (the field whose contents are to be exported). The second allows you to specify the path (the location and name) of the file that the contents are to be exported to.

Record Script Steps

Just as the script steps listed in the Fields category are used to work with data at the field level, those listed in the Records category are used to work at the record level in Browse and at the request level in Find mode. While many of the script steps in this category have corresponding and similarly named commands available under the Records menu, a few do not and might prove to be helpful when creating scripts. Those script steps follow:

- **Delete Portal Row**—When a portal row is selected, this script step deletes the related record that corresponds with the row. This is equivalent to clicking on a portal row and clicking the Delete Record icon in the Status Toolbar.

- **Open Record/Request**—This script step can be used to determine whether the current record is available for editing. FileMaker first confirms that the user has the access privileges required to edit the record. If so, it then checks to see that the record isn't locked (meaning that it isn't already being edited by either another user or the same user in another window). If the Open Record/Request script step is successful, FileMaker essentially locks the record, which prevents other users from editing or deleting it until the user releases it by either committing or reverting any changes that she made to it.

 TIP You learn how to handle script errors later in this chapter. However, it is worth noting that when using the Open Record/Request script step, FileMaker returns error code 200 if the user does not have permission to access the current record, and error code 301 if the record is in use by another user (or in use by the same user in a different window).

- **Copy Record/Request**—The Copy Record/Request script step copies all the field values from the current record to the clipboard. The values are copied as tab-delimited text, so they can be pasted into another application (such as a spreadsheet or text document). Only values in fields on the current layout are copied, and they are copied in the order in which they appear on the layout. This is equivalent to selecting the Edit > Copy command when viewing a record, and specifically when the cursor isn't in a field.

- **Copy All Records/Requests**—This script step is similar to the Copy Record/ Request step. However, it copies values from all the records in the current found set. In this case, the individual records are delimited by a carriage return. (Note that you can perform this same action manually by holding down the Option key [Mac] or Shift key [Windows] and selecting Edit > Copy when the cursor isn't in a field.)

 NOTE The Copy Record/Request and Copy All Records/ Requests script steps copy only the actual values in the fields. They do not copy any styles applied to those values.

Found Set Script Steps

As you'd probably suspect, the script steps in the Found Sets category are used to change the found set of records. All the steps in the category have corresponding commands available via the Requests menu (which is visible in Find mode) or via the contextual menu that appears when you right-click in a field when in Browse mode.

Window Script Steps

The Windows script steps can be used to open, close, select, and adjust the appearance of windows. Most of these script steps are self-explanatory and behave in ways similar to their corresponding commands in the Windows menu. However, some of those script steps provide options not available to you when running the commands manually. Let's review some of the steps.

- **New Window**—As you'd probably expect, this script step opens a new window. Like the New Window command, the window created by this script step takes on all the attributes (layout, found set, sort order, and so on) of the window that was active when the script step runs. However, the script step provides options that give you an opportunity to specify a name for the new window, as well as its height, width, and position (distance from the top and left edge of the window). In addition, the step gives you the option to specify the window's style. The styles available include Document Window (which is the same style of window that FileMaker normally opens windows in), Floating Document Window (a window that "floats" above any other windows that are open, even when the floating window is no longer considered to be the active window), and Dialog Window (or Modal window, which appears in the foreground, above any other windows that are opened, preventing the user from interacting with other windows until it is closed). Also note that, depending on the style of window that is to be opened, the script step also gives you the option to display or hide certain window controls, including close, minimize, maximize, zoom controls, and resize.

- **Select Window**—This script step can be used to make a window appear in the foreground and become the current active window. You can select a window open in the current database or one opened in another database.

- **Freeze Window**—In some cases, you might need a script to perform actions that you do not want the user to see. For example, a script might loop over the found set of records and make changes to each one. Using the Freeze Window command, you can have FileMaker perform that action without updating the active window. To the user the window appears frozen until the Refresh Window script step is reached, the script is paused (using the Pause/Resume script step), or the script completes.

- **Scroll Window**—Use this script step to scroll the window to the top (Home) or bottom (End), to page up or down, or to scroll the window so that the active field is visible.

File Script Steps

The File script steps can be used to create FileMaker database files, open and close files, and more. These script steps are powerful and can be somewhat complicated. Let's take a few moments to review them:

- **New File**—Use this script step to initiate the process of creating a new FileMaker database from scratch. It is the equivalent of selecting File > New Database. The user is asked to select the location and name of the new database file.

- **Open File**—This script step can be used to open another FileMaker database file. You can use the step's Open hidden option to open the database without a window being visible to the user. (The database's window appears in the Windows menu.)

- **Close File**—Use this script step to close either the current database file or another FileMaker database that is also opened.

- **Convert File**—With this script step, you can automate the conversion of a file in a supported file format into a FileMaker Pro database file. Supported file formats include delimited text files, dBase files, HTML tables, merge files, Microsoft Excel files, and XML files. You can optionally choose to have the new FileMaker database opened after it has been created.

- **Set Multi-User**—Use this script step to allow or disallow other users from accessing the database across your local network. You learn how to share a database in Chapter 16, "Sharing a Database."

- **Set Use System Formats**—The format in which a FileMaker database stores dates, times, and numbers is determined by the regional settings of the computer in use when the database was created. Those settings might differ from those being used by the database's users. For example, suppose that a database is created on a computer using the English language and one of the users of that database is using a computer whose language is set to Japanese. Using the Set Use System Formats script step, you can allow a user to enter values using a format that corresponds to the settings of the user's computer. The values actually saved in the database are formatted according to the settings used when the database was created. This script step is particularly helpful when users of the database are in geographically diverse areas.

- **Save a Copy as**—You can use this script step to automate the process of creating a copy of the current database. For example, you might use it to create a backup of the database (including all its data). You can also use the step to create a clone of the database, which is a copy of the database that does not include any of its data. Other options that this script step provides include creation of a compacted copy of the database (which includes the data but in a manner that potentially makes the file's size smaller) as well as a self-contained copy of the database (which embeds any externally stored container contents within the copy).

- **Recover File**—It is possible for a FileMaker database to become damaged. For example, if a database isn't closed properly, it is possible that some of its data might not be saved. In cases where a file is damaged, you can use Recover File to help automate the recovery of another database. When the step runs, FileMaker does as much as it can to recover the information stored in the damaged file. If the process is successful, a new, recovered database is created, and the damaged FileMaker database file will remain. This script step is equivalent to the File > Recover command.

- **Print Setup**—You can use the Print Setup script step to set the options used during printing, including the paper size, page orientation, and scale. You can choose to set all these options automatically, or allow the user to make adjustments to the settings. The step is equivalent to the File > Page Setup command, or clicking the Page Setup icon in the Status Toolbar when viewing a layout in Preview mode.

- **Print**—With this script step, you can automate the process of printing a report, labels, and so on. Like the Print Setup script step, you can either have

FileMaker perform the print command without any interaction with the user, or you can let the user make adjustments to the print command as needed. This step is equivalent to selecting the File > Print command, or clicking the Print icon in the Status Toolbar when viewing a layout in Preview mode.

Account Script Steps

Using the script steps in the Accounts category, you can automate several tasks that involve the security of a FileMaker database. For example, you can use these script steps to automate the creation and deletion of accounts, to reset an account's password, to change the password of the current user, to enable or disable an account, or to re-login using a different account. We discuss database accounts and other security-related topics in Chapter 14, "Protecting a Database."

Spelling Script Steps

The Spelling script steps can be used to check the spelling of words in a selected block of text, in the current record, or across the found set of records. You can also use the following script steps to automate other spelling-related tasks.

- **Spelling Options**—Use this script step to open the database's File Options dialog and specify how you want FileMaker to indicate potentially misspelled words.

- **Select Dictionaries**—FileMaker can use alternative dictionaries to perform spell checking. With this script step, which is equivalent to Edit > Spelling > Select Dictionaries, you can automate the process of opening the Select Dictionary window, which allows the user to select one of the alternative dictionaries available.

- **Edit User Dictionary**—In some cases, you might find that a word you use regularly in your database isn't in FileMaker's dictionary. With the Edit User Dictionary script step, you can open the User Dictionary dialog window, which allows you to add words to, or remove words from, the dictionary. This script step is equivalent to selecting Edit > Spelling > Edit User Dictionary.

Open Menu Item Script Steps

Using the Open Menu Item script steps, you can automate the opening of some of FileMaker's dialog boxes. For example, the Open Manage Value Lists script step opens the Manage Value Lists dialog box. These scripts are useful in cases where you have restricted the menus and/or menu commands available to a user.

Miscellaneous Script Steps

The Miscellaneous script steps can be used to perform a variety of different tasks. For example, there are steps available for installing FileMaker plug-ins, sending mail, and more. Let's review the available steps:

- **Show Custom Dialog**—Using this script step, you can display a custom message in a dialog box and optionally interact with the user. We discuss this script step in depth in the "Interacting with Users" section of this chapter.

- **Allow Formatting Bar**—This step gives you the ability to enable or disable the text formatting toolbar, as well as any commands listed in the Format menu. Use this step when you want to either restrict or allow the user to apply formatting to values in a field.

- **Refresh Object**—The appearance of certain layout objects might change depending on how they have been configured. For example, in Chapter 11 you learned that you can choose to hide a layout object when a certain condition is met. With the Refresh Object script step, you can indicate that a specified object should be refreshed to reflect the current conditions. This script step is similar to the Refresh Window script step, except that it only refreshes a single object.

- **Beep**—Use this script step to have FileMaker play the system's "beep" sound. This is useful when a certain condition occurs and you want to alert the user. For example, you might choose to have FileMaker beep when a find is performed and no records are found, or when some other unexpected error occurs.

- **Speak**—This script step, which is only available to Mac users, can be used to have the computer speak specified text. For example, you can use it to have the computer speak the contents of a field, or some static text. The step gives you the option to choose from several different voices that OS X provides, as well as to have the computer either speak the text while the script continues running, or to wait for the computer to finish speaking before continuing.

- **Dial Phone**—Using this script step, along with either a computer that has phone dialing capabilities or an iPhone running FileMaker Go, you can automate the process of dialing a phone number.

- **Install Plug-In File**—In Chapter 10, "Working with Calculations," you learned that you can extend FileMaker through the use of plug-ins created by third-party developers. By placing a FileMaker plug-in in a container field, you can use the Install Plug-In File script step to fully automate the process of installing the plug-in.

- **Install Menu Set**—Developers using FileMaker Pro Advanced have the ability to set up alternative menus in their FileMaker databases. They can use that function to restrict access to certain commands, or to replace FileMaker's standard commands with their own scripts. The Install Menu Set script step is one of the ways that a developer can change the set of menus available to the user.

- **Set Web Viewer**—In Chapter 11, you learned that you can add a Web viewer object to a layout and indicate what URL that the Web viewer should use to get its contents. Using the Set Web Viewer script step, you can force the Web viewer to update its contents. For example, you can reset the Web viewer to its original URL contents, reload the Web page currently being displayed, go forward or backward based on the Web viewer's history, or specify an alternative URL to display. To use the Set Web Viewer script step, you must first name the Web viewer object on the layout and then refer to that object name in the script step.

- **Open URL**—This script opens a specified URL using the user's default Web browser. You can use the step's options to open the URL automatically, or display a dialog box that gives the user the option to either go to the specified URL, go to an alternate URL, or cancel the command.

- **Send Mail**—Sending email from within a FileMaker database is a common task, and the Send Mail script step provides several options for doing so. The first option involves specifying how the message is to be sent. You can choose to have FileMaker send the message using the user's default email client or directly through an SMTP mail server. If you choose to send the message through the user's email client, FileMaker opens the email application, creates the message, and sends the message through the application. The user then sees the message appear in the Sent Mail folder, just as if the user had written and sent the message manually. When sending mail through an SMTP mail server, the user's email client does not open, and there typically is no sign of the message in the user's Sent Mail folder. The Send Mail script step also provides options for specifying who the message should be sent to (including CC and BCC addresses), the subject, the message body, and an optional file attachment. With the exception of the file attachment, the other message options can either be entered as static text or specified using a calculation formula. In addition, you can choose whether FileMaker should send the one email message using data from the current record or multiple messages where a message is generated for each record in the found set.

- **Send DDE Execute**—This script step, available only to users running Windows-based computers, can be used to perform operations in another Windows application, and it does so by sending the application a DDE (Dynamic Data Exchange) command.

- **Perform AppleScript**—This script step is similar to Send DDE Execute described previously. In this case, the step is available only to Mac OS X users. It can be used to perform operations in another application and does so by sending AppleScript commands. Using this script step, you can automate tasks that the user would normally do manually, such as installing printers, creating folders, and so on.

- **Execute SQL**—With the Execute SQL script step, you can send a SQL command to an ODBC data source. For example, you can insert records, update records, and delete records. Depending on the type of data source being used, you can also execute stored procedures or perform other commands supported by the database platform. When using ExecuteSQL, you can either specify a (static) SQL command or create the SQL command dynamically using a calculation function.

 NOTE   The Execute SQL script step is often confused with the ExecuteSQL calculation function. The Execute SQL script step is used to send a command to an ODBC data source, and unfortunately, there is no way to use it to retrieve data from the data source. The ExecuteSQL calculation function is used to execute a SQL SELECT statement using table occurrences in the FileMaker database itself. So while the script step and calculation functions have similar names, they serve different purposes.

- **Send Event**—With this script step, you can have FileMaker start another application on the user's computer and optionally open or print a document. This is a helpful script step when the FileMaker solution is one part of a workflow that involves multiple applications.

- **Comment**—It is often helpful, especially when creating long or complicated scripts, to add comments to the script, and the Comment script step makes that possible. Comments might include general information about the purpose of the script, details about what parameters the script expects to receive, or information about what the script returns. They might be used to describe the purpose of certain script steps, or to create whitespace in the script so that groups of script steps that perform a certain task can appear to be visually grouped together. Figure 13.17 shows an example of a script that includes comments.

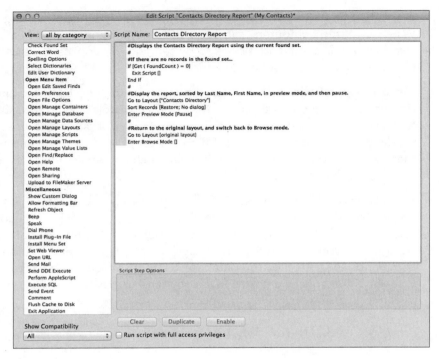

FIGURE 13.17

The Edit Script window, showing a version of the Contacts Directory Report script with several Comment script steps added.

- **Flush Cache to Disk**—FileMaker uses what it is known as a cache—a portion of data that resides in the computer's memory and can therefore be accessed more quickly. In some cases, FileMaker saves changes to data in the cache and then saves those changes to the computer's hard drive when the application is idle. This is an operation that FileMaker normally does automatically and isn't something that you need to worry about. However, in some cases, especially when many changes have been made, you might want to force FileMaker to save what it has in the cache to disk (a process referred to as *flushing* the cache). The Flush Cache to Disk script step gives you the ability to flush FileMaker's cache.

- **Exit Application**—This script step is the equivalent of the Quit command. It forces FileMaker to close all the databases that are open and then exit FileMaker Pro.

Interacting with Users

Often you will want a FileMaker script to interact with the user. For instance, you might want to display a warning or error message. In other cases, you might want the user to make a selection or provide a value for use by the script.

Earlier in this chapter, you learned about the Show Custom Dialog script step. This is the script step that gives you the ability to display a dialog box, along with a custom title and message. While this is a convenient way to display a message to the user, the script step also provides you with a way to interact with the user.

In addition to being able to specify the dialog box's title and message, Show Custom Dialog also allows you to display up to three buttons and to specify their labels. You can also choose whether each button should result in changes to the active record being committed when the button is clicked. But more importantly, after a user has clicked one of the buttons, you can use FileMaker's Get (LastMessageChoice) calculation function to determine what button was clicked, and then take appropriate action.

Let's take a look at an example of how you can use the Show Custom Dialog script step and Get (LastMessageChoice) calculation function to interact with a user. Suppose that we want the Contacts Directory Report script developed earlier in the chapter to ask the user whether she wants to print a list that includes only the current found set or one that includes all contacts. Let's modify the script to do that.

1. Open the Manage Script window (Scripts > Manage Scripts).

2. Locate the Contacts Directory Report and double-click for editing.

3. Locate the Show Custom Dialog step in the list of script steps and double-click to add it to the script.

4. Reposition the Show Custom Dialog step so that it is the first step in your script. To change its position in the script, simply click it and drag it to the top of the script.

5. Double-click the Show Custom Dialog step (or select it and click the Specify button). The "Show Custom Dialog" Options window displays.

6. For the Title field, enter **Print Contact List**.

7. For the Message field, enter **Do you want to print a list that includes the current Found Set, or all Records?**

8. Change the value of the Default Button from "OK" to "Found Set."

9. Change the value of Button 2 from "Cancel" to "All."

10. Set the value of Button 3 to "Cancel." The "Show Custom Dialog" Options window now looks like Figure 13.18.

11. Click OK to close the "Show Custom Dialog Options" window.

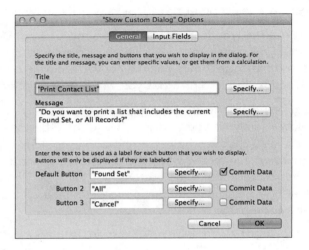

FIGURE 13.18

The "Show Custom Dialog Options" window configured to present three buttons to the user.

12. Earlier in the chapter, you added a few steps (If, Exit Script, and End If) so that if the current found set is empty FileMaker will exit the script (instead of displaying a blank list of contacts). Locate and remove those script steps. You want to remove the If, Exit Script, and End If steps.

13. Currently, the script is designed to print a contacts list using the current found set of records. However, if the user clicks the All button, it will need to find all records before printing the list. Therefore, you need to add a new set of If/ End If steps to the script. Locate the If step in the list of available script steps and double-click to add it to the script. FileMaker adds both the If and End If steps to the script. If necessary, reposition the If and End If script steps so that they are positioned after the Show Custom Dialog step.

14. Double-click the If step, and the Specify Calculation dialog window displays.

15. We want FileMaker to find all records when the user clicks the All button, which you might recall was referred to as "Button 2" in the "Show Custom Dialog" Options window. Therefore, the calculation formula that we want the If step to evaluate is Get (LastMessageChoice) = 2. Enter that formula into the Specify Calculation window, and then click OK to close the window.

16. The action that we want FileMaker to take when the All button is clicked is to find all records. Locate the Show All Records script step in the list of available script steps and double-click to add it to the script. If necessary, reposition so that it appears between the If and End If script steps.

17. When you configured the custom dialog, you added a third button, labeled "Cancel" so that the user has an opportunity to exit the script. Therefore, you also need to add a few script steps to handle that scenario. To do so, start by locating the Else If script step. You'll find it grouped in the Control category. Double-click it to add it to your script, and then, if necessary, reposition it so that it appears between the If and End If script steps, and just after the Show All Records step.

18. Double-click the Else If step, and the Specify Calculation dialog window opens.

19. We want FileMaker to exit the script if the user has clicked the Cancel button, which was referred to as Button 3 in the "Show Custom Dialog" Options window. Therefore, the calculation formula that we want the If step to evaluate is: Get (LastMessageChoice) = 3. Enter that formula into the Specify Calculation window and then click OK to close the window.

20. Locate the Exit Script step in the list of available script steps and double-click to add it to the script. If necessary, reposition it so that it appears after the Else If step.

21. Your script should now look similar to the script displayed in Figure 13.19. Close the Edit Script window and save the changes made to the script.

 NOTE The Else If script step, which you are using in the updated version of the Print Contact List script, is used to evaluate another calculation and take an alternative action when an If step (or another Else If step that appears before the step) evaluates to False. A script can have as many Else If steps as needed, so that FileMaker can take alternative steps depending on a number of different conditions.

Run the Print Contact List script, and the Print Contact List dialog box appears as it does in Figure 13.20. Experiment by running the script and clicking "Found Set" when the found set of records doesn't include all of the records in the Contacts table. Then run the script by clicking the "All" and "Cancel" buttons. As you will see, the script will behave differently depending on what button you click.

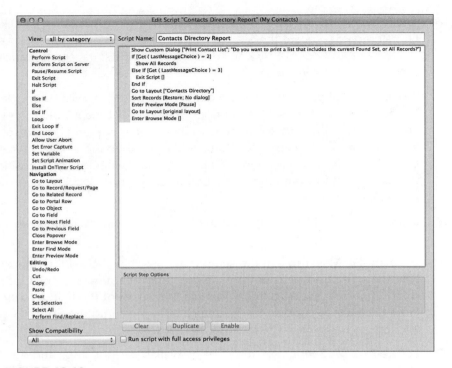

FIGURE 13.19

The Edit Script window, with a version of the Contacts Directory Report script that uses the Show Custom Dialog script step to interact with user, and a set of If, Else If, and End If script steps that respond based on the button clicked.

FIGURE 13.20

The Print Contact List dialog box, prompting the user to click on a button based on how she wants the report to be run.

Using the Show Custom Dialog script step and the optional buttons that it provides is a simple way to have a script interact with a user. However, the Show Custom Dialog script step also provides other options that you can use to interact with users and get additional information from them. Those options are referred to as *input fields*, and they can be configured via the "Show Custom Dialog" Options window, as shown in Figure 13.21.

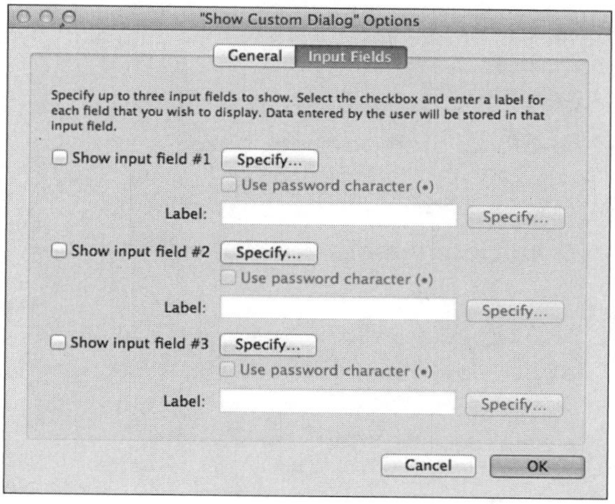

FIGURE 13.21

The "Show Custom Dialog" Options window, showing the Input Fields tab. This feature of the script step provides another method for interacting with the user by allowing them to enter values into fields.

You can use the input fields to ask the user to provide additional information. These fields appear in the custom dialog window in much the same way that fields appear on layouts. You can use up to three input fields and specify an optional label to appear next to each one. To use an input field, you must also indicate what field in the database you want the values that a user enters to be saved to. (Otherwise, the user would enter a value, and FileMaker wouldn't know where to store it.)

Let's modify the Print Contact List script so that it uses input fields. We use an input field to ask the user what title he wants to use for the Contacts List.

Before modifying the script, you need to make a few additional changes to the database. Let's start by adding a new field to the Contacts table. You use this new field to store the value that a user types into the input field.

To add the field, follow these steps:

1. Open the Manage Database window (File > Manage > Database).

2. If necessary, click on the Fields tab, so that the list of fields in the Contacts table is displayed.

3. Enter **Contact List Title** into the Field Name field.

4. Select Text as the field's Type.

5. Click the Create button.

6. Click the Options button. The Options for Field dialog window appears.

7. Select the Storage tab.

8. Check the Use Global Storage check box.

9. Click OK to close the Options for Field dialog window.

10. Click OK again to close the Manage Database window.

NOTE   We set up this new field as a global field, which you learned about back in Chapter 9, "Working with Fields." We set it up as a global field so that the dialog box can use it regardless of which record the user is on when the script runs.

Next, you need to modify the Contacts Directory layout so that instead of using static text for the report's title, it uses the new Contact List Title field. Here are the steps to take to make this change:

1. Navigate to the Contacts Directory layout.

2. Enter Layout mode.

3. Select the Contacts Directory text object, located in the Header layout part.

4. Double-click the text object. A cursor appears in the object, indicating that you can change its value.

5. Select the entire Contact Directory text. (An easy way to do so is to triple-click.)

6. From the Insert menu, select the Merge Field command. The Specify Field dialog box appears.

7. Scroll down to locate and select the new Contact List Title field.

8. Click OK to close the Specify Field dialog box. The text object now reflects the use of the Contact List Title field. (If necessary, resize the text object so that it is wide and appears in its proper location in the header.) Your layout should look similar to Figure 13.22.

9. Enter Browse mode, and save the changes that you made to the layout.

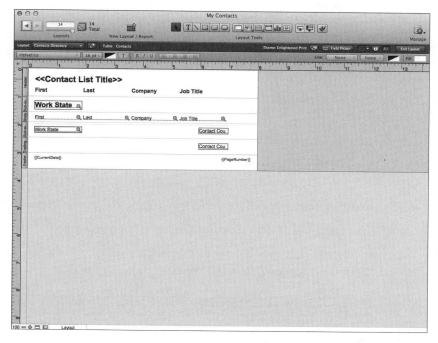

FIGURE 13.22

The updated Contacts Directory layout displayed in Layout mode with the report's title displayed as a merge field.

Now that you have the new Contact List Title field set up and the changes to the Contacts Directory layout have been made, you are ready to update the Contacts Directory Report script. Here are the steps that you need to take:

1. Open the Manage Script window (Scripts > Manage Scripts).

2. Locate the Contacts Directory Report and double-click for editing.

3. Locate the Show Custom Dialog step in the list of script steps, and double-click to add it to the script.

4. Reposition the new Show Custom Dialog step so that it appears just after the End If script step.

5. Double-click the Show Custom Dialog step (or select it and click the Specify button). The "Show Custom Dialog" Options window appears.

6. For the Title field, enter **Contact List Title**.

7. For the Message field, enter **What title do you want to use for the Contact List?**

   8. Remove the text from the Button 2 field. (For this dialog box, we are only going to provide the OK button.)

   9. Click the Input Fields tab, located at the top of the "Show Custom Dialog" Options window.

   10. Click the check box for the Show Input Field #1 field. The Specify Field dialog box appears.

   11. Scroll down to locate and select the new Contact List Title field.

   12. Click OK to close the Specify Field dialog box and return to the "Show Custom Dialog" Options window.

   13. In the Label field located below Show Input Field #1, enter **Report Title**.

   14. Click OK to close the "Show Custom Dialog" Options window.

   15. Your script should now look similar to the script displayed in Figure 13.23. Close the Edit Script window and save the changes that you made to the script.

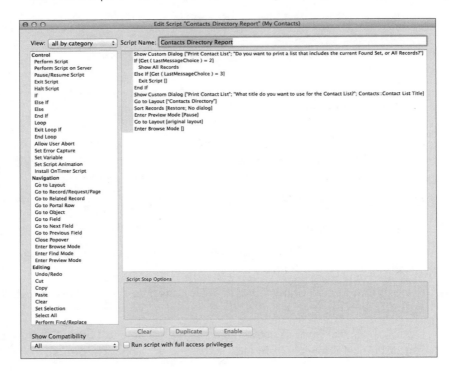

FIGURE 13.23

An updated version of the Contacts Directory Report script. This version includes a second Show Custom Dialog script step, which the user uses to provide a title for the report.

Run the updated Print Contact List script. After clicking the All or Found Set button on the first dialog box, the newly added Print Contact List dialog box appears, as shown in Figure 13.24. Enter a value into the Report Title field and click OK. The Contacts Directory layout then appears in Preview mode and displays the value that you entered into the dialog box.

FIGURE 13.24

The Print Contact List custom dialog window, which is displayed when the updated Contacts Directory Report script is performed. The user enters a title for the report, which FileMaker stores in the new Contact List Title. That field is then displayed on the layout as a merge field.

TIP   One drawback to the Show Custom Dialog's Input Field option is that you do not have much control over those fields. You cannot format them to the extent that you can format field objects on a layout. For example, you cannot set up an input field so that its Control Style is drop-down list, pop-up menu, and so on.

The only option available is to treat the input field as if the user were entering a password, in which case the text entered appears as bullets (so that the password isn't displayed as the user types it). If you need a more sophisticated dialog box, you can use create a layout to display it and then use the New Window script step, along with the Dialog Window window style option, to display it. This takes more work than simply using the Show Custom Dialog script step. However, this method also gives you considerably more control over the dialog window.

Managing Scripts

Throughout this chapter, you used the Manage Scripts window to add, edit, and perform the sample script. However, that same window gives you several options for managing your scripts. Let's take a few minutes to review some of the additional functionality that the Manage Scripts window provides, and how you can use it to better manage your scripts.

Grouping Scripts into Folders

When you created the sample Contacts Directory Report script, you clicked the New button, which is located toward the bottom-left corner of the Manage Scripts window. However, the rightmost portion of that button is a down arrow. If you click it, a pop-up menu appears, with options available for creating things other than an empty script—including a Default Script, a Folder, and a Separator. If you select Folder, the Edit Folder dialog box appears and gives you an opportunity to name a new script folder. If you proceed with the creation of the folder, it then appears in the scripts list. At that point, you can click and drag scripts into the folder. This is a great way to organize scripts and make them easier to locate.

Creating a Default Script

When you created the sample Contacts Directory Report script, you started with an empty script and then added script steps to it. However, another way to create a script is by selecting the Default Script option, which is available via the New button. When you use the Default Script option, FileMaker creates a new script and automatically adds several commonly used script steps, including Enter Browse Mode, Go to Layout, and so on. Depending on the type of script that you want to create, you might find this option to be more efficient, as it essentially "jump starts" the script for you.

Adding a Field Separator

The other option available via the New button is to add a separator. Separators can help to organize scripts that appear in the scripts menu, as they provide a visual cue that certain scripts are related in some way.

 NOTE The script separators that FileMaker creates are really just empty scripts named with a single dash. When displaying those scripts in the Scripts menu, FileMaker treats them in a special way, so that they appear as a ruled line, and so that they are not assigned a keyboard shortcut.

Duplicating Scripts

You might run into a situation where a script that you want to create is similar to one that already exists. In that case, you might want to duplicate the existing script and then modify it. The Duplicate button, located in the bottom-right portion of the Manage Scripts window, provides this capability. It duplicates the selected script and assigns it the name of the original script along with the word "Copy" added to the end. The duplicated script then acts just like any other script. You can edit it, rename it, and so on.

 TIP To rename a script, double-click it, and then use the Script Name field, located at the top of the Edit Script window.

Importing Scripts

In some cases, you might find that the script you need is similar to one that you already created in another FileMaker database. In that case, you can choose to import the script. To do so, click the Import button, located in the bottom-right corner of the Manage Scripts dialog box. FileMaker walks you through the process of importing the script. You can also choose to import multiple scripts at one time.

Deleting Scripts

To delete a script that you no longer need, select it and then either click the Delete button (located in the bottom-left corner of the Manage Scripts dialog box) or press the Delete key on your keyboard. FileMaker displays a dialog box warning you that you are about to permanently delete the script, and providing an opportunity to cancel the deletion. Note that you can also select, and then delete, multiple scripts at one time. (To select multiple scripts, Shift+click them.) Another option is to select a script folder, which when deleted also deletes any scripts that are in it.

Printing Scripts

FileMaker also provides an option for printing scripts, which can be helpful when you are working with complicated scripts and/or scripts that consist of a lot of script steps. To print a script, select it in the list and then click the Print button, located in the bottom-right corner of the Manage Scripts dialog box. You can also choose to print multiple scripts at one time, or print all scripts that are in a particular script folder.

Performing Scripts

Throughout this chapter, to perform the scripts that you have created and modified, you've done so by manually performing them from the Manage Scripts window, or by selecting them from the Scripts menu. However, there are several other ways to perform scripts.

Subscripts

Earlier we discussed the concept of creating scripts that use the Perform Script script step to perform (or "call") other scripts. The scripts called by the other scripts are known as *subscripts*. By creating general purpose scripts and then calling them as subscripts, you are able to reuse those scripts. As a result, you end up with fewer scripts in your database, making it much easier to maintain.

Buttons

Perhaps the most common method for performing scripts is to attach them to buttons. In Chapter 11, "Working with Layouts," you learned about the button layout object and created a button that used the Go To Layout script step. To create a button that performs a script, you can assign it to the Perform Script script step and then specify the script that you want to perform when the button is clicked.

Let's take a moment to add a button to your database that calls the Contacts Directory Report script. Here is what is involved:

1. Navigate to the Desktop > Contact Details layout.

2. Enter Layout mode.

3. Select the Button tool from the Status Toolbar.

4. In the header area, draw a button. The Button Setup dialog box opens.

5. Select the Perform Script script step.

6. Click the Specify button. The Specify Script dialog window opens.

7. Select the Contacts Directory Report script from the list.

8. Click OK to close the Specify Script dialog window.

9. Click OK again to close the Button Setup dialog window. A flashing cursor appears in the button, prompting you to add a label to the button.

10. Enter **Contacts Directory** and then click outside the button so that the label is applied.

Then save the change that you made to the layout, enter Browse mode, and click the new button. You see that the button performs the Contacts Directory Report script.

Script Triggers

Another method for performing scripts is to have FileMaker automatically perform them when certain events occur. We refer to those events as script triggers, and FileMaker supports a number of different script triggers.

For example, suppose that you want FileMaker to perform a script when the database is opened, or when the database is closed. FileMaker provides the OnFirstWindowOpen and OnLastWindowClose triggers to perform scripts when those events occur. In fact, the Contacts starter solution (that you used to create your Contacts database) actually uses an OnFirstWindowOpen trigger. To see it, select File > File Options, and click on the Script Triggers tab. The file's script triggers are displayed, as shown in Figure 13.25.

FIGURE 13.25

The file-level script triggers that are supported, as displayed in the File Options window.

FileMaker also provides script triggers for events that involve layouts. For example, at the layout level, you can set up script triggers to perform scripts when a record loads, when changes to a record are committed or reverted, when a user types on the keyboard, and more. You find support for these script triggers by navigating to a layout, entering Layout mode, clicking the Layout Setup button, and selecting the Script Triggers tab. The script triggers that have been set at the layout level appear as shown in Figure 13.26.

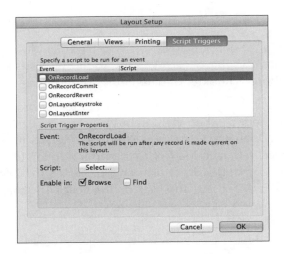

FIGURE 13.26

The layout-level script triggers that are supported, as displayed in the Layout Setup window.

NOTE When you are viewing a layout in Layout mode, and that layout has one or more script triggers assigned to it, you see a small script icon in the bottom right-hand corner of the window. This is FileMaker's way of alerting you to the fact that the layout has script triggers assigned to it.

Similarly, you can also set script triggers at the layout object level. FileMaker supports triggers for events such as entering an object, typing a key when in the object, modifying the object, and more. You can set an object's script triggers by entering Layout mode, right-clicking on an object, and selecting Set Script Triggers from the pop-up menu. The Set Script Triggers dialog box displays, as shown in Figure 13.27.

Script triggers are interesting for two reasons. First, they give you the ability to perform scripts when certain events occur, thus helping you to automate processes that you would otherwise have to remember to perform manually. And second, by using script triggers, you can set up the scripts that they call so that under certain circumstances the event that triggered them is cancelled.

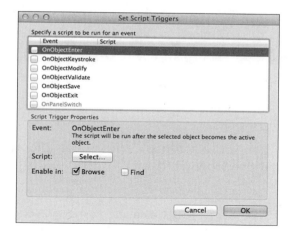

FIGURE 13.27

The field-level script triggers that are supported, as displayed in the Set Script Triggers window.

Let's take a look at an example of a script trigger that cancels an event. Suppose that when a user chooses to close the Contacts database, you want to ask the user if she really wants to do so. If the user indicates she does want to close the database, then the database closes as it normally would. But if the user indicates that she wants to remain in the database, then the event is cancelled (and the user remains in the database).

The first step in setting up this script trigger is to create the script itself.

1. Open the Manage Script window (Scripts > Manage Scripts).

2. Create a new script, and name it Confirm Close.

3. Add the Show Custom Dialog script step to the script.

4. Click the Specify button in the script step's options area. The "Show Custom Dialog" Options window appears.

5. For the title of the dialog, enter **Confirm Close**.

6. For the dialog's message, enter **Do you really want to close the database?**

7. Change the text of the Default button to Yes.

8. Change the text of Button 2 to No.

9. Click OK to close the "Show Custom Dialog" Options window.

10. Add an If script step to the script. FileMaker also adds a corresponding End If script step.

11. Select the If step, and in the step's options area, click the Specify button. The Specify Calculation window displays.

12. Enter the following calculation: Get (LastMessageChoice) = 2.

13. Click OK to close the Specify Calculation window.

14. Add an Exit Script script step to the script. If necessary, position it between the If and End If steps.

15. Select the If step, and in the step's options area, click the Specify button. The Specify Calculation window displays.

16. Enter the following calculation: **0**.

17. Click OK to close the Specify Calculation window. Your Confirm Close script should appear as it does in Figure 13.28.

18. Finally, close the Edit Script window and save the script.

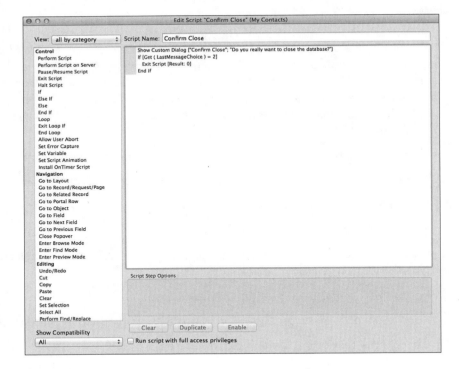

FIGURE 13.28

The Edit Script window showing the new Confirm Close script.

Now that you have the Confirm Close script created, you can assign it to a script trigger. Let's add the script trigger now.

1. From the File menu, select File Options. The File Options window displays.

2. Click on the Script Triggers tab.

3. In this case, you want the script to perform just before the last window to the database closes. Therefore, select the OnLastWindowClose event.

4. In the bottom portion of the dialog window, information about the select trigger is displayed, along with a button to select the script that should be performed when the event occurs. Click on the Select button, and the Specify Script dialog appears.

5. Select the Confirm Close script from the list.

6. Click OK to close the Specify Script dialog. You now see that the Confirm Close script is assigned to the OnLastWindowClose event, as shown in Figure 13.29.

7. Click OK again to close the File Options window.

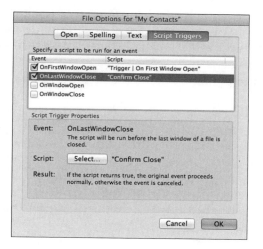

FIGURE 13.29

The File Options window, showing the "Confirm Close" script assigned to the OnLastWindowClose event.

To test the script trigger, either close the window (or all open windows, if you have more than one open) or select File > Close or Quit FileMaker Pro entirely. Regardless of what action you take, the script trigger performs the Confirm Close script, prompting you to confirm that you really want to close the database (as shown in Figure 13.30). If you choose Yes, the database closes. If you choose No, the "close" event is cancelled, and you remain in the database.

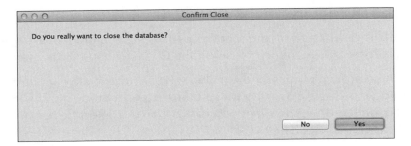

FIGURE 13.30

The Confirm Close dialog window, which now appears when the user attempts to the close the database.

The key to making this script trigger work is to use the Exit Script script step. In the Confirm Close script, the Exit Script step is called if the user selects the No button. You configured the script step so that it returns a value of zero (which is equivalent to False in FileMaker Pro). When FileMaker receives the result of the script, that False value is its indication that it should not proceed with the event that it was about to perform. In this case, that event was to close the last window.

 NOTE Some events cannot be cancelled, simply because the event has already occurred. For example, at the field level, one of the script triggers available is OnObjectEnter. When scripts are assigned to this event, they run after the selected object has become active. You cannot use the script trigger to prevent the user from entering the object, because the script will be performed after the user has entered the object. An easy way to tell whether an event can be cancelled is to select it in the Set Script Triggers dialog window and read the Event description. The description indicates whether the script attached to the trigger will run before or after the event occurs.

Install OnTimer Script

Another way to automatically perform a script is to assign it using the Install OnTimer Script script step, which we discussed earlier in the chapter during our review of the script steps that FileMaker supports. Using the Install OnTimer Script script step, you can schedule a script to run at a certain interval. Once that interval has passed, FileMaker performs the specified script.

There are several important things to note about the Install OnTimer Script script step. First, remember that FileMaker continues to perform the script on the specified interval until you tell it otherwise. To indicate to FileMaker that you no longer want the script to run on the interval, you can perform a script that includes the Install OnTimer Script step with either no script or no interval specified.

Also remember that the Install OnTimer Script script step works at the window level. Therefore, it is possible to have OnTimer events assigned to multiple windows at the same time. However, it is not possible for a single window to have multiple OnTimer events assigned to it at the same time. If the window are viewing already has an OnTimer event set, and you perform a script that includes the Install OnTimer Script step, the first OnTimer event is replaced by the new one.

NOTE   There is another way to perform scripts, but it requires FileMaker Pro Advanced. With FileMaker Pro Advanced, you can set up a database so that it uses a set of custom menus. Using that function, you can replace FileMaker's standard commands with your own scripts and also add commands to the menus.

Script Parameters and Results

Earlier in the chapter, you created a Confirm Close script and assigned it to the OnLastWindowClose script trigger. You used the Exit Script script step to return the value of False back to FileMaker, indicating that you wanted it to cancel the event that it was about to perform (closing the last window to the database). The value that the Exit Script window returned is known as a script result. In this example, the result was passed to FileMaker itself. However, in cases where a script has been called as a subscript, you could also use this technique to return a result to the calling script.

Similarly, FileMaker also supports script parameters. Using script parameters, you can perform a script and pass values to it, which it can then use. Like script results, script parameters make it possible for you to create scripts that can serve multiple purposes, thus reducing the number of scripts that you need to create and maintain.

In your Contacts database, there are fields for both a contact's office email address and a personal email address. Suppose that we want to automate the process of sending an email message to those addresses. We could create two scripts, one that sends to the office email address and another that sends to the personal email address. However, using script parameters, you can write one script to accomplish both tasks. Let's create that script.

1. Open the Manage Script window (Scripts > Manage Scripts).

2. Create a new script, and name it Send Email.

3. Add the Show Custom Dialog script step to the script.

4. Click the Specify button in the script step's options area. The "Show Custom Dialog" Options window appears.

5. For the title of the dialog, enter **Send Email**.

6. For the dialog's message, enter **Do you really want to send an email message?**

7. Change the text of the Default button to Yes.

8. Change the text of Button 2 to No.

9. Click OK to close the "Show Custom Dialog" Options window.

10. Add an If script step to the script. FileMaker also adds a corresponding End If script step.

11. Select the If step, and in the step's options area, click the Specify button. The Specify Calculation window appears.

12. Enter the following calculation: **Get (LastMessageChoice) = 1**.

13. Click OK to close the Specify Calculation window.

14. Add a Send Mail script step to the script. If necessary, position it between the If and End If steps.

15. Select the Send Mail step, and in the step's options area, click the Specify button. The Send Mail Options window displays.

16. Click on the button that appears next to the To field and select Specify Calculation. The Specify Calculation window displays.

17. Enter this calculation formula: **Get (ScriptParameter)**.

18. Click OK to close the Specify Calculation window.

19. Click OK again to close the Send Mail Options window. Your Send Email script should appear as it does in Figure 13.31.

20. Finally, close the Edit Script window and save the script.

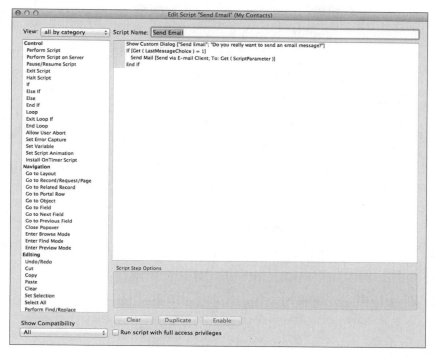

FIGURE 13.31

The Send Email script. This script sends email to an address specified as the script's parameter.

Next, you need to add two buttons to the layout, one that calls the script and passes the Office Email address as a script parameter, and a second that passes the Personal Email address as a script parameter.

1. Navigate to the Desktop > Contact Details layout.

2. Enter Layout mode.

3. Right-click on the label that appears next to the Office Email field, and select Button Setup from the menu that appears. The Button Setup dialog box displays.

4. Select the Perform Script script step.

5. Click the Specify button. The Specify Script dialog window opens.

6. Select the Send Email script from the list.

7. At the bottom of the Specify Script dialog window is the Optional Script Parameter field. Using this field, you can either manually enter a parameter

that should be passed to the selected script or click the Edit button to specify a parameter using the Specify Calculation window. Click on the Edit button, and the Specify Calculation window displays.

8. Enter this formula: **Contacts::Office Email**.

9. Click OK to close the Specify Calculation window.

10. Click OK to close the Specify Script dialog window.

11. Click OK again to close the Button Setup dialog window.

12. Right-click on the label that appears next to the Personal Email field, and select Button Setup from the menu that appears. The Button Setup dialog box displays.

13. Select the Perform Script script step.

14. Click the Specify button. The Specify Script dialog window displays.

15. Select the Send Email script from the list.

16. Click the Edit button that appears next to the Optional Script Parameter field. The Specify Calculation window displays.

17. Enter this formula: **Contacts::Personal Email**.

18. Click OK to close the Specify Calculation window.

19. Click OK to close the Specify Script dialog window.

20. Click OK again to close the Button Setup dialog window.

21. Enter Browse mode, and save your changes to the layout.

Test the script by clicking on the Office Email and Personal Email field labels. The Send Email script runs, and depending on what label you clicked, the message is pre-addressed to either the contact's office or personal email address. With one script, you have automated two tasks.

Handling Script Errors

As mentioned earlier in the chapter, one of the script steps that FileMaker supports is Set Error Capture. When this script step is used and its option is set to On, you can suppress the error messages that FileMaker normally displays. However, it then becomes your responsibility to handle any errors that occur in your script.

For example, take a look at the script displayed in Figure 13.32.

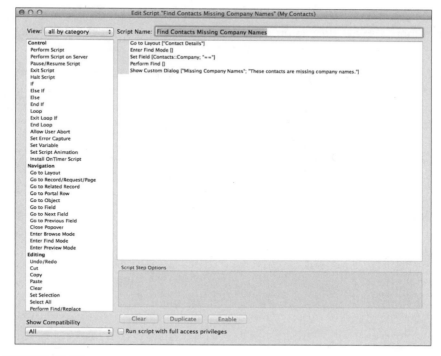

FIGURE 13.32

The Find Contacts Missing Company Names script. This script is an example of how FileMaker normally handles errors that occur when a script is performed.

The script is fairly simple. It navigates to the Contact Details layout, performs a find for contacts whose Company field is empty, and then displays a dialog box that reads, "These contacts are missing company names." The script works perfectly, as long as at least one contact record is missing its company name.

However, if no contacts are missing their company name, FileMaker displays an error message as shown in Figure 13.33. It is the standard FileMaker error message displayed when a Find is performed and no records are found. In the context of this script, that error message is a bit awkward.

FIGURE 13.33

The standard error message that FileMaker displays when a Find is performed and no records meet the find criteria.

To make matters worse, if the user clicks the Continue button, the script resumes and then displays the dialog box that reads, "These contacts are missing company names." That will potentially confuse the user.

Using the Set Error Capture, you can suppress FileMaker's standard error message and display your own message instead. Figure 13.34 shows the script with the Set Error Capture script step added, as well as a few additional script steps that display a custom error message.

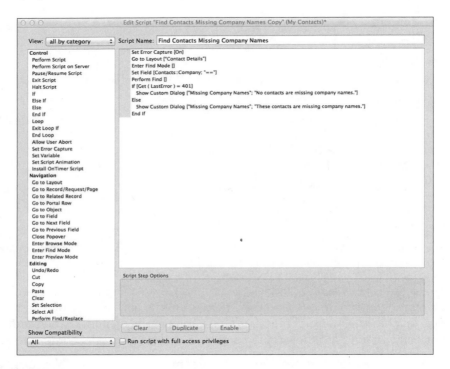

FIGURE 13.34

An updated version of the Contacts Missing Company Names script, with several steps added to capture an error if one occurs during the Perform Find script step.

In this version of the script, the Set Error Capture step is set to On, indicating that the script itself will take care of any errors that occur. Immediately after the Perform Find script step is an If step, whose calculation formula is Get (LastError) = 401. If the previous script step caused an error, then the Get (LastError) function returns a number that corresponds to that error. (It returns a 0 if the script step is successful.) In this case, the If statement is checking to see whether the Perform Find script step resulted in a "401" error, which indicates that "No records match the request." If so, then a dialog message is displayed that indicates to the user that "No contacts are missing company names." Otherwise, the original "These contacts are missing company names" message is displayed. The updated script handles the error much more gracefully, and the custom error message displayed is less confusing than FileMaker's standard error message.

NOTE   For a complete list of FileMaker error codes, refer to the FileMaker Pro Help function (Help > FileMaker Pro Help). In the Reference section, select the FileMaker Pro error codes option.

Running Scripts with Full Access

Throughout this chapter, as you edited scripts you might have noticed an additional option located in the bottom-left corner of the Edit Script window—the Run Script with Full Access Privileges check box. In Chapter 14, "Protecting a Database," we discuss security and access privileges in more detail.

For the moment, think of access privileges as the set of actions that a group of users is allowed to perform. For example, you might set up a group of users who can only look at the database but cannot change anything in it. Or you might set up a group of users that can add and update records in the database but cannot delete records. As you see in Chapter 14, FileMaker provides a number of options when it comes to setting up access privileges.

In cases where a user is assigned access privileges that prevent him from performing a certain action and he performs a script that attempts to take that action, FileMaker enforces that restriction and displays an error message. However, in some cases, you might want to allow the user to perform that action only when it is being taken as part of a script. By enabling the Run Script with Full Access Privileges option for the script, the script will run as though the user has full access to the database.

NOTE   When a user performs a script that has the Run Script with Full Access Privileges option enabled, the special privileges the user is granted during the execution of the script are revoked as soon as the script completes. In other words, the script only grants full access to the database temporarily.

THE ABSOLUTE MINIMUM

In this chapter, you learned how to create scripts to automate functions in a FileMaker database. Here are the key points to remember:

- Scripts can consist of one or more script steps and can be as simple or as complicated as you need them to be.

- There are several different ways to perform a script. You can perform a script manually (via the Manage Script window or by selecting it from the Scripts menu), you can attach a script to a button, or you can use a script trigger to perform a script when a certain event occurs. Also, scripts can perform other scripts, in which case the other scripts become subscripts.

- Using the Show Custom Dialog script step, a script can interact with the user.

- You can pass a value to a script (known as a script parameter). Similarly, a script can return a value (known as a script result).

- It is possible for script steps to cause errors, and normally FileMaker displays a standard error message. Using the Set Error Capture script step, along with the Get (LastError) function, you can replace FileMaker's error messages with your own messages.

- It is possible to allow a user who normally doesn't have full access to a database to run a script as though she does have full access.

PROTECTING A DATABASE

While working on the examples in this book, you've been using sample (or "fake") contact data. Therefore, there hasn't been a need to worry about the security of the Contacts database that you've created. However, when you start creating databases to manage "real" data, you'll want to be sure that the data is safe and secure.

In this chapter, you learn why it is important to secure FileMaker databases and how to use FileMaker's security features to do so. You learn about important FileMaker security concepts, including accounts, privilege sets, and more.

The Importance of Security

These days, we frequently hear about companies whose systems have been hacked and their data stolen or compromised. These security breaches often result in multiple types of damages—from financial losses, to identity theft, and in some cases a loss of confidence from customers and investors. Without a doubt, security is a growing concern. As someone who plans to create or use FileMaker to manage data, it should be of concern to you, too.

In addition, depending on the type of data that you plan to manage, you might actually be required to secure your data. In some industries, regulations are in place that are intended to ensure that the data being collected is secure. For example, if you are in an industry that collects medical data, financial data, information about students, or any data that can be used to identify a specific individual, you might be legally required to take certain steps to secure that data. Failing to do so might result in fines or other penalties.

Thankfully, the FileMaker platform provides functionality that you can use to secure the data that you have stored in your databases. In the following sections, you learn about FileMaker's security model and actions you can take to secure your databases.

The FileMaker Security Model

To fully understand FileMaker's security model, you first need to be familiar with two important concepts: accounts and privilege sets.

In the FileMaker platform, *accounts* are used to identify the person accessing a database. Typically, when you open a FileMaker database, you are required to identify yourself using an account name, which FileMaker uses to identify your account. Further, to ensure that you are who you claim to be, you are also asked to provide the password associated with the account. This process of identifying yourself, and having FileMaker confirm that you have provided both a valid account name and corresponding password, is known as *authentication*.

Another important FileMaker security concept is *privilege sets*. FileMaker uses privilege sets to determine what a database user is allowed to see and do in the database after the user has been authenticated. Every account is associated with one, and only one, privilege set. However, a privilege set may be assigned to one or more accounts. Think of a privilege set as a group of database users who have been assigned the same privileges. For example, you might set up privilege sets for users in various departments, or for users who perform specific tasks. For instance, you might set up a privilege set for users in the Accounting department and configure the privilege set so that those users have access to only the accounting-related data and functionality of the database. You might set up a second privilege set for users in the Sales department, configured so that the users have access to only customer information, orders, and so on. And finally, you might set up a privilege set for Management, configured so that those users can access all the data in the database.

A related FileMaker security concept is known as extended privileges. FileMaker uses extended privileges to determine the methods by which users in a privilege set can access a database. For example, you might allow users in a certain privilege set to access the database over a network via FileMaker Pro, while users in another privilege set cannot.

FileMaker's Default Security Settings

When you create a new FileMaker database, a few default accounts and privilege sets are created for you. One of the accounts created is assigned the account name of Admin, along with a blank password. This account is assigned to a privilege set that has Full Access to the database, allowing the user to access all the data in the database and to make changes to the database's structure, scripts, and so on. In addition, FileMaker configures the new database so that when you open it, the Admin account is used automatically. As a result, when you open a new database, you are not required to log in to it, and you have the ability to make any changes that you want.

The other account that is automatically created is assigned the account name of Guest. It is a special type of account that allows users to access the database without needing to authenticate. The account is assigned to a Read Only Access privilege set, which allows the guest only to view the data in the database. Guests are not allowed to add, update, or delete records. In addition, they cannot make changes to layouts or scripts, or change the database's settings in any way. By default, FileMaker disables this account. If you want to make the Guest account available to your users, you must first enable it. (You learn how to enable accounts shortly.)

New FileMaker databases also include three default privilege sets: Full Access, Data Entry Only, and Read-Only Access.

Accounts assigned the Full Access privilege set can access all the data in the database, make structural changes to the database (add tables, fields, and so on), and manage layouts, scripts, accounts, privilege sets, and so on.

Accounts assigned to the Data Entry Only privilege set can view and change data in the database but cannot make changes to the database's structure, nor can they make changes to layouts and scripts.

The Read-Only Access privilege set allows users to view all the data in the database but prohibits them from making any changes to the data. And like the Data Entry Only privilege set, these users cannot changes layouts, scripts, and so on.

 NOTE While accounts assigned to the Read-Only Access privilege set are prohibited from making changes to data, they do have the ability to change values stored in global fields.

When new databases are created, FileMaker automatically creates six extended privileges, which can be used to indicate how users can access the database. The default extended privileges include

- fmxdbc (to control access via ODBC or JDBC)

- fmapp (to allow remote access to database via a network connection)

- fmreauthenticate10 (a special FileMaker Go-related access setting, which is discussed in Chapter 17, "Taking Data with You")

- fmxml (to control XML Web publishing access to databases hosted using FileMaker Server)

- fmphp (to control PHP Web publishing access to databases hosted using FileMaker Server)

- fmwebdirect (to control access to a database using the new FileMaker WebDirect feature of the FileMaker platform)

The security settings that FileMaker assigns to new databases are intended to make it easy for you to get started with the new database. However, as a result of that convenience, new databases are not particularly secure. Later in this chapter, you learn to make a few quick changes that help you secure a new FileMaker database.

The Manage Security Window

The primary interface to a FileMaker database's accounts, privilege sets, and extended privileges (and a few other security features as well) is the Manage Security window. To access the Manage Security window, select File > Manage > Security. (Note that there is no keyboard shortcut for this command.) The Manage Security window opens, as shown in Figure 14.1.

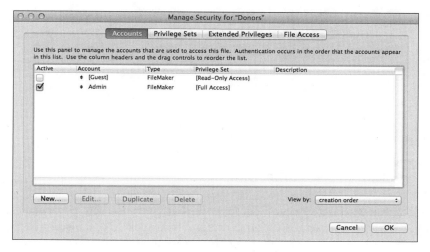

FIGURE 14.1

The Manage Security window, showing the Accounts tab and the two default FileMaker accounts listed.

As you've seen with several other FileMaker windows, the Manage Security window uses a tabbed interface to separate its functionality. In this case, the tabs are Accounts, Privilege Sets, Extended Privileges, and File Access. The window opens to the Accounts tab. Let's take a moment to review that tab.

The Accounts tab includes a list of all the accounts that have been set up in the database. As mentioned earlier, new databases are automatically configured with default Admin and Guest accounts, and you see those listed here.

The leftmost column, Active, indicates whether the account is active. Notice that the Admin account is active, and the Guest account is not. When an account is set to inactive, it cannot be used to log in to the database. You can easily change an account from active to inactive, and vice versa, by simply checking or unchecking the check box for an account.

To close the Manage Security window, you must have at least one active account assigned to the Full Access privilege set. Otherwise, you are presented with an error message as displayed in Figure 14.2.

Continuing our exploration of the Accounts tab, the Account column itself includes the account names assigned to the accounts in the database. You also see columns indicating each account's type, the privilege set assigned to it, and an optional description of the account. The two default accounts are both FileMaker account types, indicating that the accounts are authenticated by FileMaker itself.

FIGURE 14.2

The error message displayed if you attempt to close the Manage Security window without an active Full Access account in place.

If a database is hosted on a FileMaker Server, and a directory service (Windows Active Directory or Apple Open Directory) is available, you also have the option of setting up accounts so that they are authenticated by those services. For those types of accounts, the Type column will be listed as External Server.

Also, note that the Admin account is assigned to the Full Access privilege set, and the Guest account is assigned to the Read-Only Access privilege set.

Below the list of accounts are buttons that can be used to add a new account, edit an existing account, duplicate an account, and delete an account. A pop-up menu, located in the bottom-right corner of the tab, changes the order in which the accounts are listed. This can be helpful in databases that contain many accounts.

The Privilege Sets tab, displayed in Figure 14.3, is used to manage the privilege sets in a FileMaker database. As mentioned earlier, you can think of a privilege set as a group of users assigned the same privileges. Notice that the three default privilege sets, discussed earlier, are listed on this tab. Also, like the Accounts tab, buttons located at the bottom of the list of privilege sets can be used to add a new privilege set, edit an existing privilege set, duplicate a privilege set, and delete a privilege set.

NOTE FileMaker will not allow you to delete the three default privilege sets, nor will it allow you to delete a privilege set if one or more accounts are assigned to it.

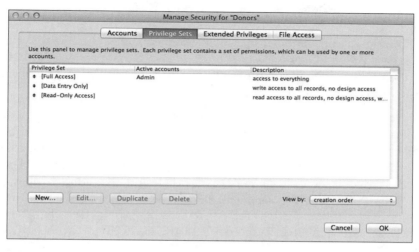

FIGURE 14.3

The Manage Security window, with the Privilege Sets tab displayed and the three default privilege sets listed.

Creating Privilege Sets

Let's learn more about privilege sets by creating one. If you do not already have your Contacts database opened, do so now. Then open the Manage Security window by selecting File > Manage > Security, and change to the Privilege Sets tab.

To create a new privilege set, you can click the New button located in the bottom of the window. However, new privilege sets are, by default, created with no privileges assigned to them. Therefore, using this approach, you would need to carefully work your way through all the privilege set's options and assign those that you want to grant to the users in that set. A faster and easier approach to creating a privilege set is to pick one of the default privilege sets that most closely matches the one that you want to create and then make modifications to it.

For this example, let's suppose that we are going to give read-only access to the Contacts database for all the employees in the company. We want the employees to be able to view all the information with one exception: We want to prevent them from viewing the Income field (which we added back in Chapter 9, "Working with Fields").

Here's how you would create this type of privilege set:

1. The default privilege set that most closely matches the one that we want to create is Read-Only Access. Therefore, locate that privilege set in the list and then click the Duplicate button (located below the list). A new privilege set named Read-Only Access Copy is created.

2. We need to make changes to the newly created privilege set. To do so, select the new privilege set and then click the Edit button (also located below the list). The Edit Privilege Set window appears, as shown in Figure 14.4. The name and description of the privilege set are displayed first, and other options are grouped logically (Data Access and Design, Extended Privileges, and Other Privileges). We review these options.

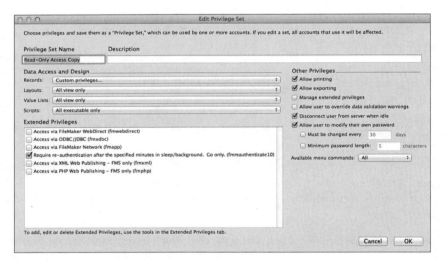

FIGURE 14.4

The Edit Privilege Set window, displaying the attributes of the Read-Only Access Copy privilege set.

3. Change the privilege set's name from Read-Only Access Copy to Employees. To do so, click in the Privilege Set Name field to make the change.

4. Give the new privilege set a Description. The description is optional, but it can sometimes be helpful to describe the intent of the privilege set, especially if you need to make changes to it in the future. Let's add this description: **Allows all employees to view contact information. The Income field is not viewable.**

5. In the Data Access and Design area of the window, options are presented that can be used to limit access to records, layouts, value lists, and scripts. The Read-Only Access privilege set, which we based this new privilege set on, is set up so that users in the set can view all the layouts and value lists and can run all the scripts. However, notice that with regard to records, these users have custom privileges. To see what those custom privileges are, click on the Custom Privileges. Notice that this is actually a pop-up menu, with options that include Create, Edit, and Delete in All Tables; Create and Edit in All Tables; View Only in All Tables; All No Access; and Custom Privileges. (See Table 14.1 for an explanation of these options.) The changes that we want to make to the privilege set involve the records (we want to restrict access to the Income field), so select the Custom Privileges option. The Custom Record Privileges window appears, as shown in Figure 14.5.

TABLE 14.1 Privilege Set Options for Records

Option	Description
Create, Edit, and Delete in All Tables	Users can add, edit, and delete all records in all the tables in the database.
Create and Edit in All Tables	Users can add and edit records in all the tables in the database. However, they cannot delete records from any of the tables.
View Only in All Tables	Users can view records in all the tables in the database. However, they cannot add, edit, or delete any of the records.
All No Access	Users do not have access to the records in the tables.
Custom Privileges	Users have limited access to the data, depending on how the custom privileges are defined.

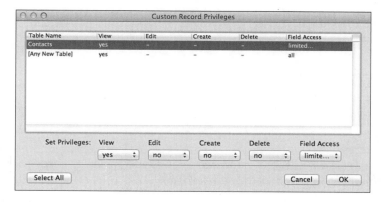

FIGURE 14.5

The Custom Record Privileges window, showing the record privileges for the privilege set.

6. The Custom Record Privileges window provides a table that you can use to set the record privileges for the tables in the database. Our database currently has only one table in it (Contacts). If the database were to include multiple tables, you would see them listed here as well. (Also note that the last row of the table can be used to specify the permissions assigned to any new tables added in the future.)

    In addition to the table name, columns are shown indicating whether users in the privilege set can view, edit, create, or delete records in each table. A value of "yes" in each of those columns indicates that users have been granted the permission; a dash indicates that the permission has not been granted. In this example, users can view data in the existing Contacts table and also are granted the same privilege for any table added in the future. They cannot edit, credit, or delete records in the tables.

    The last column, Field Access, is used to specify permissions that users have for specific fields in each table. The default value, All, indicates that users have access to all fields in the table. However, in this example, we want to restrict access to the Income field of the Contacts table. To do so, select the Contacts row in the table. The row becomes highlighted, and the Set Privileges options, located at the bottom of the list of tables, becomes active. Click on the Field Access menu and select Limited. The Custom Field Privileges window appears, as shown in Figure 14.6.

FIGURE 14.6

The Custom Field Privileges window, which gives you the ability to specify how users in a privilege set can work with data at the field level.

7. The Custom Field Privileges window lists all the fields in the table that you selected. In this case, you are presented with the list of fields in the Contacts

table. For each field, the name is listed along with the privilege that users in the privilege set have on the field. For all the fields, the privilege is set to Modifiable. As a result, it appears as though users have the ability to modify values in all the fields.

However, this is a bit misleading. Remember that at the table level, this privilege set is configured to view records in the table. The Edit, Create, and Delete privileges were not set. So even though the field-level privileges indicate that users in this privilege set can modify values in all the fields, the table-level privileges prevent them from doing so. The users can only view the values in the fields.

For this example, we want users assigned to this privilege set to be able to see all data in all the fields, except for the Income field. To enable this, scroll through the list of fields, locate the Income field, and select it. The Privilege radio button, located below the list of fields, then becomes active. Change the value from Modifiable to No Access. Then click OK to close the Custom Field Privileges window, bringing the Custom Record Privileges window back to the foreground.

 TIP When creating new privilege sets, be sure to test them thoroughly. To do so, set up a test account, assign it to the privilege set, and then log in using the account. You want to confirm that the account has permission to see and do the things that it should be able to do, and that it cannot see or do things that should be restricted. It is better to discover any problems with how the privilege is configured early, before the privilege set has been put to use. Otherwise, you might end up inadvertently giving users access to something that they shouldn't have access to.

While no additional changes need to be made to the Employees privilege set, this is a good opportunity to explore some of the other options available. Again, the Custom Record Privileges window includes columns that indicate whether users in the privilege set have permission to View, Edit, Create, or Delete records in each table, and the Field Access column indicates what type of permission the users have at the field level. You saw that the options for the Field Access column are All, Limited, or None. However, the options for the other columns are a little different. For example, the options available for the View, Edit, and Delete privileges are Yes, Limited, and None. The options for the Create privilege includes only Yes and No. While the Yes and No options are self-explanatory (users either can or cannot perform those actions on the specified table), the Limited option can be a little confusing.

Using the Limited option for the View, Edit, and Delete privileges, you can use a calculation formula to programmatically determine whether a user can or cannot perform an action on records in the table. For example, suppose that the Contacts database is being used by salespeople to manage their customers and prospects. You might want to set up a Sales privilege set such that users assigned to it are only able to view the contact records that they create or that are assigned to them. You might also use the Limited option to indicate when records can be edited. For example, you might add a field that indicates whether a contact record is active or inactive, and then prohibit changes to records where this Status field is set to Inactive.

Similarly, you might prevent users from being able to delete a contact record if that contact has had recent activity. By selecting the Limited option, the Specify Calculation window, which you've now used in a number of different ways, appears. Indicating whether users can view, edit, or delete records in a table is simply a matter of representing your business rule as a calculation formula. If the result of the calculation is true, the user has the privilege. Otherwise, the user does not.

Let's continue to explore the privilege set options available. First, click OK to close the Custom Record Privileges window, and the Edit Privilege Set window is visible once again. In the Data Access and Design area of the window, we explored the options that pertain to Records. The options for layouts, value lists, and scripts are a little different, and Table 14.2 explains what those options are and what they do.

TABLE 14.2 Privilege Set Options for Layouts, Value Lists, and Scripts

Option	Description
All Modifiable	Users can modify all of this type of entity, whether it is a layout, a value list, or a script.
All View Only/ All Executable Only	Users can view the layouts or value lists, but cannot make any changes to them, add new layouts or value lists, or delete layouts/value lists. Similarly, with regard to scripts, users can execute the scripts, but cannot add, change, or delete scripts.
All No Access	Users cannot view the layouts or value lists. With regard to scripts, they cannot execute any of the scripts.
Custom Privileges	With this option, you can specify permissions in more detail. For example, with regard to layouts, you can indicate for each layout whether users can view or modify the layout, or whether they simply have no access to the layout. You can also indicate whether users can modify, view, or have no access to records displayed on a layout. (Note that there is also an option that can be used to indicate whether users are allowed to create new layouts.)

Option	Description
	With regard to value lists, for each value list, you can indicate whether users can modify or view the list, or whether they have no access to the list. Also, an option is provided so that you can indicate whether users in the privilege set are allowed to create new value lists.
	Similarly, with regard to scripts, you can indicate whether users can modify or execute a script, or whether users are not allowed to run the script. Again, an option is provided that you can use to indicate whether users are allowed to create new scripts.

So far, you've seen how FileMaker allows you to specify privileges that pertain to records, layouts, value lists, and scripts. However, there are several additional options that you can set. Let's take a quick look at those now.

Earlier in the chapter, you learned that extended privileges can be used to indicate how users can access a FileMaker database. The six default extended privileges, which FileMaker creates automatically when a new database is created, are displayed in the Extended Privileges area of the Edit Privilege Set window. You can grant or revoke these privileges by simply toggling the check box next to each privilege.

The rightmost area of the Edit Privilege Set window includes several other privileges, including the options for allowing users to print, export records, and more. See Table 14.3 for a list and descriptions of these privileges.

TABLE 14.3 Additional Privilege Set Options

Option	Description
Allow Printing	Allows users to both print and save records to a PDF file.
Allow Exporting	Allows users to export records, to save records to an Excel file, to copy found sets of records (to the clipboard), and so on.
Manage Extended Privileges	Allows users to make changes to extended privileges without needing to give them full access to the database.
Allow User to Override Data Validation Warnings	Allows users to enter values into fields, even if those values do not meet validation rules. This only applies to fields that have been configured to allow overriding of validation rules.
Disconnect User from Server When Idle	For databases being hosted with FileMaker Server, users are disconnected after a certain amount of inactivity. The details as to when a user is considered to be idle are managed by FileMaker Server.

TABLE 14.3 (continued)

Option	Description
Allow User to Modify Their Password	Allows users to change their passwords. Additionally, you can specify that passwords must be changed after a certain number days, as well as the required minimum length of the passwords. Unfortunately, you cannot require that users set "strong" passwords.
Available Menu Commands	This option gives you the ability to specify what set of menu commands are available to users. All, which is the default option, makes all the commands available, unless a command is not available due to other privileges and security options. (For example, the Delete Record command would appear in the menu but might be inaccessible if the user does not have permission to delete records.) Editing Only allows users access to a limited set of editing-related commands when they are in Browse mode. Minimum provides users access to a limited set of commands, including open, close, windows, scripts, help, and so on.

That completes our review of the available privilege set options. Be sure to click OK to close the Edit Privilege Set window. You should see the new Employees privilege set in the list, and it is now ready to be put to use. Next, you learn how to create an account, and we assign one to the Employees privilege set.

 TIP FileMaker includes support for the Get (AccountPrivilegeSetName) function, which gives you the ability to get the current user's privilege set. You might use this, along with the Hide Object When layout object option, to prevent users from seeing buttons (or other objects) that call scripts that they don't have permissions to run. However, don't use this to implement security. You still want to set up the privilege sets so that users who should be able to run a certain script have permission to do so, and those who should not, cannot run it. In other words, don't use the Hide Object When function to implement security.

Privilege Sets and Scripts

Privilege sets are enforced at all times, including when scripts are being performed. For example, if a user is assigned to a privilege set that prohibits him from exporting records and he runs a script that includes the Export Records script step, FileMaker will not perform that step. It simply skips the step and continues on to any steps that follow it. (It is possible to use FileMaker's error handling functionality, which you learned about in Chapter 13, "Automating Tasks with Scripts," to check for and gracefully resolve this condition.)

However, it is possible to configure a script so that when it is performed, it acts as though the user has Full Access privileges. You can specify that a script should run in this manner by selecting the Run Script with Full Access Privileges option, which is located toward the bottom of the Edit Script window. (When the script completes, the user's original, assigned privilege set will be enforced.)

As an example of when this feature might be useful, consider the following scenario. You want users of your Contacts database to be able to view all the information about the contacts stored in it. You also want certain users to be able to export records from the database. However, you do not want those users to be able to export all the details of the contacts. (Otherwise, a disgruntled employee might export all the data and provide it to a competitor.) Perhaps their role within their organization is marketing related, and they need to be able to export fields such as contact names and addresses, but nothing more.

In this scenario, you start by setting up a privilege set for the users where the Allow Exporting option is disabled (thus preventing them from exporting all the data). Next, you create a script that those users have permission to run. It would include an Export Records script step, with the Specify Export Order option enabled (so that only the name and address fields will be exported). You enable the Run Script with Full Access Privileges script option so that, when the script step is reached, it is performed. This solution allows authorized users to export only those fields that they need to do their job.

Creating Accounts

Earlier, you created a new privilege set and learned about the many different options available when doing so. Now, you create an account. Thankfully, significantly fewer steps and options are involved.

If you don't already have the Contacts database opened, open it now. Then follow these steps:

1. Open the Manage Security window (File > Manage Security). The window opens to the Accounts tab.

2. Click the New button, located at the bottom of the window. The Edit Account window opens, as shown in Figure 14.7.

FIGURE 14.7

The Edit Account window, which is used to add new accounts and update existing accounts.

3. Earlier in the chapter, you learned that when databases are hosted with FileMaker Server, it is possible to authenticate users via external services. The first option on the Edit Account window (Account Is Authenticated Via) can be used to indicate whether the account should be authenticated via an external server or via FileMaker itself. The default value is FileMaker, and for this example, we use that setting.

4. Specify an Account Name. The name can be any value that you want. However, FileMaker does not let you assign duplicate account names, so the value has to be unique. When selecting an account name, you might want to use a value that the user will be able to remember, such as the user's email address. For this example, let's use tester1 as the account name. Note that account names are not case-sensitive, so "tester1" and "Tester1" are treated as equals.

5. Provide a Password for the account. If you want, you can provide a temporary password and then select the User Must Change Password on Next Login option. When the user logs in to the account, she does so with the temporary password that you provided, and she is required to select a new password at that time. Unlike account names, passwords are case-sensitive.

6. The Account Status field is used to indicate whether the account is Active or Inactive. In this case, we are creating a new account and want it to be active.

7. Assign the account a privilege set. This field is a menu that lists all the active privilege sets. When you click on it, you see the three default privilege sets that FileMaker provides, as well as the Employees privilege set that you created earlier. Select the Employees privilege set.

8. The Description field is optional. You might want to use it to keep track of the user's real name, or to make a note about the account. Let's enter **Test Account**.

9. Click OK to save the new account. The Edit Account window closes, and you should then see the new tester1 account in the account list.

Next, click OK to close the Manage Security window. When you do so, you might see the dialog box displayed in Figure 14.8. The dialog box alerts you to the fact that one or more active accounts, which have been assigned to the Full Access privilege set, have not been assigned passwords, and that this is a potential security problem. Earlier, you learned that when a new database is created, an Admin account is created, assigned to the Full Access privilege set, and is not assigned a password. If you see this dialog box, chances are that is why it is being presented to you.

FIGURE 14.8

The dialog box that appears if one or more active Full Access accounts have not been assigned a password.

To address this issue, click Cancel to dismiss the dialog box. The Manage Security window remains open. Locate the Admin account, and double-click it to edit it. The Edit Account window, which you used to create the new account, opens. Enter a password and then click OK.

Click OK to close the Manage Security window. This time, the Confirm Full Access Login window appears, as shown in Figure 14.9.

FIGURE 14.9

The Confirm Full Access Login window, which appears when you have modified accounts and attempt to close the Manage Security window.

The Confirm Full Access Login window displays whenever you make changes to accounts and then attempt to close the Manage Security window. FileMaker wants to be certain that you know the account name and password of at least one active account that has been assigned to the Full Access privilege set. It does this so that you don't accidentally lock yourself out of your database. To proceed, enter **Admin** for the account name and the password that you assigned to it, and then click OK. If you provide the correct password, then both the Confirm Full Access Login and Manage Security windows close.

Now, let's take a moment to test both the new account that you created, as well as the privilege set that you created. To do so, close the database and reopen it. The Open dialog box displays, as shown in Figure 14.10.

FIGURE 14.10

The Open dialog box, which appears when you attempt to open a password-protected database.

Previously, the database had been configured so that it automatically opened using the Admin account, and because it had no password, you were not required to log in to the database. Now that the Admin account has been assigned a password (and the password has not been set in the file's Open options), you are required to log in.

Let's log in using the tester1 account that you created. Enter **tester1** in the Account Name field and whatever password you chose in the Password field. (Note that when you type in the Password field, the characters that you enter are displayed as bullets.) Click OK to continue, and the Change Password dialog box displays, as shown in Figure 14.11.

Change Password

You must change the password for your FileMaker account before opening this file.
Please enter your old password once and your new password twice.

Account Name: tester1

Old Password: ••••

New Password:

Confirm New Password:

Cancel   OK

FIGURE 14.11

The Change Password dialog box, which is used to replace a temporary password or to set a new password if the password has expired.

The Change Password dialog displays if the account that is being used to log in with has the User Must Change Password on Next Login option selected, or if the account has been assigned to a privilege set that requires that passwords be changed after a certain number of days. Three fields are displayed. The Old Password field is used to confirm that you have permission to change the password for the account (and because you just logged in, it has been preset for you). The New Password field is used to enter your new password, and the Confirm New Password field is used to confirm that you truly know the password that you entered in the New Password field.

 NOTE   For security reasons, both the New Password and Confirm New Password fields replace characters typed into them with bullets. And because you cannot see what you have typed in the New Password field, entering the password a second time in the Confirm New Password field helps to ensure that you know what you've entered.

To continue, enter a new password in the New Password field and enter it a second time in the Confirm New Password field. If the values match, the new password is applied, the Change Password dialog window closes, and you are given access to the database.

Finally, to confirm that the Employees privilege set is working properly, you should be able to view everything in the Contacts database with the exception of the Income field. Change to a layout that the field is on, and you should see that it appears with a "?" symbol in it. This is FileMaker's way of indicating that while the field is on the layout, you are using an account that does not have permission to see its value.

NOTE If you want to log in to the Contacts database with full access, close the database and log in using Admin as the account name and the password that you assigned earlier.

TIP It is possible for multiple users to share a single account, and in cases where a database is being hosted (a concept that you learn about in Chapter 16, "Sharing a Database"), it is even possible for multiple users to be logged in to a database using the same account at the same time. However, it is highly recommended that you do not allow users to share accounts. Every user should have his own account, and you should encourage users not to share their credentials with other users. Otherwise, if users do share accounts, it will be difficult to determine who has made changes in the database and to keep track of who has access to the database.

Resetting an Account's Password

Often, users forget their passwords, and if you are serving as the manager of the database, they will turn to you for help. The easiest way to handle these types of requests is to log in to the database using your Full Access account, open the Manage Security window, pull up the user's account, and then assign a new temporary password. Be sure to check the User Must Change Password on Next Login option, which forces the user to select a more permanent password when he logs in.

Securing New Databases

As mentioned earlier in the chapter, the default security settings that FileMaker applies to a new database are intended to make it easy for you to get started as quickly as possible. However, to ensure that your new database is secure, you should do a few things immediately.

First, you might want to consider changing the name of the Admin account to something else. Changing the name makes it significantly more difficult for people to attempt to "break into" your database, because they will not only need to guess the account's password but the account name as well.

Next, assign the full access account a strong password. For guidance on selecting a strong password, you might want to search online for "strong passwords." You'll find suggestions for creating strong passwords, as well as sites that can be used to generate them for you. (In addition, several third-party applications, such as 1Password, can be used to both generate strong passwords and help you manage all your passwords.)

Finally, disable the auto-login feature of the database. To do so, open the database with an account that has Full Access and select File > File Options. On the Open tab, uncheck the Log In Using option.

Additional Security Features

We've already discussed some of the most commonly used and important security features that FileMaker provides. However, because security is so important, FileMaker provides a number of other somewhat advanced features as well. Some of the features require the use of FileMaker Pro Advanced or that the database be hosted using FileMaker Server. In this section, we briefly review these features so that you are aware of them. (If you want additional information about them, I encourage you to explore FileMaker's Web site and product documentation.)

Custom Extended Privileges

Earlier in the chapter, you learned about the extended privileges that FileMaker adds to newly created databases. These are special privileges that can be used to control how users can access a database. Using the Extended Privileges tab of the Manage Security window, you can create your own custom extended privileges. Then, through the use of the Get (AccountExtendedPrivileges) function in calculation formulas, you can determine whether a user has been assigned a certain custom extended privilege. You can use this technique to implement additional security based on your business rules.

File Access Control

In Chapter 20, "Expanding Your Database," you learn how you can add additional tables to a database and that you can also refer to tables located in other databases. To do these things, a user needs to have accounts in both databases, and so to that extent, these techniques are secure. However, it is possible for a user to create an external reference in one database to a table in another, and then create a layout based on that external table. If the user does so, it is also possible that he might bypass business rules that you have implemented in the source database, especially those implemented using script triggers. In other words, using this external file technique, a user might end up manipulating data in ways that you want to prevent. You can prevent unauthorized external references to a database's table through the use of the File Access tab of the Manage

Security window. It provides an option for requiring that external references be made using accounts assigned to the Full Access privilege set. It also provides a way for you indicate specific databases that you want to allow external references to be made from.

Encryption at Rest

Encryption at Rest (EAR) is a new feature introduced with the FileMaker 13 platform. It provides a way for developers to encrypt the physical database file itself, so that if someone were to obtain a copy of the database, it would be extremely difficult for them to "break into" the file, or to use some sort of utility to look at the raw file and try to make sense of what it contained. To implement EAR, you use FileMaker Pro Advanced to assign an encryption key to a database file. Thereafter, to open the database (whether opening it locally or opening it for sharing via FileMaker Server), you need to provide the key.

FileMaker Server Security Options

When databases are hosted using FileMaker Server, several additional security features become available. For example, with FileMaker Server, you have the option of using the Secure Sockets Layer (more commonly known as SSL) protocol to encrypt data as it is sent back and forth from the server to clients. This makes it difficult for someone to access the data while it is in transit. When this option is enabled, all traffic is encrypted, regardless of whether the data is being accessed via FileMaker Pro, FileMaker Pro Advanced, FileMaker Go, WebDirect, or the FileMaker Server's Web Publishing Engine (WPE).

Earlier in this chapter, you learned that it is possible to authenticate a database's users via an external system, such as Active Directory (Windows) or Open Directory (OS X). To use this feature, the database must be hosted with FileMaker Server, which provides the functionality for sending the remote authentication requests to an external server.

These are just a few of the additional security options available when FileMaker Server is used to host databases. In Chapter 15, "Backing Up a Database," you learn about some of FileMaker Server's other features that make implementing a robust backup plan possible. Those features, along with FileMaker Server's security features, create a compelling argument for investing in and using FileMaker Server.

THE ABSOLUTE MINIMUM

In this chapter, you learned about the importance of security and how the FileMaker platform provides options for making your databases secure. Here are the key points to remember:

- The FileMaker security model uses accounts to authenticate users who are attempting to access a database, and privilege sets to determine what users can see and do after they have been authenticated.

- Accounts must be assigned to one and only one privilege set. However, you can assign multiple accounts to a single privilege set, thus providing a way to easily implement security across a number of accounts.

- Many of FileMaker's security functions are accessible via the Manage Security window. It provides tools for managing accounts, privilege sets, and more.

- Through the use of privilege sets and the options that FileMaker provides, it is possible to implement detailed business rules. You can control access to tables, specific records in a table, and even specific fields. Similarly, you can control access to layouts, value lists, and scripts.

- Extended privileges can be used to determine how users can access a database (via the network, ODBC, and so on). You can also create your own custom extended privileges to easily implement your own business rules.

- Through the use of FileMaker Pro Advanced and FileMaker Server, several additional and more advanced security options are available, including Encryption at Rest, SSL, and external authentication.

BACKING UP A DATABASE

In Chapter 14, "Protecting a Database," you learned about the importance of securing your databases and the features that FileMaker Pro provides to secure them. While implementing security is an important part of protecting your databases, you should also have a plan in place for backing up your data, so that it can be restored should something go wrong.

In this chapter, you learn why it is important to back up your FileMaker databases, how to properly back up database files, and how to create a comprehensive backup strategy. You also learn how to restore from a backup, how to recover a damaged FileMaker Pro database, and more.

The Importance of Backing Up

As mentioned at the start of Chapter 14, you have been using sample data to work on the examples in this book. If something were to happen to the example database that you have created, you could recreate the database and reload the sample data. Doing so would be inconvenient but not a terrible loss.

However, you will eventually use FileMaker to create databases that manage "real" data—data that is important and valuable to you. At that point, you are going to need to have a backup plan in place so that, should something terrible happen, you have a way to recover the data.

You might be wondering what would cause you to need a backup. It's possible that the computer that the database is being hosted on will crash, or FileMaker Pro itself might crash. In those cases, the FileMaker file will not be closed properly, possibly damaging the file. Another possibility is that a user might damage or alter the data, whether intentionally or accidentally. For example, a user might delete one or more records or incorrectly set field values in many records. In those cases, having access to a reliable and current backup file will save you a lot of time and trouble.

Challenges of Backing Up Databases

Hopefully, you are already backing up the important files stored on your computer. On both the Mac and Windows platforms, the process of backing up files has never been easier. Software provided by the operating systems themselves, as well as third-party products and services, can assist you in backing up your files. Many of these programs and services fully automate the backup process, so that you don't even have to remember to perform the backup.

However, while backup software and services are ideal for backing up most types of files, they are not necessarily a good way to back up FileMaker database files. In fact, in some cases, they can do more harm than good. The primary reason for this is that, unlike other types of files, many databases are constantly in use. As a result, the database files are nearly always open, and backing up open files often provides unexpected results. For example, maybe changes that have been made to a database have not yet been saved to disk, or worse, have only been partially saved. In those cases, the database might appear to have been backed up properly, but should you ever need to restore it, you might find that that the backup is unusable.

Backing up large database files, such as those used to store large amounts of digital data (photos, movies, and so on), poses other challenges. Backing up these large files can take a long time. As a result, it is entirely possible that changes will have been made to the database during that time. In this scenario, you might find that the backup includes incorrect or incomplete data.

In addition, using backup software and services to back up "live" FileMaker files not only poses the risk of creating unusable and unreliable backups, but it also has the potential to cause problems with the live files as well. During the process of backing up a live file, the backup software might lock the file. If FileMaker tries to write changes to the locked file, it will likely encounter an error and cause it to crash. Therefore, you want to be sure that your backup solution is configured in such a way that it excludes live FileMaker database files.

Performing Backups

The key to properly backing up a database is to back it up using FileMaker, and then let your backup software "back up the backup." In other words, don't back up the live database. Instead, use FileMaker to create a backup file first, and then let your backup software back up that file.

If you alone are using a FileMaker database, and it is stored locally on your computer, then backing up the database is a matter of closing the file and then making a copy of it. Another option is to close the file and manually run your backup software, allowing it to back up the closed database file. (Just be sure that you allow the backup process to complete before reopening the database.)

If you are hosting a FileMaker database and other users are accessing it remotely (a topic that we cover in Chapter 16, "Sharing a Database"), then you have two options: You can ask the other users to log out of the database (so that you can close the file and back it up), or you can use FileMaker's Save A Copy As command to create a backup file. Whenever possible, you want to avoid interrupting and inconveniencing database users. Therefore, using the Save A Copy As command is probably the better choice.

To use the Save A Copy As command, follow these steps:

1. Select File > Save A Copy As. The Create a Copy Named dialog box opens, as shown in Figure 15.1.

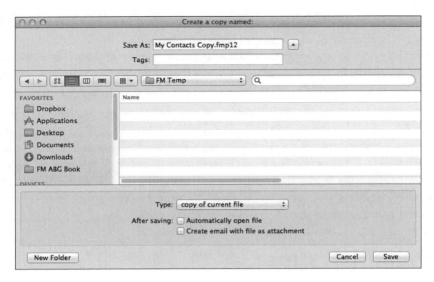

FIGURE 15.1

The Create a Copy Named dialog box.

2. Specify the name of the file that you want to create. You might want to include the date, and possibly the time as well, in the name so that you can easily identify it; for example, Contacts Backup - 20140906 - 0915.fmp12.

3. Select a location to which you want to save the file.

4. For the Type of file to create, select Copy of Current File.

5. Click Save.

When the process has completed, you should look in the location that you specified in step 3, to be sure that the file was actually created. You might also want to take a moment to try to open the file and confirm that it opens properly.

Here are a couple of things to consider when using the Save A Copy As command:

- Depending on the size of the database, it may take a few moments for the backup to complete. During that time, users connected to the database might see it appear to be "paused" or slow in responding.

- The Save A Copy As command is only available to the user who has the FileMaker database opened locally. For users accessing the database remotely, the command appears to be grayed out.

NOTE In the previous instructions, I indicated that you should set the backup file type to Copy of Current File. However, another option, Compacted Copy (Smaller), can also be used. With this option, a more compact file is created, which takes up less space on your hard drive. However, with this type of backup, the process might take a little longer to complete, because FileMaker needs to take extra steps to compact the file's contents.

Backing Up with FileMaker Server

In Chapter 16, you learn how to share a FileMaker database with multiple users. You learn that while it is possible to share databases using FileMaker Pro itself, another alternative is to use FileMaker Server, the server component of the FileMaker platform. FileMaker Server provides a number of options for sharing databases that FileMaker Pro does not provide and several other features as well.

One of FileMaker Server's features is the capability to perform fully automated, scheduled backups—and to do so with little to no impact on a database's users. Using FileMaker Server, you can create robust backup plans, create efficient "progressive backups" (that back up only changes made since the last backup was performed), verify the integrity of backups, send email alerts if problems are encountered during a backup, and more. As your FileMaker databases become more important to you, you might want to consider using FileMaker Server to host your files.

Creating Backup Strategies

Regardless of how you back up your FileMaker databases, you need to have a good strategy in place for managing the backups. Here are a few things to consider as you put together a backup strategy:

- **Schedule backups properly**—The frequency with which you perform backups is important, and the frequency that you need depends on your situation. For example, if you are working in a database consistently throughout the day, then backing up only at the end of the day is probably not sufficient. You'll likely want to back up hourly, or every few hours at the least.

- **Retain backups properly**—You also need to consider how long you want to maintain backups. For example, do you need to be able to recover from a backup that is more than a month old? Should you maintain your daily backups for a year or more? In some cases, you might need to retain your backups based on regulations or your company's policy.

- **Rotate external hard drives**—If you are backing up to external hard drives, consider rotating them. For example, if you are backing up to an external drive on a weekly basis, you might want to use multiple external drives and alternate them each week. That way, should one of the drives fail, you still have access to the backups on the other drive.

- **Store your backup drives in a safe location**—If you are storing them in your home or office, consider investing in a water and fireproof media safe.

- **Include offsite backups in your plan**—For example, you might want to store physical backups in safety deposit box. Or, consider using a cloud storage service, such as DropBox (https://dropbox.com) or Box (https://www.box.com).

- **Be sure that your backups are secure**—Consider password protecting any external drives that you are backing up to. Also, as discussed in Chapter 14, if you are using FileMaker Pro Advanced, you might want to use the new Encryption at Rest (EAR) feature to encrypt the database files themselves.

- **Test your backups**—Periodically test your backups to ensure that they are working properly. To do so, open up a backup file and take a look around. Is all of the data in the file? Are the layouts working properly?

Restoring from Backups

Hopefully, you will never need to use your backups. However, in the event that you do run into problems with a database, you need to know how to use them.

In most cases, the process of restoring from a backup involves replacing a damaged database with a backup file. In this scenario, be sure that you close the damaged database before replacing it with a backup. I also recommend that you copy the damaged file to a safe place before replacing it.

In other cases, the restoration process might be a bit more complicated. For example, suppose that your last backup was at 9:00 a.m. At 9:45 a.m., a user accidentally deletes a number of records. In this scenario, restoring might be a simple matter of replacing the database with the 9:00 a.m. backup file.

However, if other changes had been made to the database between 9:00 a.m. and 9:45 a.m. (new records were added, records were changed, and so on), then you're going to have to make a decision. Should you restore from the 9:00 a.m. backup file and have your users redo the work that they had done? (Will they even remember all the work that they had done?) Or should you pull the 9:00 a.m. backup, locate the records that were deleted, and import them into the live database?

There are no hard and fast rules with regard to how you recover. My only advice is this: Don't panic, take your time, think things through, and be careful. And remember, it is for situations like these that you've created backups in the first place.

Recovering Damaged Databases

In some cases, you may be able to recover information from a damaged FileMaker file. It will largely depend on the nature of the damage and how the file was damaged.

For example, suppose that you are working in a local FileMaker database, and your computer crashes. It is entirely possible that when you attempt to reopen the file later that it will open without any problems whatsoever.

However, if a database file isn't closed properly, the next time that it is opened FileMaker runs a test on the file (known as a *consistency check*) to ensure that it is safe to use. If FileMaker finds a problem with the file, it displays a dialog box (as shown in Figure 15.2) indicating that the file "is damaged and cannot be opened. Use the Recover command to recover this file."

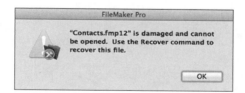

FIGURE 15.2

The dialog box that FileMaker displays when a file is found to be damaged.

The Recover command that the dialog box is referring to is located under the File menu (File > Recover). When you run the Recover command, the process starts by asking you to select the file that you want to recover, as shown in Figure 15.3.

Next, you are asked to provide the name and location of the file that you want the recover file to be saved to, as shown in Figure 15.4.

FileMaker then attempts to recover information from the file. It does as much as it can to recover the tables, records, layouts, scripts, and more from the damaged file and recreate them in the "recovered" file. When the process is complete, another dialog box, similar to that shown in Figure 15.5, displays, indicating the results of the recovery process.

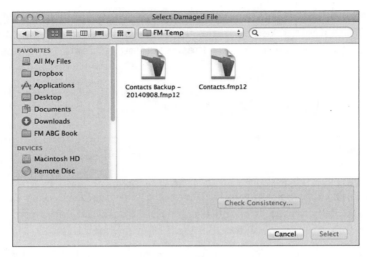

FIGURE 15.3

The first dialog box that appears when you attempt to recover a damaged file.

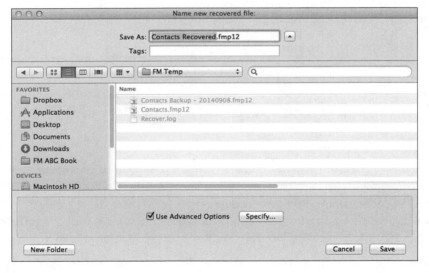

FIGURE 15.4

The second dialog box that appears when you attempt to recover a damaged file.

In cases where the damage to the file is extensive, FileMaker might not be able to recover anything from the damaged file. In cases where FileMaker can recover information from the file, it is important to note that you should not use the recovered file directly. Instead, you should pull a backup of the database, and then apply recent data from the recovered file to the backup.

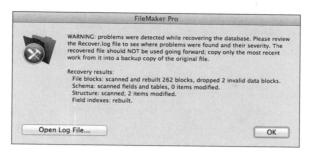

FIGURE 15.5

The third dialog box that appears during the recovery process, showing the results of the recovery attempt.

The Recover command also provides several advanced options, giving you the opportunity to give detailed instructions on what you want FileMaker to try to recover from the damaged file. To use these advanced options, select File > Recover, locate the database that you want to test, and on the Name New Recovered File dialog box, check the Use Advanced Options button. The Advanced Recover Options dialog appears, as shown in Figure 15.6. Once you have specified the options that you want the Recover command to use, click OK, and then click Save. FileMaker then attempts to recover the file and generates a recover file as it normally would.

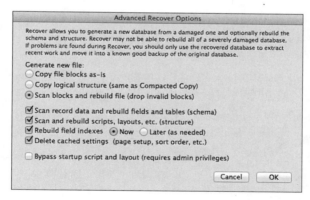

FIGURE 15.6

The recovery command's Advanced Recover Options dialog box.

Performing Consistency Checks

FileMaker automatically performs a consistency check whenever a file isn't closed properly. However, if you want to do a consistency check on a file at any time, you can use the Recover command to do so.

To use the feature, select File > Recover, locate the database that you want to test, and then click the Check Consistency button. A dialog box similar to that shown in Figure 15.7 is displayed indicating any errors detected.

FIGURE 15.7

The results of a file consistency check.

THE ABSOLUTE MINIMUM

In this chapter, you learned why it is important to back up databases and the unique challenges that backing up database files presents. Here are the key points to remember:

- You should never use backup software to back up "live" database files. Doing so can result in backups that are corrupt or incomplete, and can even damage the live files themselves.

- To back up a database being hosted with FileMaker Pro, you can use the Save A Copy As command.

- For additional backup options, including fully automated, scheduled backups, consider using FileMaker Server.

- It is important to create a strategy for both backing up your databases and maintaining those backups. A good backup plan includes a well-thought-out backup schedule, retention policy, the rotation of external backup drives, offsite backups, and more.

- FileMaker provides a recovery function that can be used to attempt to recover damaged files. It also provides a tool for performing a consistency check of a database, which can be helpful when diagnosing a problematic file.

16

SHARING A DATABASE

As you've worked through the examples in this book, you've seen just how powerful databases can be and how easy FileMaker Pro makes it to both create and work with databases. A well-designed database can truly empower an individual.

That power is multiplied when a database is shared with others, allowing multiple people to access and work with data simultaneously. Not surprisingly, FileMaker makes the process of sharing a database easy and convenient. With just a few minor changes to a FileMaker database, you can begin to share it with colleagues.

In this chapter, you learn how to share a database using FileMaker Pro. You also learn about FileMaker Server and the additional methods that it provides for sharing databases.

Hosting with FileMaker Pro

Using FileMaker Pro or FileMaker Pro Advanced, you can host a database and allow up to five other users to connect to it concurrently. In FileMaker terms, the computer that has opened the FileMaker database is acting as the *host*, and the computers connecting to the host are called *clients*. The clients must also be running FileMaker Pro, FileMaker Pro Advanced, or FileMaker Go, and they must be connected to the same local area network as the host. This form of sharing is known as *peer-to-peer sharing*.

When a database is shared, FileMaker handles all the work involved in keeping things running smoothly. It ensures that changes made by users are saved to the hosted file and, when applicable, that those changes are immediately visible to the other users who are also looking at that data. For example, if User A and User B are both looking at the same contact record, and User A makes changes to the record and commits the changes, then User B will see those changes. FileMaker also prevents two users from attempting to change the same record at the same time. For example, if User A starts to make changes to a record but hasn't committed them yet, and User B attempts to change the same record, FileMaker displays a message to User B indicating that the record is in use by User A. Figure 16.1 shows an example of the message that User B would receive.

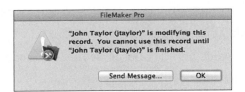

FIGURE 16.1

The dialog box displayed when a user attempts to edit a record that is in use by another user.

When it comes to tables, fields, layouts, scripts, and so on, FileMaker works in much the same way. For example, it allows only one user at a time to make changes to a certain script or layout. It also prevents users from making changes to tables, fields, value lists, accounts, and privilege sets simultaneously.

To configure a FileMaker database for sharing, follow these steps:

1. Open the FileMaker database as you normally would using FileMaker Pro. You need to log in to the file with an account associated with a privilege set that has Manage Extended Privileges enabled (such as a Full Access account).

2. From the File menu, select Sharing > Share with FileMaker Clients. The FileMaker Network Settings dialog box displays, as shown in Figure 16.2.

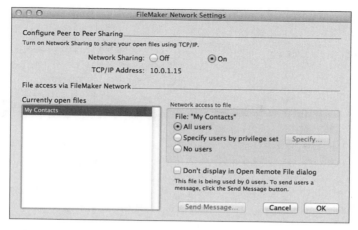

FIGURE 16.2

FileMaker Network Settings dialog box.

3. Set the Network Sharing option to On. This configures your copy of FileMaker Pro so that it can host databases over the network.

4. Locate and select the database that you want to host in the list of Currently Open Files. The Network Access to the File area becomes active, displaying the access settings for the selected database.

5. To allow all users to access the database, select the All Users option. Users still need to have an active account in the database and be associated with a privilege set that includes the Access Via FileMaker Network (fmapp) extended privilege. To limit access to specific privilege sets, use the Specify Users by Privilege Set option.

When users connect to FileMaker on your computer, they normally see a list of any databases that you have available for sharing. If you would prefer that they not see this database in that list, check the Don't Display in Open Remote File Dialog option.

Once users have connected to a database that you are hosting with FileMaker Pro, you can see the number of users connected in the FileMaker Network Settings dialog box, as shown in Figure 16.3.

In addition, the Send Message button becomes active. If you want to send a message to the users connected to the database, click the button and the Send Message to Guests dialog appears, as shown in Figure 16.4.

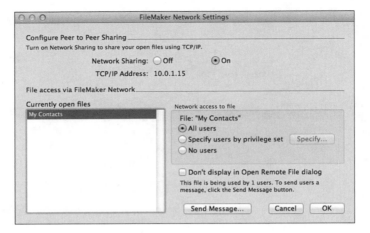

FIGURE 16.3

The FileMaker Network Settings dialog box, showing the number of users connected to the hosted database.

FIGURE 16.4

The Send Message to Guests dialog box, which can be used to send a message to guests of a hosted database.

To send a brief message to the database's users, enter the message into the text box and click OK. For example, you might want to send a message indicating that you are planning to close the database, and asking that users wrap up their work and log out. That message appears to the users in a dialog box, similar to that shown in Figure 16.5.

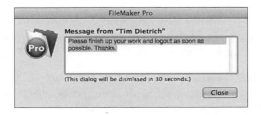

FIGURE 16.5

The dialog box that appears to users of a hosted database when the host has sent a message.

NOTE The remote users of the database see any message that you send to them, but they do not have the ability to reply to the message.

When you have finished configuring the database for sharing, click OK to close the FileMaker Network Settings dialog box.

Connecting with FileMaker Pro

To connect to a shared database using FileMaker Pro or FileMaker Pro Advanced, follow these steps:

1. Select File > Open Remote. The Open Remote File dialog box appears, as shown in Figure 16.6.

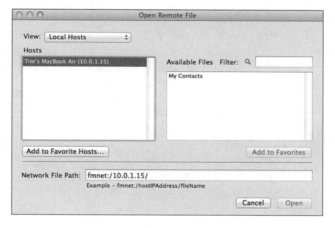

FIGURE 16.6

The Open Remote File dialog box, which is used to connect to a hosted database.

2. Set the View option to Local Hosts. The list of local hosts should refresh, showing the names and IP addresses of any computers on your local area network that are hosting FileMaker databases.

3. In the Hosts list, select the computer that is hosting the database that you want to access. The list of Available Files refreshes, showing the names of the databases that the selected Host has available.

4. Click on the database that you want to log in to, and then click the Open button. The Open dialog box opens, as shown in Figure 16.7.

FIGURE 16.7

The Open dialog box, which is used to log in to a FileMaker database.

5. Enter your Account Name and Password, and then click OK to log in to the database.

 TIP Once you've connected to a hosted database for the first time, connecting again in the future will be significantly easier. To reconnect, you can either select the database from the list of Recent Files on the FileMaker Quick Start screen or select the database from the File > Open Recent menu.

 TIP If you are acting as the host of a FileMaker database, you can email users a link to the database, thus making it even easier for them to connect. To send a link to the database, select File > Send > Link to Database. The email appears in your email client. Both the subject and body of the message are set for you, so all that you need to do is address the message and send it to your users. When a user receives the email, she can simply click the link to connect to the hosted database.

Remember that you can also connect to hosted databases using FileMaker Go, the FileMaker app that runs on iOS-based devices (including iPhones, iPads, and iPod Touches). In Chapter 17, "Taking Data with You," we walk through the process of connecting to hosted databases with FileMaker Go.

Closing Hosted Databases

As the host of a shared FileMaker database, there may be times when you need to close the database. To do so, close the file as you normally would, by selecting File > Close. If users are connected to the database at that time, you see a dialog box listing those users, as shown in Figure 16.8.

FIGURE 16.8

The dialog box that displays when you attempt to close a hosted database that is still opened by other users.

If, after reviewing the list of users, you decide to keep the hosted database open, click Cancel. Otherwise, click the Ask button. A dialog box displays on each user's machine, requesting that they close the database. Figure 16.9 shows an example of the message users receive.

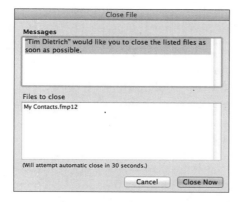

FIGURE 16.9

The message received by users of a hosted database when the host is attempting to close the database.

When the message displays, users have the option of clicking the Close Now button, which logs them out of the database immediately. If the user clicks Cancel, then the user can continue to use the file until they manually close the file. If the user does not respond to the dialog box within 30 seconds, FileMaker automatically logs the user out of the database.

Sharing Via ODBC

In addition to being able to share databases with other FileMaker users, FileMaker Pro can also share data with other applications via a standard known as ODBC. FileMaker can act as both an ODBC data source (meaning that it can share its data with other applications) and as an ODBC client (meaning that it can access what is being shared by other applications).

We do not cover all the details involved in setting up ODBC connections here. However, if you are interested in this topic, see the "FileMaker 13 ODBC and JDBC Guide," which can be found on the FileMaker Web site.

Hosting with FileMaker Server

During our discussions of security in Chapter 14, "Protecting a Database" and backing up databases in Chapter 15, "Backing Up a Database," we mentioned that the server component of the FileMaker platform includes features that FileMaker Pro lacks. For example, in terms of security, with FileMaker Server you can use an external server to authenticate users. With regard to backing up databases, FileMaker Server has the capability to run fully automated, scheduled backups.

When it comes to sharing databases, FileMaker Server provides additional functionality as well. It is capable of hosting databases for larger groups of users and can do so using additional sharing methods.

Increased Support for Concurrent Users

Where FileMaker Pro is limited to hosting up to five concurrent users, FileMaker Server can support as many as 250 simultaneous connections from FileMaker Pro clients, and as many as 50 simultaneous connections from FileMaker Go clients. So if you need to make your databases available to a large number of concurrent users, you need to host using FileMaker Server.

Support for FileMaker WebDirect

Starting with FileMaker 13, FileMaker introduced FileMaker WebDirect, a technology that makes it easy to publish databases to the Web. You can think of FileMaker WebDirect as a browser-based FileMaker client, providing a convenient way for users who do not have FileMaker Pro to connect to hosted databases. Without installing any additional software, these users can connect to hosted databases and perform many of the same tasks that FileMaker Pro and Go can perform. They can work with data, perform finds, and much more.

FileMaker WebDirect does a fantastic job of replicating the FileMaker experience in a browser environment. Figure 16.10 shows the Contacts Details layout (from the Contact database) as it appears in WebDirect.

FIGURE 16.10

An example of a FileMaker database being accessed using FileMaker WebDirect.

FileMaker WebDirect does have some limitations that you should be aware of, including

- FileMaker WebDirect can only be used by databases being hosted with FileMaker Server.

- Only a handful of modern Web browsers are supported: Safari 6.1.x, Safari 7.x, Internet Explorer 10.x or 11.x, and Chrome 27.x.

- FileMaker WebDirect does not support FileMaker functions such as printing, PDF generation, and layout mode.

- Connections to databases made with FileMaker WebDirect (as well as from FileMaker Go) are considered to be concurrent connections, and FileMaker treats these connections differently than other types of connections. For details about concurrent connections, see the FileMaker Web site.

FileMaker WebDirect is a new technology that will evolve in the future. If you need to make your databases available to users who do not have FileMaker Pro, FileMaker Pro Advanced, or FileMaker Go, you might want to consider FileMaker WebDirect.

Custom Web Publishing

FileMaker Server also provides support for two web publishing technologies (XML and PHP), which make it possible to integrate FileMaker databases with Web sites and Web services.

FileMaker Server's support for XML makes it possible for Web applications to send requests using special URLs. Those URLs specify the type of command to be run by the server and any necessary parameters. FileMaker Server evaluates the XML request and returns the result in XML format, which the calling Web application can use.

FileMaker provides support for PHP via its FileMaker API for PHP. This API allows Web developers to interact with FileMaker Server via the popular PHP programming language. Developers can use the API to retrieve data in a FileMaker database, add records, update records, delete records, run scripts in the database, and more.

Using FileMaker Server's Custom Web Publishing technologies, you can integrate your FileMaker databases with advanced Web applications, giving you more control over how the data appears, how it is accessed, and so on. These technologies require experience with Web programming. For more information, see "Custom Web Publishing with XML" and "Custom Web Publishing with PHP," which are available on the FileMaker Web site (http://www.filemaker.com).

ODBC/JDBC Connections

Like FileMaker Pro, you can use FileMaker Server to make the data stored in FileMaker databases available via ODBC and JDBC (two standards often used to facilitate communication between two applications). Unlike FileMaker Pro, ODBC client applications that want access to databases do not need to be on the same machine, or even on the same network, as FileMaker Server. Also, where FileMaker Pro limits the number of simultaneous ODBC connections to nine, FileMaker Server supports an unlimited number of simultaneous connections.

With all the advantages that FileMaker Server provides, you might be wondering why some FileMaker users don't use it. Without getting into specifics, FileMaker Server can be costly. You need to invest in the FileMaker Server software itself, a server to run it on, and possibly concurrent connections (depending on the number of FileMaker WebDirect and FileMaker Go users that will be accessing the hosted databases). In addition, setting up and maintaining FileMaker Server requires knowledge of networking and experience setting up and configuring servers. In any case, if you are at a point where you need the capabilities that FileMaker Server provides, I encourage you to look into it. You can find detailed information about FileMaker Server on FileMaker's Web site.

TIP If you have a need for FileMaker Server but lack the budget or experience needed to purchase and configure it, you might also want to consider using services provided by FileMaker database hosting companies. These companies provide a number of different plans, from shared database hosting (where your database is hosted on the same server as several other hosting clients) to dedicated database servers. This is a great way to get the advantages that FileMaker Server provides and to do so in an affordable way. For a list of companies that provide FileMaker hosting services, visit the FileMaker Web site, select Solutions > Consultants, and select Show Only Hosting Providers.

THE ABSOLUTE MINIMUM

In this chapter, you learned about the options available for sharing a FileMaker database with multiple users. Here are the key points to remember:

- You can host FileMaker databases using FileMaker with up to five additional users. Those users can access the file using FileMaker Pro, FileMaker Pro Advanced, or FileMaker Go. This form of sharing is known as peer-to-peer sharing.

- You can also use FileMaker Pro to server as an ODBC data source, making it possible for other applications to access data stored in your FileMaker databases.

- The server component of the FileMaker platform, FileMaker Server, can also be used to host FileMaker databases. With FileMaker Server, you can provide access to many more users than you can with FileMaker Pro.

- FileMaker Pro provides several additional methods for sharing FileMaker databases, including FileMaker WebDirect and custom Web publishing with PHP and XML.

17

TAKING DATA WITH YOU

Mobile devices—especially smartphones and tablet computers—have forever changed the way that we use technology. This is especially true with regard to how and where we work. The expectation is that we always have access to the information we need to make business decisions and respond to customer requests, regardless of whether we are working in an office, a coffee shop, or from an airport as we prepare to hop on a plane.

For years now, the FileMaker platform has provided the tools and functionality that knowledge workers need to create databases that can be accessed via mobile devices. Key to this is FileMaker Go, an iOS app that runs on iPads, iPhones, and iPod Touches.

In this chapter, you learn about FileMaker Go's role in the platform, discuss how you can use your knowledge of FileMaker to create solutions that work well with FileMaker Go, and explore the options for deploying solutions to FileMaker Go users.

The Role of FileMaker Go

FileMaker Go is the mobile component of the FileMaker platform. It is an iOS-based app, meaning that it runs on Apple's iPads, iPhones, and iPad Touches. It is a free app, available for download from the iOS App Store.

You can think of FileMaker Go as a "lite" version of FileMaker Pro. It can be used to access FileMaker databases; to add, update, and delete records; to export data; and much more. However, unlike FileMaker Pro, FileMaker Go is not capable of creating new FileMaker databases, nor can it be used to update a database's schema (its tables, fields, and relationships) or to create or update layouts or scripts. The functionality that FileMaker Go provides is limited to what a user needs to use a FileMaker database.

Designing for FileMaker Go

You can use FileMaker Go to view any layout, and it fully supports all the FileMaker layout object types that you learned about in Chapter 11, "Working with Layouts." In fact, you can open a FileMaker database with FileMaker Go and for the most part use it without needing to make any changes.

However, to provide the best experience for your mobile users, you might want to consider creating special "mobile-friendly" layouts. These layouts are sized in such a way that mobile users do not need to spend a lot of time scrolling vertically and horizontally to see the full contents of the layout. In addition, the layout's objects, especially text and fields, are sized so that users can easily read the text. And finally, you might find mobile users do not need access to the full set of data that desktop users normally see. In other words, you might be able to simplify the layouts for mobile users. This helps you to create layouts that fit well on the mobile devices and might also improve the performance of the database, especially for mobile users connecting to hosted databases over slower Wi-Fi or cellular connections.

With FileMaker Pro 13, creating mobile-friendly layouts has never been easier. As you learned in Chapter 11, when you create a new layout, one of the first steps involved is to specify what type of device the layout is intended to be used on. Selecting Touch Device brings up a menu of devices that you can choose from (as shown in Figure 17.1). By choosing one of the touch devices, FileMaker automatically creates a layout whose dimensions work nicely on the specified device.

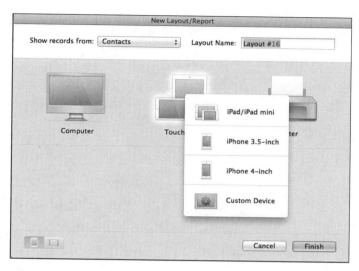

FIGURE 17.1

The New Layout/Report window with the Touch Device options displayed.

In addition, when you choose to create a layout for a touch device, FileMaker also automatically chooses a layout theme specially designed for mobile devices. These themes (which include Enlightened Touch, Luminous Touch, Sophisticated Touch, Tranquil Touch, and so on) take into account the challenges that using mobile devices pose. For example, layouts based on touch themes include larger text (for improved readability), slightly larger fields and portals, and more. Figure 17.2 shows an example of a FileMaker database as it appears on an iPad using FileMaker Go.

FileMaker also provides a tools and script step that can be used to make layouts appear to be responsive in much the same way that many Web sites are today. Specifically, you can use the Stencil layout tool, along with auto-sizing layout objects, and the OnLayoutSizeChange script trigger to create layouts that adjust automatically depending on whether the device is being used in landscape or portrait mode. Many of the databases created via Starter Solutions include examples of these types of layouts. (For an example, take a look at the layouts in the iPad and iPhone layout folders of the Contacts database.)

FileMaker also includes script steps and calculation functions that enable you to use the full capabilities of iOS devices. For example, with the Insert from Device script step, you can collect content from a device's music library, photo library, camera, or microphone. In addition, you can collect signatures or scan barcodes, and you can use the special Location and LocationValues functions to determine the latitude and longitude of the device.

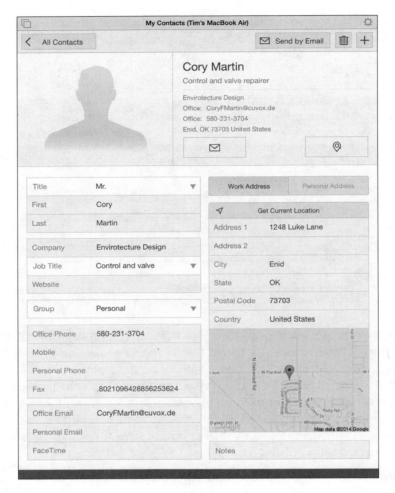

FIGURE 17.2

An example of a FileMaker database as it appears in FileMaker Go.

Using a combination of FileMaker's layout design tools, special "touch" themes, script steps, and functions, you can use FileMaker Pro to create elegant and user-friendly solutions for your mobile users.

Deployment Options

With FileMaker Go, you can access both hosted and local FileMaker databases. Let's take a few minutes to review these options.

Accessing Hosted Databases

To connect to a database being hosted with FileMaker Pro, the iOS device must have a Wi-Fi connection to the same network that the host is on. If the database is being hosted with FileMaker Server, the iOS device must have either a Wi-Fi or cellular connection.

To connect to a hosted database, follow these steps:

1. Open the FileMaker Go app on the mobile device and click the Hosts icon located in the left column of the window. A list of hosts displays, as shown in Figure 17.3.

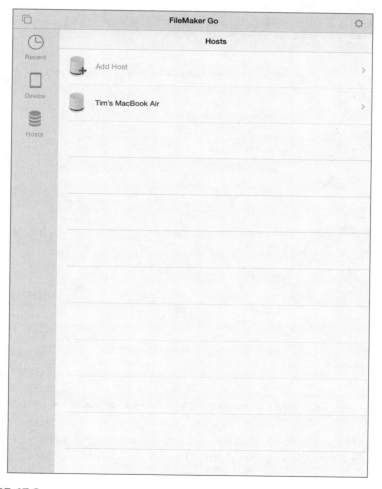

FIGURE 17.3

The FileMaker Go window showing a list of local hosts.

2. Click on the name of the computer that hosts the database that you want to connect to. The screen refreshes and lists any databases being hosted on the selected computer, as shown in Figure 17.4.

FIGURE 17.4

The FileMaker Go window showing a list of databases available on the selected host.

3. Locate the database that you want to connect to, and click on the database name. The Opening File dialog displays, as shown in Figure 17.5.

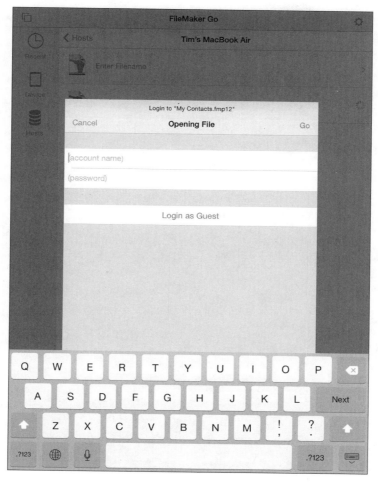

FIGURE 17.5

The Opening File dialog window, as shown in FileMaker Go.

4. Enter your FileMaker account name and password. Then click the Go button, located in the top-right corner of the window.

That's all it takes to connect to a hosted database from FileMaker Go.

When you are finished with the hosted database, you can log out by following these steps:

1. Click the icon located in the top-left corner of the FileMaker Go window. A pop-up menu displays, as shown in Figure 17.6.

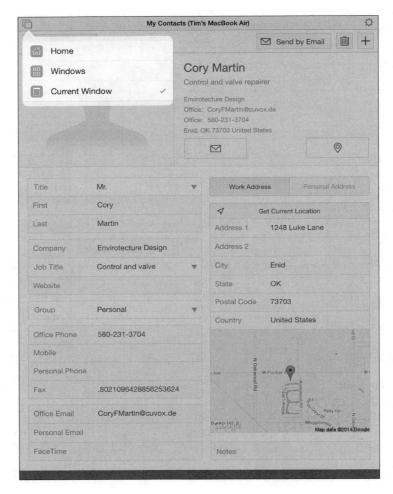

FIGURE 17.6

The menu that appears, allowing you to return to the home screen, view open windows, or return to the current window in FileMaker Go.

  2. Select Windows from the menu. The database window shrinks in size, as shown in Figure 17.7.

FIGURE 17.7

FileMaker Go, with the active window minimized. You can close a window by clicking the X icon at the top of the window preview.

3. Click the red X close icon, located in the top-left corner of the database window. This closes the connection to the database and returns you to the FileMaker Go window.

Using Local Databases

In some cases, you might need to access a database that either is not hosted or in a location where your ability to connect to a hosted database is unreliable. For example, suppose that your business involves servicing large HVAC systems, which are often located in the basements of large buildings. In that environment, it might be difficult to get a reliable Wi-Fi or cellular connection.

In that type of scenario, users need to have local copies of the FileMaker database stored directly on their mobile devices. That way they have access to the database regardless of whether they have a reliable connection. These users work on their local databases, and when they are finished and have a reliable network connection they synchronize with a hosted copy of the database.

There are several ways to get a FileMaker database onto an iOS device. One method is to connect the device to a computer via a USB cable and then use iTunes to transfer the file to the device. Another option is to put a copy of the database on a server and then use Safari to open a link to the file. When Safari attempts to open the file, it recognizes the file as being a FileMaker database and asks whether you want to open it in FileMaker Go. Yet another solution is to email the file to an account that the device has access to. In this case, you need to take into consideration the size of the file, as you would not want to email a particularly large database.

The process of synchronizing data between local and hosted databases can be tricky, depending on what type of data needs to be synced, how much data is being synced, and so on. Several solutions are available that can help you to add sync functionality to your solutions. Some are commercially available, while others are provided free of charge.

Security Considerations

Regardless of whether you will provide mobile users with access to hosted or local databases, you must take into consideration a few security-related issues.

If mobile users are going to connect to a hosted database, consider assigning the fmreauthenticate10 extended privilege to their privilege set. This extended privilege specifies what happens when a user switches from the FileMaker Go app to another app and then returns to FileMaker Go. When the fmreauthenticate10 extended privilege is enabled, users who switch from FileMaker Go and return within 10 minutes are not required to re-log in to the hosted database. By disabling this extended privilege, users are required to re-log in to a hosted database, regardless of how long ago they switched from FileMaker Go.

 NOTE   You can also set up custom extended privileges to create your own fmreauthenticate privileges. To do so, create an extended privilege with a name like fmreauthenticate followed by the amount of time (in minutes) that you want to give users before requiring that they re-log in. You can specify a value as high as 10,080 minutes (7 days).

If you are going to provide mobile users with a copy of the database for local use, you might want to consider using the FileMaker Pro Advanced new function to apply Encryption at Rest (EAR) to the database. We discussed this new feature in Chapter 14, "Protecting a Database." Using EAR, you can encrypt the actual database file itself. As a result, should the mobile device (and the database file on it) fall into the wrong hands, it will be difficult for someone to "break into" the file.

Other Considerations

One last thing to consider before deploying FileMaker Go solutions is cost. While FileMaker Go itself is free, concurrent connections to FileMaker Server are not. We briefly discussed the concept of concurrent connections in Chapter 16, "Sharing a Database." With databases hosted on FileMaker Server, connections made via FileMaker Go and FileMaker WebDirect are limited based on the number of concurrent connection licenses purchased. Therefore, if you are planning to deploy a FileMaker Go-based solution to a large number of mobile users, you should do some research to determine the number of concurrent licenses that you are going to need, and how much the licenses are going to cost.

THE ABSOLUTE MINIMUM

In this chapter, you learned about the mobile component of the FileMaker platform, FileMaker Go. Here are the key points to remember:

- FileMaker Go is a free app that runs on iOS devices, including iPhones, iPads, and iPod Touches.

- FileMaker Go can be used to work with FileMaker databases. However, it cannot be used to make design or development changes to databases.

- Using FileMaker Go, mobile users can both connect to hosted databases and use databases stored locally on their devices.

- FileMaker provides a number of tools and features that make creating mobile-friendly database solutions easier, including special layout themes, script triggers, and layout object attributes to automatically resize layouts when devices are rotated and more.

- Before deploying mobile solutions, a few security-related features should be considered, including the fmreauthenticate extended privilege and Encryption at Rest (EAR).

18

PLANNING YOUR DATABASE

In this chapter, you learn how to design a database that meets your specific needs. You learn to create a database model by identifying the entities that the database keeps track of, as well as their attributes. In Chapter 19, "Creating Your Database," you use that database model to create your own FileMaker database.

Defining Your Goals

As you would with any project, when you set out to create a new database, the first step is to define your goals. That may seem like common sense, but you would be amazed at how often I see users start a database project by jumping right into FileMaker Pro and creating a new database, without giving any thought as to what they hope to accomplish. In those cases, it is common to find out later that the database they created is incomplete, incorrect, or both.

So, before you do anything else, ask yourself what problems you are hoping to solve and what goals you want to achieve with the new database. This is an important first step in creating your database, and you should not skip it. Without knowing what you are hoping to accomplish, it is difficult to develop an effective database. It's like an architect drawing up plans for a house without knowing what type of house the client wants. The client might end up with plans for a dog house instead of the single family home she was hoping for!

Let's look at an example. A local private school wants to raise funds for a new building and wants to use a database to keep track of fundraising efforts. The database will be used by members of the fundraising committee to store information about possible donors and to send out a mass mailing to ask for donations. The plan is to send out a mass mailing to the parents of students currently enrolled in the school, as well as alumni of the school.

In this example, the goal is to create a database that committee members can use to build a list of potential donors and to generate letters and labels for their mass mailing.

 TIP In many cases, the databases that you create will be used by multiple people. Therefore, as you define your goals, think about what those other people's goals and needs are. It could be that they need the database to keep track of additional information or to be able to generate additional reports or other types of output. To ensure that your database is a success, take those goals into consideration as well.

Identifying Tables

Now that you know what your goals are, you need to determine what your database needs to keep track of to achieve those goals. First, you need to identify and create a list of the things that need to be tracked. We refer to those things as *entities*, and when we actually create the database using FileMaker Pro, those entities become tables.

To identify the entities that your database needs to model, start by looking at your notes and at the description of the goals you are trying to achieve. You will see clues that help you identify the entities, and certain words (usually nouns) will stand out.

In our example, the words *committee members*, *donors*, *letters*, and *labels* stand out. Let's consider each of those as possible entities for the time being. Table 18.1 lists the potential entities and a description/analysis of each.

TABLE 18.1 Potential Entities in the Donors Database

Entity	Description/Analysis
Committee Members	These are the people who will actually use the database. We certainly need to keep track of the people using the database. However, FileMaker includes built-in tools for managing database users, and we can use those to track committee members. So let's remove committee members from the entity list.
Donors	These are people who the committee thinks are potential donors. We certainly need to track them, so let's keep donors on the entity list.
Letters	One of the functions of the new database will be to print letters used for the mass mailing. This is an important aspect of the database. However, it isn't really an entity that we need to keep track of. Instead, it is one of the things that users will get out (an "output") of the database. So let's remove this from the entity list.
Labels	Like letters, labels are something that users will get out of the system. So let's remove this from the entity list as well.

We narrowed the list down to a single entity: Donors. That was easy!

NOTE Not all database models are as simple as the one we're using in this example. Often, the goals of a database are numerous, and as a result what is being modeled is complex. In those cases, the list of entities is long. In Chapter 20, we add some goals to our example, and as a result, add support for additional entities.

Identifying Fields

Now that we have a list of the entities that the database needs to keep track of, the next step is to identify the important characteristics of those entities that need to be tracked. We refer to those characteristics as *attributes*, and when we create the database using FileMaker Pro, these attributes become the fields that make up the tables.

Continuing with our example, we narrowed our list of entities down to donors. Some obvious characteristics of a donor are name and address. However, we might also want to "think ahead" a little and add some characteristics that we are likely to need in the future. For example, we might want to track donors' phone numbers and email addresses, so that we have alternate ways of contacting them. Also, the fundraising efforts will be targeted to parents of students currently enrolled in the school, as well as alumni of the school. Therefore, we might want to categorize the donors.

Our list of potential attributes is now: Name, Address, Phone Number, Email Address, and Category. A good next step is to review that list to see whether the attributes should be broken down into smaller, more granular attributes. Table 18.2 lists the potential attributes of a donor and a description/analysis of each.

TABLE 18.2   Potential Attributes in the Donors Table

Attribute	Description/Analysis
Name	The donor's name is actually composed of several things. There are the first and last names and possibly a middle name (or initial). A prefix or salutation is also important, especially when it comes to addressing letters and labels. We also want to be able to keep track of any suffixes (for example, "Jr." or "Sr.").
Address	Like the name attribute, the address can also be broken down into a number of smaller attributes. There's the street address and possibly a second line of the street address (to be used to store an apartment or suite number, for example). The address is also made up of a city, state, and ZIP code. (In our example, we assume that all the potential donors live in the United States. Otherwise, we'd also need to add attributes to track the province, country, and other things that make up foreign addresses.)
Phone Number	You could argue that a phone number can be broken up into individual attributes as well, since it is composed of an area code, a prefix, and number. However, for our needs, breaking up the phone number into those smaller attributes isn't necessary. So let's keep Phone Number as it is.
Email Address	Like the Phone Number attribute, it is possible to break the email address down into smaller attributes. For example, you could break "someone@acme.com" into the username ("someone") and the domain name ("acme.com"). However, this is not only unnecessary, but also causes the database users more work when they are entering data. So we leave Email Address as it is.
Category	This is the attribute we added to help distinguish between the two types of potential donors that will be targeted (parents of current students and alumni). There's no need to break this attribute down any further.

Our list of attributes for Donors has been narrowed down to First Name, Last Name, Middle Name, Prefix, Suffix, Street Address One, Street Address Two, City, State, ZIP Code, Phone Number, Email Address, and Category. Again, these attributes will become the fields that make up the Donors table in our database.

If your database model consists of multiple entities, you need to repeat this process for each entity. The end result is a list of the entities that the database will model and the attributes of each.

 NOTE The formal name for the process of identifying a database's entities and attributes is *data modeling*, and entire books have been written on the subject. My goal in this chapter is to provide you with a simplified, logical approach to what can easily become a complicated and time-consuming process.

Identifying Relationships

In Chapter 1, "Welcome to FileMaker Pro," we defined a database as a collection of related information. The key word here is *related*. In many cases, databases need to track multiple related entities. In cases where multiple entities are involved, a good next step in the planning process is to review the list of entities and try to determine the relationships between them.

The Donors database example that we have been using consists of only a single entity (Donors). Therefore, for this example, this step isn't necessary. However, in Chapter 20, "Expanding Your Database," we expand the scope of the database and add an additional entity to the database model. We then explore relationships in greater depth.

 TIP As you design your database, try to keep the database model as simple as possible. If you don't need to keep track of an entity, remove it. If there are attributes that you have no need for, remove them as well. I often find that users add unnecessary entities and attributes to their database models because they think they might need them someday. Keep in mind that you can always expand your database model in the future.

THE ABSOLUTE MINIMUM

In this chapter, we started the process of creating a database from scratch. Here are the key points to remember:

- Like other types of projects, the first step in creating a new database is to identify the goals that you are trying to achieve with it.

- Once you know what the goals of the database are, the process of designing the database begins. It starts with identifying all the things (the entities) that the database needs to keep track of. The entities that you identify will become the tables in your database.

- Once a list of entities has been created, the next step is to identify the characteristics (the attributes) of those entities. The attributes will become the fields that your tables consist of.

- Some database models consist of a single entity. However, many databases are more complex, and their models consist of multiple related entities. In cases where a database model is made up of multiple entities, the next step is to determine how they are related (a concept that we explore in Chapter 20).

- It is possible to expand a database's model as needs change. Therefore, you should always strive to keep your databases as simple as possible, and only include the entities and attributes that you actually need. You can always add additional tables, fields, and so on when it becomes necessary.

IN THIS CHAPTER

- Creating Databases from Scratch
- Adding Fields Using the Field Picker
- Changing a Table's Name
- Naming Tables and Fields

19

CREATING YOUR DATABASE

In Chapter 2, "Creating Your First Database," you created your first FileMaker Pro database using a Starter Solution. One of the advantages to using a Starter Solution is that FileMaker does a lot of the work that goes into creating a database. It creates the tables and fields, establishes relationships between tables, creates layouts, scripts, and more.

The process involved in creating a database from scratch is a little different. In this case, you are essentially starting from a blank slate. You need to create the tables, add their fields, and in cases where the solution involves multiple tables, establish any relationships between them. That's where the database model that you created in the Chapter 18, "Planning Your Database," comes into play.

In this chapter, you create a FileMaker Pro database from scratch, using your database model as a blueprint for the database. You learn how to create tables in the database and add fields to the tables.

Creating Databases from Scratch

1. To get started, open FileMaker Pro. You should see the FileMaker Quick Start screen. If not, select Quick Start Screen from FileMaker's Help menu.

2. In the top-left corner of the Quick Start screen, click the Create a New Database option.

3. A dialog box displays (as shown in Figure 19.1) prompting you to name the new database file and to specify the location to save it to. By default, FileMaker sets the filename to Untitled.fmp12. However, you should select a name that reflects the nature of the database that you are creating. For example, if your database will be used to track a collection of comic books, you might want to name the file Comic Books.fmp12.

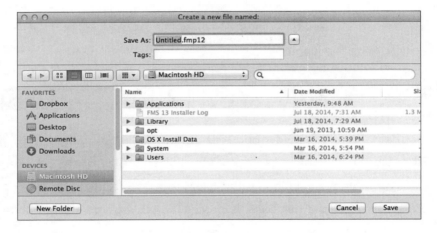

FIGURE 19.1

The dialog box that displays when you create a new FileMaker database.

 NOTE The fmp12 file extension is used to identify FileMaker Pro 12 and 13 databases. When creating a new database, be sure that the filename includes the fmp12 extension so that your database is easily identified as a FileMaker database, which makes it easier to open the database in the future.

4. After you have selected a filename and location for your database, click the Save button. The database file is created and opened. The window that appears (as shown in Figure 19.2) is a little odd looking because the database is, for the most part, empty.

FIGURE 19.2

The window that appears when a new database is created from scratch. A blank layout is presented and opened in Layout mode, and the Field Picker is opened so that you can quickly add fields to your first table.

When you create a new database from scratch, FileMaker does several things:

- It creates the FileMaker Pro database file and saves it in the location that you specify.

- It configures the security-related settings that you learned about in Chapter 14, "Protecting a Database."

- It creates the first table in your database and gives that table the same name as your database file. FileMaker does this because it assumes that one of the tables in your database will be named the same as the database itself. (That might not be the case. If so, don't worry. You see in a moment that you can easily change the name of that table.)

- It creates a layout that also has the same name as the database file. You can change this, too, should you want to do so.

When FileMaker completes those tasks, it opens the new database and presents the window that you see now. The layout created is displayed in Layout mode, and the Field Picker is opened. At this point, the database is a essentially a blank canvas that you can now begin to work with.

Adding Fields Using the Field Picker

In Chapter 9, "Working with Fields," you learned how to add fields to a table in a database created using a Starter Solution, and you used the Manage Database function to do so. While you can certainly use that same method to add fields to the table in this new database, FileMaker opens the Field Picker so that you can add new fields using an alternative method.

 NOTE If you want to work with the Manage Database function, you can easily do so by clicking on the small gear icon located in the top-right corner of the Field Picker window. This makes it easy for you switch between using the Field Picker and the Manage Database function.

You learned about the Field Picker in Chapter 11, "Working with Layouts," and used it to select and add fields to a layout. The Field Picker can also be used to quickly add fields to tables. Let's use the Field Picker to do that now.

First, refer to your database model to see what entities the database will keep track of. Those entities will become tables in your new database, and their attributes will become the fields. Let's assume that the table that FileMaker has already created for you is the first entity on your list. Let's take one of the attributes of that entity and set it up as a field in the table.

To do so, click the + New Field button located toward the bottom of the Field Picker window. FileMaker adds a new field to the table named Field and sets the field's type to Text. The field name is highlighted, allowing you to simply type to change the name of the field. Change the field's name from Field to the name of the attribute. For example, if your entity involves people, the first attribute might be First Name. (We discuss some techniques for naming both tables and fields in a few moments.) Type **First Name** to replace Field as the field's name.

The field's type is set to Text. You learned about field types in Chapter 9. If the entity that you are adding to the table is one that would be better represented as another type of field (Number, Date, and so on), you can easily change the new field's type in the Field Picker. To do so, click on the word "Text" that appears to the right of the new field's name. A pop-up menu appears, giving you the ability to change the field type from Text to Number, Date, Time, Timestamp, and so on.

To continue setting up the first entity in your database model as a table, you would repeat the process described previously, adding additional fields for each of the attributes of the first entity. In Chapter 20, "Expanding Your Database," you learn how to add tables for any additional entities in your database model and to establish relationships between those tables.

You are now well on your way to creating your own database. After you have finished adding the fields to the first table, you can use the tool techniques that you learned about in Chapter 11 to add the fields to the layout. You now have a solid foundation to build your database on and can begin to add other layouts, scripts, and more.

NOTE As you can see, compared to the process of creating a database using a Starter Solution, a lot more is involved when creating a database from scratch. Depending on the type of database that you want to create, you might find it easier to select a Starter Solution that is somewhat like the database that you want, create a database using that Starter Solution, and then modify the database. In other words, use the database created from the Starter Solution to "jump start" the process of creating your database.

NOTE In Chapter 14, we discussed the importance of security and some steps that you can take to secure a new FileMaker database. I recommend that you take a few moments to take those steps now.

Changing a Table's Name

As mentioned earlier, when FileMaker creates a new database from scratch, it creates the first table in the database and gives it the same name as the database itself. In some cases, that name might not be applicable.

Thankfully, FileMaker makes it easy for you to change a table's name. Here are the steps involved:

1. Open the Manage Database window (File > Manage > Database).

2. Click on the Tables tab.

3. Locate the table whose name you want to change. The table's name displays in the Table Name field, located at the bottom of the window.

4. Change the name of the table.

5. Click the Change button, located to the right of the Table Name field.

6. Click OK to close the Manage Database window and apply the change.

You can change a table's name at any time, and doing so does not cause any problems with regard to calculation formulas, layouts, and so on.

Naming Tables and Fields

When naming tables and fields, it is important to use descriptive and meaningful names. Sometimes names might make sense to you now, but will they still make sense a few months from now when you need to make a change to the database? And will they make sense to someone else using or modifying the database?

Every developer has his or her own preferred way to name tables and fields, as well as the other things that make up a FileMaker database (including layouts and scripts). There is no "right" way to name things, and no rules that you need to stick to.

That being said, here is how I prefer to name tables and fields.

I use table names that are short and plural. For example, in a database created recently, I set up tables with names like Products, Orders, Customers, Suppliers, and Notes. In cases where I need to set up a join table (a special table sometimes required to establish more complex relationships between entities), I name it by using a combination of the names of the tables being joined. For example, a join table between a Students table and a Classes table would be named Students_x_ Classes. Also, notice that I use underscores where you normally expect spaces to be. I avoid using spaces, both in table and field names, because they tend to cause problems with calculations.

I name fields in much the same way that I name tables, with one big exception: The names that I use for fields are normally singular. For example, in a Students table, you would see fields named First_Name, Last_Name, Middle_Initial, City, State, and Zip_Code. And while I strive to use short names, I also try to avoid using abbreviations as much as possible.

Again, those are just a few of the ways that I prefer to name tables and fields. In time, you'll likely find a naming method that works best for you.

Also keep this in mind: FileMaker makes it easy to change the names of things in a database, whether a table, field, layout, or script. So if you decide to rename things later on, it won't be a problem.

One last note regarding names: FileMaker is flexible with regard to the names that it allows you to use. However, if you try to use a name that FileMaker doesn't support, or one that it can use but might be troublesome, it alerts you. In those cases, a dialog box similar to that displayed in Figure 19.3 appears.

When this occurs, it is usually best to change the name. Otherwise, you might run into problems later, especially when it comes to using the table and/or field in calculations.

FIGURE 19.3

The dialog box that appears if you attempt to name a field that might cause problems in calculations.

NOTE A group of developers put together a collection of suggested FileMaker coding styles and best practices. This includes suggested naming conventions. You can learn more about this initiative at http://filemakerstandards.org.

THE ABSOLUTE MINIMUM

In this chapter, we continued the process of creating a database from scratch and learned more about the tables and fields that make up a database. Here are the key points to remember:

- The model that you create when you plan your database becomes important when you actually create the FileMaker database itself. The entities that you identify become tables, and their attributes become their fields.

- The Field Picker can be used to quickly and easily add new fields to tables in the database.

- There are no hard-and-fast rules with regard to how you must name tables and fields. However, FileMaker warns you if a name you have selected might cause problems.

20

EXPANDING THE DATABASE

The database you created in Chapter 19, "Creating Your Database," included only one table, and that's a good start. However, many databases are made up of multiple tables, each of which is used to store records related to records in other tables.

In this chapter, you learn how to add additional tables to your database, and how to create relationships between related tables. You also learn about some important and somewhat technical topics, including primary and foreign keys, FileMaker's Relationship Graph, and more.

Adding Additional Tables

In Chapter 19, you learned that when you create a new FileMaker Pro database file from scratch, FileMaker automatically creates the first table in the database. FileMaker's goal is to make it as easy and as fast as possible for you to get started with the new database, and that is why it creates that first table for you.

Adding additional tables to a database requires the use of the Manage Database function that you used in previous chapters. Let's take a moment to look at what is involved in adding additional tables.

If you don't already have the database that you created in Chapter 19 opened, open it now. Then open the Manage Database window (File > Manage > Database) and click on the Tables tab. You see a list of the tables in your database, as shown in Figure 20.1.

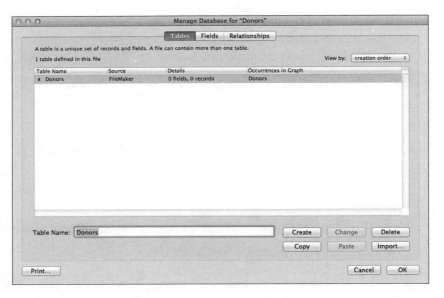

FIGURE 20.1

The Manage Database window, opened to the Tables tab.

To create a new table, enter the table's name in the Table Name field (which is below the list of tables), and then click the Create button. The table is then added to the list of tables. Repeat this process to add tables for the other entities that you identified in your database model.

NOTE The changes that you make using the Manage Database window aren't applied to your database until you click OK, located in the bottom-right corner of the window. Also, if you make changes in the Manage Database window and don't want to commit those changes for any reason, you can click Cancel, and the changes are ignored.

Understanding the Relationship Graph

Throughout this book, you used the Manage Database window to manage tables and fields. The Manage Database window also provides access to an important tool known as the Relationship Graph, which is used to establish relationships between tables. The Relationship Graph can be accessed via the Relationships tab of the Manage Database window, as shown in Figure 20.2.

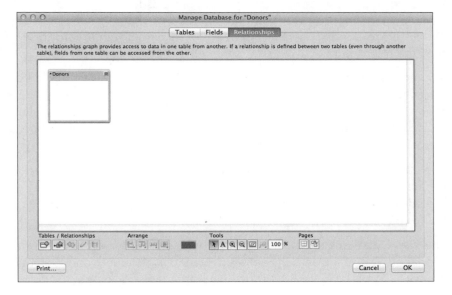

FIGURE 20.2

The Relationship Graph, as seen in the Manage Database window.

To help explain how the Relationship Graph works and the concept of relationships in general, let's return to the example used in Chapter 18, "Planning Your Database." The example involves the creation of a database used by a private school to do fundraising. After reviewing the goals of the database, we narrowed the list of the tables needed to a single Donors table.

Suppose that those fundraising efforts are starting to pay off, and the school is now receiving donations. The school wants us to expand the database so that it can keep track of those donations. Specifically, the school wants to keep track of when the donations were received, who made them, their amounts, and the check numbers. (For the sake of simplicity, let's assume that all the donations are made by check.) The school also wants to be able to send thank you letters to the donors that have made donations. Ideally, when a new donation is received, the school wants to be able to locate that donor in the Donors table and record the information about the donation that was received.

An easy way to add support for these donations is to add a few new fields to the existing Donors table. We could add fields for Donation_Date, Donation_Amount, and Check_Number. However, that only works if a donor makes a single donation to the school. If a donor were to make multiple donations, there would be no way to record the details of those donations.

While we could easily add additional sets of fields for the second, third, and fourth donations, that approach presents problems. For example, when sending thank you letters to donors, users would need to be careful with regard to the donation they are referring to.

Additionally, generating reports about the donations received would become difficult. For example, suppose that school administrators wanted to generate a report showing donations received during a specified date range. With potentially multiple donations stored in fields in the Donors table, many with different dates, it would be difficult to generate that report.

The correct way to add support for donations is to store that information in a separate table. That way, donors can make as many donations as they want, and the school can easily record them. It also makes generating reports, including thank you letters, much easier.

This new Donations table consists of fields to store the date of the donation (Donation_Date), the amount donated (Donation_Amount), and the check number (Check_Number). Figure 20.3 shows what that table looks like.

When you add a new table to a database, FileMaker automatically adds it to the Relationship Graph. Figure 20.4 shows an example of what the Relationship Graph looks like after the Donations table is added.

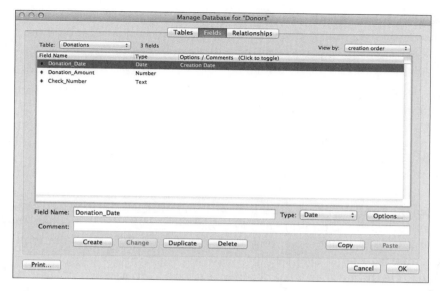

FIGURE 20.3

An example of what the new Donations table might look like, as seen in the Manage
Database window.

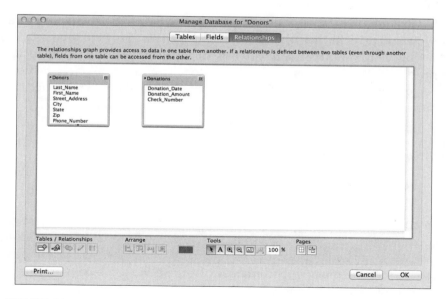

FIGURE 20.4

The Relationship Graph, as seen after you add a Donations table to the database.

As you can see, our original Donors table and the new Donations table now appear on the graph. However, there is no relationship between those two tables—at least not yet. We work on that in a moment. But first, let's explore the Relationship Graph a little more.

You may have noticed a number of buttons at the bottom of the graph. The buttons appear in four groups, and a color selection button is available as well. Let's review what each of these icons does, and why you might want to use them.

 TIP If you hover over an icon on the Relationship Graph, a tooltip appears to describe what the icon does.

The leftmost buttons are used to work with tables and relationships. You can use these to add a table to graph, add a relationship, duplicate a table on the graph, edit a table or relationship, or remove a table or relationship from the graph. It is possible for a table to appear on the graph multiple times. FileMaker developers often refer to these as *table occurrences* and to groupings of related tables as *table occurrence groups* (TOGs). Going forward, we'll refer to the objects that appear on the relationship graph as table occurrences.

The four Arrange buttons can be used to clean up the Relationship Graph by aligning, distributing, and resizing the tables on the graph. To use these buttons, you must first select one or more tables on the Relationship Graph. The easiest way to do that is to click on the graph and drag to select the table occurrences that you want to work with, or you can Shift+click to select multiple tables individually. Then click on one of the buttons to arrange, align, or resize the selected tables. You can align the left edges of the selected table occurrences, distribute three or more tables horizontally or vertically, and so on.

 TIP If you want to be able to see more of the Relationship Graph, you can resize the Manage Databases window. To do so, click on the left, right, or bottom edge of the window and drag to resize it.

The color selection button can be used to set the color of one or more table occurrences on the graph. To use it, select one or more table occurrences and then click on the color button to select the desired color. Some developers use this tool to make multiple occurrences of a table the same color, so that they can be easily identified and located on the relationship graph. (This is particularly helpful in databases that have complicated Relationships Graphs, with a large number of table occurrences.)

There are six Tools buttons. The leftmost button is used to select table occurrences on the relationship graph. The Text Note button can be used to add notes or comments to the relationship graph. The two magnifying glass buttons are used to reduce or increase the magnification of the graph, or you can manually enter a magnification percentage into the magnification field. (The relationship graph can be viewed at a maximum of 400%.)

And finally, the two Pages buttons can be useful when you want to print the relationship graph. The leftmost button is used to toggle between displaying or hiding the page breaks that would occur if you print the relationship graph. The rightmost button opens the Page Setup dialog window, so that you can select a paper size, orientation, and so on. To print the graph, simply click the Print button, which is located in the lower-left corner of the Manage Database window.

Setting Up Relationships

Before we continue, let's discuss why we are interested in creating a relationship between the two tables in the Donors database—and why you might want to set up similar relationships between tables in your database. There are several reasons.

First, remember that the school committee members need to be able to keep track of who has made donations. When looking at a donation, they want to be able to see the donor who made it. It would also be nice to be able to look at a donor and see the donations that the donor has made, and perhaps the total amount of the donations as well. So one reason for establishing the relationship is to be able to look at data in one table and see related data from the other table. And with regard to the request to see total donations made by each donor, we can add a calculated field to the Donors table that uses the relationship to sum up the related donations.

Another reason for setting up the relationship is that we want to reduce the amount of data that the users have to enter into the database. For example, the fundraising committee wants to be able to send thank you letters to donors as donations are received. We don't want the users to have to record both the donation information as well as the name and address of the donor every time a donation is received. Instead, we want the users to be able to identify the donor and record only information about the donation itself. That way, the process of receiving a donation is streamlined, and it is less likely that the information will be duplicated, inconsistent, or incorrect.

To set up a relationship between tables, you need fields in the tables that can be used to uniquely identify their records. In database terms, these fields are known as *primary keys*. For a field to serve as a primary key, it needs to be set up so that the values in it are unique, the field is never empty, and ideally the values in the field never change.

In some cases, a table already has a field that can serve as the primary key. In database terms, these are known as natural primary keys. For example, in a table used to track employees, a natural primary key might be a Social Security Number field in an Employees table. (Or would it? Remember that, ideally, the value being used as a primary key should never change. It is possible that an employee might end up being assigned a new Social Security Number if the employee's identity is stolen.)

In cases where no natural primary key is available, a new field needs to be added to the table to serve as the primary key. These are sometimes referred to as *artificial* or *surrogate* primary keys. My advice is this: Regardless of whether a table has a natural primary key, always add a field that can serve as the primary key. That way, you can be absolutely certain that every record has a unique value in that field and that those values will not change.

Let's take a look at what would be involved in adding primary key fields to the Donors and Donations tables.

Figure 20.5 shows the updated Donors table, and you can see that I added a field named Donor_ID. Notice that I used the Auto-Number field option so that every new record is assigned a unique, sequential number, and the value cannot be changed. I also set up the Validation options for the field, so that the field is always validated, is a number, is not empty, and is unique.

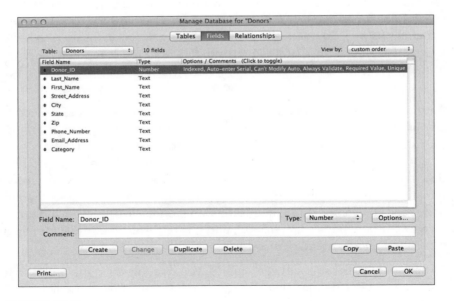

FIGURE 20.5

The Donor_ID field, which was added to the Donors table to serve as a primary key.

Figure 20.6 shows a similar field that would be added to the Donations table. Its primary key field is named Donation_ID.

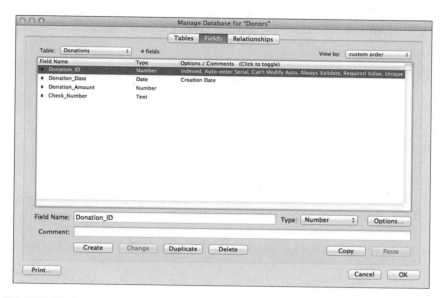

FIGURE 20.6

The Donation_ID field, which was added to the Donations table to serve as a primary key.

We are close to being able to establish a relationship between the two tables. We have primary keys set up on both the Donors and Donations tables, so we can uniquely identify the records in those tables.

However, something is still missing. In the Donations table, we do not yet have a field that indicates who made a donation. We need a field that can be used to store the primary key of the donor who made a donation. In database terms, this type of field is known as a *foreign key*. Foreign keys are fields in one table whose values are the primary keys of another table.

Figure 20.7 shows the Donations table with a new Donor_ID field added, which serves as a foreign key field to the Donations table. Notice that I have not set any of the Auto-Enter options for this field. (Later in the chapter, you learn how the value for this field can be set automatically using a relationship.) I have, however, set a few of the Validation options. The field is set to validate always, to be a numeric value, and to never be empty. Also notice that I did not set the Unique Value validation option for this field. Had I done so, we would not be able to add multiple Donation records for a donor.

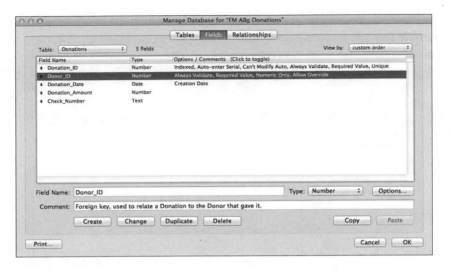

FIGURE 20.7

The Donor_ID field, which was added to the Donations table to serve as a foreign key to the Donors table.

NOTE Chapter 19, "Creating Your Database," mentioned that there are no rules about naming tables and fields. However, some developers prefer to name fields that are serving as primary and foreign keys in a special way, so that they are easy to identify. For example, you might choose to add a "__pk_" prefix to a field name when it is a primary key and "__fk_" to a field if it is serving as a foreign key. (Personally, I like to keep all the field names as simple as possible. Therefore, I use names like Customer_ID, Order_ID, and so on.)

Now that there is a field that can be used as a foreign key in the Donations table, we can set up a relationship between the Donors and Donations tables. To do so, let's return to the Relationship Graph by clicking the Relationships button at the top of the Manage Database window.

To create a relationship between table occurrences, click a field in one of the table occurrences and drag to a field in the other table occurrence. As you drag, a line appears and connects the two table occurrences. Figure 20.8 shows what the Relationship Graph looks like after a relationship is created between the Donors and Donations table occurrences.

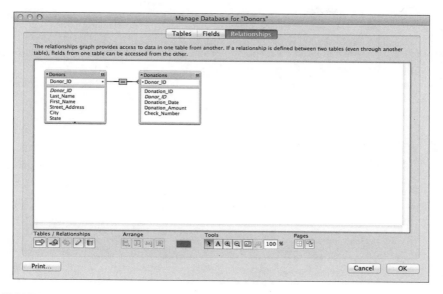

FIGURE 20.8

The Relationship Graph after a relationship is created between the Donors and Donations table occurrences.

Notice that the fields used to create the relationship now appear at the top of the list of fields for each table occurrence and that a line connects them. The line represents the relationship between the two table occurrences. The equals sign that appears in the middle of that line indicates that records in the Donations table occurrence are related to records in the Donors occurrence when the values in their Donor_ID fields are equal.

Note that you can edit a relationship by double-clicking on the equals sign that appears on the line. This opens the Edit Relationship window (as shown in Figure 20.9), which you can use to make changes to the relationship and set additional options.

The top part of the Edit Relationship window is used to change the relationship itself. You can change the fields used in the relationship, add additional fields, make changes to the relationship criteria, or remove criteria. It is also possible to set up more complicated relationships. For example, you might set up a relationship between two tables where the records are related in cases where the value in a field on one side of the relationship is less than, greater than, or not equal to a value on the other side. You can also set up criteria involving two or more fields.

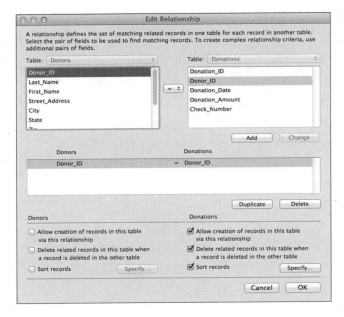

FIGURE 20.9

The Edit Relationship window, showing the relationship between the Donors and Donations table occurrences.

The bottom part of the Edit Relationship window is used to set some interesting options available when table occurrences are related. Table 20.1 lists and explains several of those options.

TABLE 20.1 Relationship Options

Option Name	Description
Allow Creation of Records in This Table Via This Relationship	Allows users to create related records in one table while working on a record in the other table. (We use this option when we discuss portals later in the chapter.)
Delete Related Records in This Table When a Record Is Deleted in the Other Table	Can be used to prevent related records from being orphaned when a related record is deleted. For example, suppose that you are working with a database used to track orders. The order information is stored in an Orders table, and the items on each order are stored in an Order_Items table. When an order is deleted, you want any related records in the Order_Items table to be deleted as well. Otherwise, the related records in the Order_Items table would have no related Order record to refer to.

Option Name	Description
Sort Records	There are several different ways to sort records in FileMaker, and this option is one of them. In this case, by setting the sort order for related records, you can specify the order in which any related records appear when they are being viewed through the relationship. For example, in the Donors database, when viewing a donor, we might want the donations that they have made to be listed in reverse order based on the date that the donations were made (so that the most recent order appears at the first).

As mentioned earlier, once you have established relationships between table occurrences, you can use the relationships to reference related data in a number of different ways. For example, you can create calculations in one table that reference related data in another table. You can also create layouts that display related data, and add a layout object known as a *portal* to make it easier and more efficient for users to add, change, and delete related data. We talk more about portals in a moment. But first, let's discuss a concept known as *context*.

The Importance of Context

One of the reasons for establishing relationships is that they allow us to create calculations in one table that are based on values stored in a related table. Using the Donors database scenario, when a relationship is established between the Donors and Donations table occurrences, we can add a field in the Donors table to calculate the total amount of donations that an individual donor made. Similarly, we can add calculations to determine the most recent donation that a donor made, the total number of donations a donor made, and so on. Figure 20.10 shows an example of a calculation formula used to determine the date of the most recent donation that a donor made.

Suppose that for some reason we add a second occurrence of the Donors table to the relationship graph as shown in Figure 20.11. This second occurrence of the Donors table is named Donors_2, and it does not have a relationship with the Donations table.

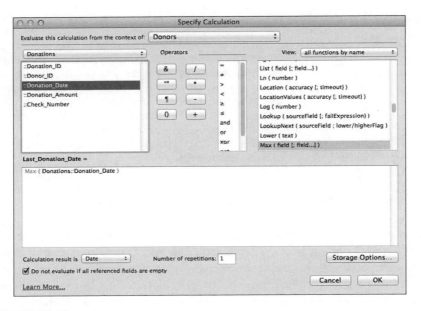

FIGURE 20.10

The calculation formula used to determine the date of the most recent donation made by a donor.

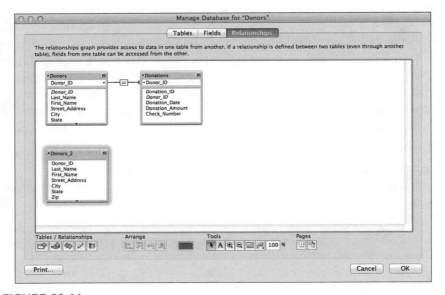

FIGURE 20.11

The relationship graph showing a second occurrence (Donors_2) of the Donors table. Note that Donors_2 has no relationship to the Donations table occurrence.

In this scenario, if we were to set up a calculated field in the Donors table, we would need to specify the table occurrence that we want FileMaker to use when evaluating the formula. In FileMaker terms, that table occurrence is referred to as the *context* in which the formula is to be evaluated. If you were to set up a calculation formula that references data in a table occurrence that is not available via the selected context, the formula would not evaluate correctly. Thankfully, when you enter a calculation formula, FileMaker alerts you if any of the fields in the formula are from unrelated table occurrences and prevents you from saving the invalid formula. (One exception is global fields, which can be referenced regardless of context.)

So, how do you indicate what context a calculation should be based on? At the top of the Specify Calculation window is a drop-down menu labeled Evaluate This Calculation from the Context Of. The options listed are the table occurrences of the table that the field is being added to.

Context also comes into play when you set up layouts. When you create a layout, you are asked what table occurrence the layout should be based on. That decision has an impact on what fields can and cannot be displayed on the layout. For example, if we were to create a layout based on the Donors_2 table occurrence, we would not be able to display related Donations records properly.

 NOTE   You can change the table occurrence that a layout is based on via the Show Records From field, located on the Layout Setup window. Refer to Chapter 11, "Working with Layouts," for more information about the Layout Setup window.

Context is also important when it comes to exporting data. When exporting records, the table occurrence that the current layout is based on determines whether data in related tables can also be exported.

In summary, if your database includes tables represented multiple times on the relationship graph, be careful with regard to context.

Working with Related Records Via Portals

As mentioned earlier, one of the other benefits of establishing relationships between table occurrences is that it allows us to create layouts that can both show and allow editing of related data. FileMaker supports a layout object known as a *portal* that makes this possible.

For example, suppose that in our Donors database, we want to create a layout that displays a donor and any donations that a donor has made. We create a layout based on the Donors table occurrence and then add a portal to that layout.

To add a portal, enter Layout mode, click on the Portal icon in the Status Toolbar, and then click and drag on the layout to both position and size the object. The Portal Setup dialog box, displayed in Figure 20.12, displays.

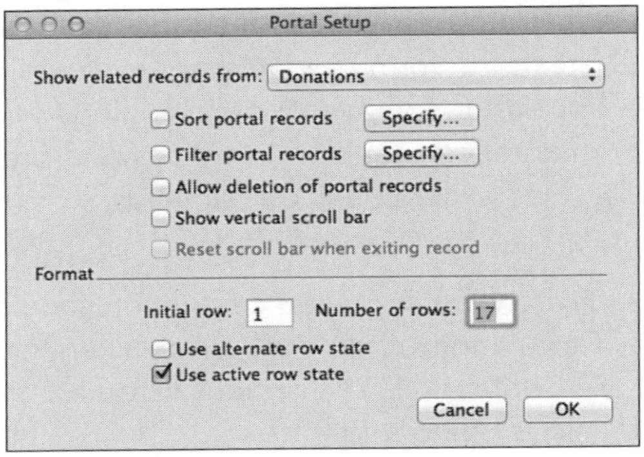

FIGURE 20.12

The Portal Setup dialog box.

Using the Show Related Records From drop-down menu, you can specify the related table occurrence that you want to display records from. The list includes only table occurrences that the layout's base table occurrence has a relationship to.

Several additional portal options are supported, allowing you to specify how the related records should be sorted, to filter the related records displayed, and more. Table 20.2 lists those options and describes what they do.

TABLE 20.2 Understanding Layout Types

Option	Description
Sort Portal Records	This option allows you specify the order in which you want the related records to appear. (If the relationship to the table occurrence has a sort order specified, this portal option overrides that sort order.)
Filter Portal Records	The relationship between the table occurrence that the layout is based on and the table occurrence used for the portal automatically filters the records displayed in the portal. In other words, only related records are displayed. However, with this option, you can use a calculation formula to further filter the records, thus preventing you from having to add additional table occurrences and relationships to the relationship graph.

Option	Description
Allow Deletion of Portal Records	This option makes it possible for users to delete related records directly from within the portal (assuming, of course, that they have the required privileges to do so). By enabling this function, a user can highlight a portal row and click the Delete icon in the Status Toolbar (or a button in the portal that references the Delete Portal Row script step) to delete the related record.
Show Vertical Scroll Bar	When this option is enabled, the user can scroll through the portal and view rows that might not otherwise be visible. For example, if there are 12 related records and the portal is set up in such a way that only 10 rows are visible, enabling this option allows the user to scroll down to see the additional 2 rows that were not immediately visible.
Reset Scroll Bar When Exiting Record	This option is available only when the Show Vertical Scroll Bar option is enabled. When enabled, and when a user exits a record, the position of the scroll bar is reset to the top of the portal.

Four formatting-related options are also available for portals. You can specify what row the portal should display first (Initial Row), the number of rows that should be displayed, and whether alternate and active rows should be displayed differently. (When the alternate and active row states are enabled, you can specify how they should be styled, which makes it easier for users to view the portal rows and to determine which row is active.)

Once a portal is placed on a layout, you can use the Field Picker to select fields from the related record and position them in the portal. Those fields act just like any other fields, and you can style them, use the Inspector tool to specify control styles, and more.

Here are a couple of additional notes about portals:

- As mentioned earlier, you can configure a portal so that related records can be deleted. It is also possible to allow users to add related records via a portal. To do so, the relationship to the table occurrence that the portal is based on must be configured so that the Allow Creation of Records in This Table Via This Relationship option is set.

- When a new record is added through a portal, the foreign key of the new related record automatically is set based on the primary key of the record in the table that the layout is based on. In other words, when you add related records via a portal, FileMaker automatically sets the foreign key for you.

Understanding External Data Sources

Before we wrap up this chapter, let's discuss one additional concept that involves relationships—external data sources. In the example used earlier, two tables were involved (Donors and Donations). Those tables were a part of the Donations database itself. However, it is also possible to use tables that reside in other databases. FileMaker refers to these as external data sources.

External data sources might be other FileMaker databases or SQL databases that use an entirely different technology, such as Microsoft SQL Server, Oracle, or MySQL. FileMaker refers to those types of external data sources as External SQL Sources (ESS).

You can use the tables in external data sources in much the same way as tables stored in the local database itself. You can even add them to your relationship graph to create relationships between your local tables and external tables.

The process involved in setting up external data sources can be tricky and certainly is beyond the scope of this book. However, it is important to know that this is a possibility, and depending on how you plan to use FileMaker, you might want to investigate this functionality further.

NOTE FileMaker Inc. provides a technical brief that explains External SQL Sources in detail. The document, "Introduction to External SQL Sources," is located here: http://www.filemaker.com/downloads/documentation/techbrief_intro_ess.pdf.

THE ABSOLUTE MINIMUM

In this chapter, you learned how to expand a FileMaker database so that it supports multiple tables. We discussed relationships, why they are important, and the process of creating relationships in FileMaker Pro using the Relationship Graph. We covered a lot of ground, but here are the key points to remember:

- You can use the Manage Database function to work with the tables, fields, and relationships in a FileMaker database. You can easily add, rename, and delete tables, and you can also work with fields.

- The Manage Database function provides access to the Relationship Graph, which is the tool used to define relationships between related tables.

- Primary keys are fields used to uniquely identify a record in a table, and they are required to set up relationships. Foreign keys, which are fields in one table whose values are the primary keys of another table, are also required.

- When working with data in related tables, context becomes important. Context is essentially the table occurrence that we want FileMaker to use to resolve references to related records, whether those records are being referenced in a calculation formula, displayed on a layout, and so on.

- It is possible to use tables that reside in external data sources, including other FileMaker databases and certain types of SQL databases.

Index

G